THE SACRED SCROLLS

COMICS ON THE PLANET OF THE APES

THE SACRED SCROLLS

COMICS ON THE PLANET OF THE APES

EDITED BY

RICH HANDLEY

JOSEPH F. BERENATO

SEQUART ORGANIZATION   EDWARDSVILLE, ILLINOIS

The Sacred Scrolls: Comics on the Planet of the Apes
edited by Rich Handley and Joseph F. Berenato

Cover by Patricio Carbajal. Book design by Julian Darius. Interior art is © their respective owners.

Published by Sequart Organization. Edited by Rich Handley and Joseph F. Berenato.

For more information about other titles in this series, visit sequart.org/books.

Contents

I've Never Met an Ape I Didn't Like: An Introduction

by Rich Handley

Welcome to this stinkin' book, you damn dirty ape.

As a young child in the 1970s, I developed an early fascination with science fiction from watching repeats of television shows spawned before my birth – something I inherited from my sci-fi-loving mother. As I devoured one episode after another on our family's black-and-white TV set, there was something about the sci-fi genre's message that immensely appealed to my sense of wonder, though I was probably too young, at that point, to articulate the reasons why.

It wasn't just entertaining – it was illuminating. When *Star Trek* showed two angry aliens, black on one side and white on the other, locked in irrational race hatred after countless eons of warfare, I absorbed the lesson that racial differences were only skin-deep. When *The Twilight Zone* featured a lonely man finding solace in a library following a nuclear war, only to break his eyeglasses, leaving him alone and blind in a building full of books, I learned more about irony and twist endings than Alanis Morissette could ever comprehend. And when *The Outer Limits* introduced an amnesiac with a glass hand, from a future in which mankind had been dominated by non-human invaders, I became intrigued by time travel and post-apocalyptic fiction.

So you can imagine my reaction the first time I saw *Planet of the Apes* in 1977 at age nine. A sci-fi film highlighting the irrationality of bigotry and war, featuring a lead character isolated from his fellow man, an ironic twist ending, time travel, and a post-apocalyptic setting in which mankind was dominated by a non-human force – and written, in part, by the same guy who created *The Twilight Zone*, to boot?

I had no choice but to fall in love.

A panel from *Planet of the Apes* magazine #6 (Mar 1975).

Like many people living in New York, I avidly enjoyed a daily film showcase called *The 4:30 Movie*, which aired on Channel 7, a local ABC affiliate. Thanks to its theme weeks, my eyes were opened to such classics as the *Pink Panther* films, *Westworld* (and its lesser sequel, *Future World*), the *Godzilla* franchise, and so many other movies that, to this day, remain a staple in my home-video library. But my most vivid memories were of *Planet of the Apes* Week, which lasted for five glorious years, from 1977 to 1981, before ABC inexcusably cancelled *The 4:30 Movie* and replaced it with *The People's Court*. (Damn you, Judge Wapner! Goddamn you all to hell!)

Having never watched the *Apes* films in theaters (I was born in 1968, the same year the first one was released), I was absolutely enthralled when that original movie (split in half over a two-day period) launched the first-ever *Apes* Week, sparking in this young viewer a lifelong fascination with the upside-world discovered by Charlton Heston's grizzled astronaut, George Taylor.

That passion continued during my teen years, and on into adulthood. Although home-viewing options were extremely limited until the heyday of the video rental store in the 1980s, I was ever on the lookout for an opportunity to view those amazing *Apes* films, with their wonderful John Chambers makeup and their jaw-dropping final scenes. Each time, I sat mesmerized by the performances of Heston, Roddy McDowall, Kim Hunter, Maurice Evans, Linda Harrison, Eric Braeden, Hari Rhodes, Ricardo Montalbán, Paul Williams, and so many other fine actors.

Like a pesky human scavenger netted in the hunt, I was drawn in and held helplessly captive.

My *Apes* addiction waned as I attended college, began my career, and got married – but it never ended. I eventually explored the live-action television series and the cartoons on Sci-Fi Channel, which weren't quite the same but were nonetheless *Apes*. I read Pierre Boulle's original source novel, *La Planète des Singes* (*Monkey Planet*), as well as the film and TV novelizations. And I survived Tim Burton's remake (that should be a T-shirt slogan), then delighted a decade later when the current films wiped clean all memory of *that* mishap.

And then there were the comics. I didn't discover those until the early 1990s, when my wife Jill and I traveled to California to celebrate our wedding anniversary. While there, I stopped at a comic shop (my wife is a very forgiving soul) and found nearly the entire run of Malibu Graphics' *Planet of the Apes* comics in a four-for-a-dollar bin.

For about twelve bucks, I snagged all but four or five issues – which I found in the very next town we visited. A few days later, as we waited at the airport to fly back to New York, and then during the flight itself, I devoured the series from start to finish. It wasn't necessarily *Apes* as I knew it,[1] but it provided new

---

[1] See my essay about the Malibu series later in this book.

stories beyond the films, and it had me intrigued. To this day, I have a major soft spot for those Malibu tales.

Back on Long Island, I did some research, learned about the 1970s Marvel magazines, and hit the local comic shops to start tracking them down. I was blown away when, after completing that brilliantly trippy run, I finally sat down to read it. And then I started over again. Once I'd finished re-reading both the Malibu and Marvel stories, I suffered an immediate onset of withdrawal.

Eventually, I acquired Power Records' book-and-record sets, the British annuals, Gold Key's *Beneath the Planet of the Apes* one-shot, and Marvel UK's wonderfully dreadful "Apeslayer" storyline. That California trip had given me something new to obsess about – and (sorry, Jill) to fill up space alongside my vast *Star Trek* comics collection. Since then, I've grabbed up the more recent issues from Dark Horse, Mr. Comics, and BOOM! Studios (all of which have been great fun), found numerous rarities along the way, and even enjoyed a number of fan-generated comics, chief among them *Beware the Beast* and *Return to Yesterday*.[2] My *Apes* comics hold a valued place on my shelves, and I frequently re-read them (even the Apeslayer issues... what the hell is wrong with me?).

Thanks to online fandom, I became involved, several years back, with a project to translate some 1970s Spanish-language *Apes* comics into English.[3] This led to my writing a pair of *Planet of the Apes* reference guides[4] and co-authoring a licensed *Apes* novel.[5] So when the opportunity arose to return to the madhouse once more and co-edit a pair of books about the *Apes* universe (the second volume, *Bright Eyes, Ape City: Examining the Planet of the Apes Mythos*, is currently in the works), how could I not answer the calling? I'm no bloody baboon, no chump of a chimp.

Compiling this anthology has been more fun than (dare I say it?) a barrel full of monkeys (yes, I apparently dare). The best part has been the opportunity to work with a number of good and wise apes: Joe Berenato, who invited me to write for his anthology, *New Life and New Civilizations: Exploring Star Trek*

---

[2] *Beware the Beast* (2004): Dave Ballard, Neil T. Foster and Michael Whitty. *Return to Yesterday* (2005): Mike McColm.

[3] Published only in Argentina, these are available for download at potatv.kassidyrae.com/simios.html.

[4] *Timeline of the Planet of the Apes: The Definitive Chronology* (2008) and *Lexicon of the Planet of the Apes: The Comprehensive Encyclopedia* (2010), for Hasslein Books

[5] *Conspiracy of the Planet of the Apes*, with Andrew E. C. Gaska, Christian Berntsen, and Erik Matthews (Archaia Publishing and BLAM! Ventures, 2011)

Comics – and whom I, in turn, asked to join me in helming this one; Sequart's Julian Darius and Mike Phillips, who proved they have impeccable taste by signing us up to co-edit a half-dozen other upcoming volumes covering several franchises (stay tuned!); Pat Carbajal, an immensely talented illustrator whose cover paintings always seem as though he reached into our heads and plucked out exactly what we were picturing; and Malibu Graphics co-founder Tom Mason, who agreed to be interviewed about his company's *Apes* comic line, and who took no offense at the resultant essay's honesty.

I also consider myself privileged to have worked with the book's amazing contributors: Corinna Bechko, Gabriel Hardmann, and Dafna Pleban, from BOOM! Studios' *Planet of the Apes* team, who provided insider insights in the book's foreword and afterword; Joe Bongiorno, a close friend for two decades, with whom I've spent countless hours dissecting films, TV shows, comics, and books – including, of course, *Planet of the Apes*; Dayton Ward, a prominent *Star Trek* novelist whom I've known since the 1990s, when both of us were just geeky fanboys establishing ourselves as writers (we're still geeky); *Simian Scrolls* co-editor John Roche and *Sacred Scrolls* editor Zaki Hasan, whose respected *Apes* fanzines helped to keep fandom alive during the lean times; Jim Beard, who stepped up when we needed someone to write a last-minute essay, and did a great job of it; Joseph Dilworth Jr., Lou Tambone, and Dan Greenfield, who have been among the movers and shakers of online sci-fi fandom, via their respective websites and blogs; Sam Agro, who contributed to Mr. Comics' *Revolution on the Planet of the Apes*, writing two terrific back-up stories for that miniseries; and Edward Gross, who co-wrote the acclaimed behind-the scenes book *Planet of the Apes Revisited*, which many consider to be **the** *Apes* bible.

Nearly two hundred *Planet of the Apes* comics have been published as of press time – and they're all covered in this volume, which pleases me to no end. (To find out if you're missing any, download an exhaustive index by yours truly at www.hassleinbooks.com/pdfs/POTAComics.pdf.) The essay writers have each done a phenomenal job of exploring the vast world of *Apes* comics, and I'm exceedingly proud to have each and every entry in this book.

The creators of those comics have explored the settings and concepts of the films and TV series, while introducing an array of new characters and scenarios. Back stories have been revealed, plot holes filled in, and histories extrapolated upon. The comics have employed multiple genres and styles; have taken readers to distant villages, ruined cities, and oceanic civilizations; and have even crossed over with *War of the Worlds*, *Alien Nation*, and *Star Trek*. It's been a mixed bag, to be sure. But by and large, the *Apes* funnybooks have remained true to Boulle's simian spirit, and with the recent announcement of a new film, *War of the Planet of the Apes*, coming in 2017, it's pretty much a given that there will be more to come, which makes this *Apes* fan happy indeed.

A lot has changed since I was a child. But inside me still lives that nine-year-old who gleefully explored strange new worlds and new civilizations, who traveled through a dimension not only of sight and sound but of mind, who never attempted to adjust the picture because there was nothing wrong with my television set – and who, for one week every year, stared in awe as thirteen-inch-tall talking apes inherited the Earth while humanity fell from evolution's ladder.

I Love You, Doctor Zaius!: An Introduction

by Joseph F. Berenato

I've loved fictional primates for a long, long time. King Kong (original, of course), Son of Kong, Mighty Joe Young, Bonzo, Clyde the orangutan, Goliath the chimp, King Louie, Magilla Gorilla, Donkey Kong, and even Grape Ape; I've delighted in their monkeyshines for as long as I can remember.

(Ooh – let's add The Monkees to that list too, while we're at it. True, monkeys aren't apes, but they *are* simians...)

Yes, sir. I love every ape I see, from chimpan-a to chimpan-z. And yet, for all that hominoid affection, I didn't have much time for *Planet of the Apes*.

Sure, I was aware of it, inasmuch as it was about a planet full of apes. I caught a few episodes of the cartoon when I was a kid. I chuckled when a couple of apes came upon Dark Helmet and Colonel Sandurz at the end of *Spaceballs*. I laughed when newly minted astronaut Homer Simpson finally figured out that (spoiler alert!) the Planet of the Apes was, in fact, Earth of the future.

And I can sing every line from *Stop the Planet of the Apes, I Want to Get Off!*, the musical starring *The Simpsons*'s Troy McClure.

But it was never really a franchise that interested me.

It should have, for sure – not only was it sci-fi full of apes, but it also starred Charlton Heston, a guy who delighted me in everything from *The Ten Commandments* and *The Agony and the Ecstasy* to *The Omega Man* and *Soylent*

They finally made a monkey out of Troy McClure in *Stop the Planet of the Apes, I Want to Get Off!* from *The Simpsons* episode "A Fish Called Selma" (20th Century Fox, 24 Mar 1996).

Green; and Roddy McDowall, whose time as the villain Bookworm on *Batman* was one of my favorite storylines.

Apes. Chuck Heston. Bookworm. A recipe for success, surely.

But it still didn't grab me. Not until I was twenty years old.

On September 12, 1998, I was just beginning my junior year at Rowan University. My romantic interest at the time had invited me over for dinner, and we flipped through the channels as we ate. That's when we came upon it: the 30th anniversary *Planet of the Apes* marathon on AMC, hosted by Heston, McDowall, and Kim Hunter. It was right at the start of the first flick, so we sat back, relaxed, and tuned in. Despite the protestations of my innamorata, we watched the first and moved on to the second. I went home shortly thereafter and watched the rest of them.

That marathon changed my life in two distinct ways: I now had A) a newfound love for the *Apes* franchise, and B) plenty of time to indulge that love, since I was also now single.

Over the course of the last two decades (my God, has it really been that long?), I've come to love the original films as well as the two most recent offerings, *Rise* and *Dawn of the Planet of the Apes*. (I'm told that there were some rumblings about a movie in 2001 starring Marky-Mark and Michael

Jackson, but I think that's just a damn dirty rumor, like the ridiculous notion that George Clooney was once Batman.)

Also during that time I've come to know Rich Handley, one of the founders of Hasslein Books and an *Apes* expert extraordinaire. After handing in an excellent essay for *New Life and New Civilizations: Exploring Star Trek Comics*, Rich approached me with an offer I couldn't refuse.

"Joe!" he said. "What do you know about *Planet of the Apes*?"

"Eh," I said, "the movie? Or the planet?"

"The brand-new book I'm pitching examining all of the *Apes* comics, and I want *you* as my partner."

Planet of the Apes comics, huh? This was an area I'd been looking to explore for ages. I'd been intrigued about the history of the apes after the end of *Conquest* but before the beginning of the '68 flick. I had been looking for a reason to delve into the Malibu comics from the 1990s. And I was itching for a reason to work with Rich again.

Without hesitation, I replied, "It's the book I was born to co-edit, baby!"

And thus was born the anthology that you now hold in your hands.

This is actually the first volume in a long collaboration between me and Rich, and more specifically part one of a two-book set. The second – *Bright Eyes, Ape City: Examining the Planet of the Apes Mythos* – will cover all other iterations of the *Apes* franchise, and is due out in 2016. The rest of our works? You'll have to stay tuned to Sequart.org for that.

In his introduction, Rich has done an excellent job of thanking many of the same people for many of the same reasons that I wish to do so, but I would be remiss if I did not as well, so I hope you'll indulge the repetition. I would, of course, like to thank Rich for asking me along on this ride; Julian Darius and Mike Phillips of Sequart Organization, for greenlighting this and all of our upcoming projects; and Pat Carbajal, for continuing to hand in absolutely inspired covers.

I'd also like to thank novelist and friend Jim Beard, for jumping in at the last minute, and for introducing Rich and me in the first place; Corinna Bechko, Gabriel Hardman, and Dafna Pleban of BOOM! Studios; Dayton Ward, the acclaimed *Star Trek* novelist and fellow geek who continues to sign on to projects Rich and I helm, no matter how far-fetched; Sam Agro, Joe Bongiorno, Joseph Dilworth, Jr., Dan Greenfield, Edward Gross, Zaki Hasan, John Roche, and Lou Tambone, for all handing in absolutely wonderful essays and making the book the definitive look at *Apes* comics; and Rachael Stott, David Tipton, and

Scott Tipton of IDW Publishing, for agreeing to be interviewed about their trek to the year 3978.

In addition, I would like to thank the professors in Rowan University's Writing Department, particularly Ron Block, Lisa Jahn-Clough, and Dr. Jeff Maxson; my fellow 2015 grads from Rowan's Master of Arts in Writing program, especially Jason Cantrell, Jennifer Martin, Steve Royek, and Christina Schillaci; and my father Anthony and step-mother Heidi, for encouraging me to seek pursuits beyond the confines of our family farm.

Last, but certainly not least, I would like to thank my wife Helena, for continuing to support my endeavors to write about imaginary spacemen in the future. Take a bow, sugarbeet.

Fiction for Thinking Apes: A Foreword

by Corinna Bechko and Gabriel Hardman

A planet where comics evolved from films? There's got to be an answer!

After all, isn't it supposed to be the other way around? The comic first, filled with action and bravado, then the movie, giving motion and sound to those still panels? After eight films stretching all the way back to 1968, what could there possibly be left to say about talking apes?

To the uninitiated, then, the setup to the original *Planet of the Apes* film (written by Michael Wilson and Rod Serling and directed by Franklin J. Schaffner) and the novel on which it was based (*La Planéte des Singes*, written by Pierre Boulle) is deceptively simple. Apes control the world, while humans are relegated to the status of vermin and lab monkey. How could such a straightforward premise support one novel or film, let alone a whole series, as well as cartoons, television shows, and comics? Therein lies the beauty of science fiction in general, and of the *Planet of the Apes* franchise in particular.

When science fiction is working, it transcends the genre trappings of space flight and tough-talking guys toting laser guns. It simplifies things, adding and subtracting elements from our own world so that the focus is narrowed enough to really examine some aspect of culture or human nature. And if it's really good, it does so with pathos and drama, giving us memorable characters to whom we can relate all the more because of their exotic situations.

The first three issues of *Betrayal of the Planet of the Apes* (Nov 2011-Jan 2012).

Planet of the Apes does all of this in spades. It creates a rich world that's immediately easy to understand, even if we don't see the twist of the first film coming. It gives us layered characters personified by primates both human and non-human, and it makes us care about them. And because we care about them, we want to understand their world and their struggles. That's the key that opens the door to talking about all manner of things relevant to our own society, from animal rights to class warfare to nuclear or biological Armageddon. This is not light entertainment and escapism. This is fiction for thinking apes.

Like the genre of science fiction, the medium of comics is sometimes derided as catering to those who just want to see stuff blow up. Serious comics fans know that this couldn't be farther from the truth. From Batman's complicated relationship with firearms to the X-Men's subtle (and sometimes not so subtle) commentary on race and class, comics have always had something to say to those who cared to hear it.

So when comics and *Apes* meet, something magical is bound to happen. There are obvious themes to explore, given the stratified society that the different species inhabit alongside the persecuted human minority. There are sci-fi twists to be had, given the nature of the mysterious Forbidden Zone and its bizarre mutant citizens. Then there's the weight of history, both the real history of the 20th century and all of the history that must have come between the end of the old world and the start of the new. And if all that isn't enough, there is also the supposition of time travel, with all its inherent contradictions and temptations.

Maybe this setup isn't so simple after all.

When we set out to create our first *Planet of the Apes* comic, *Betrayal of the Planet of the Apes*, with BOOM! Studios, we were suddenly confronted with the myriad ways that our story could go. Having proposed a one-shot because we were fans of the original films (this was before the new movies came out), we hadn't truly considered all of the ideas that could be incorporated, given enough space. And we were given a lot of space, when BOOM! countered with the offer of a miniseries, followed by a second miniseries, and finally an ongoing series. By the time our *Planet of the Apes* run ended, we had written 20 issues. We were truly lucky with our artists, since Marc Laming worked with us on *Exile on the Planet of the Apes* and Damian Couceiro stuck with us through the entirety of *Planet of the Apes: Cataclysm*. During that time, we explored themes of social violence, religious dogmatism, military honor, family dynamics, racial and class tensions, sentient rights, feminism, and the role of ethics in both science and government. We incorporated tropes related to thrillers, horror, war stories, espionage stories, disaster flicks, romances, and science fiction.

But the thing is, we are not unique in this. Just about every comic set in the world of *Planet of the Apes* touches on one or more of these elements. It may be buried under a lot of thrilling adventure, or it may be dressed up and approached in a lighthearted manner, but rest assured, it is there. In the same way that a prism appears to be a simple lump of glass until it is held up to produce visible rainbows from invisible clear light, the seemingly simplistic setup of a world where apes evolved from men allows us to view every facet of society from a different angle with a fresh perspective.

So go on, get reading. There is a long, rich history of comics on the Planet of the Apes. And here, for the first time, you can explore some of the many threads that make up that complex tapestry, with *Apes* experts as your guide.

Like Doctor Zaius, you may find something to confirm your biases. Or like Zira and Cornelius, you may find yourself thinking about your own world in a completely different way. But unlike Taylor, you are bound to like what you find.

From Technicolor to Four-Color: The Film and Novel Adaptations

by Zaki Hasan

In this age of movies being handcuffed to elaborate, often unwieldy, *Defiant Ones*-style marketing and merchandising campaigns practically from their inception, it comes as a bit of a shock to realize that the original *Planet of the Apes* film didn't have much in the way of tie-ins or other licensed paraphernalia in the marketplace to herald its triumphant theatrical arrival. Rather, *Apes* found its audience the old-fashioned way: It presented a compelling story anchored by a compelling cast, and the rest, as they say, was (future) history.

Perhaps most surprising of all is that, despite the obvious and apparent crossover audience, there was no pre-planned *Planet of the Apes* comic book to clue the sci-fi set into this "unusual and important motion picture event," as the film was first pitched to wary cinema-goers in 1968. Rather, it wasn't until two years later, well after the movie's out-of-this-world critical and box office reception had made a filmic sequel all but inevitable, that the *Apes* brand finally made its first, tentative foray into the uncharted world of newsprint and four-colors. Or, at least, that's how it was for the English-speaking audience.

As it happens, the first steps had actually come by way of a 1968 Japanese *manga* adaptation of the original film that appeared in the long-running

Bessatsu Bôken'Ô ("Adventure King") magazine. Titled *Saru no Wakusei* ("Planet of Monkeys"), this comic was written and drawn by Jôji Enami, and although the story was compressed into a breezy 63 pages, it's still the very first *Planet of the Apes* comic ever made. Another Japanese telling of the first film would follow in 1971, this one by Kuroda Minoru, and serialized over 250 pages in *Tengoku Zôkan* magazine.

Taylor and his crew encounter... a dinosaur? Yes, wackiness ensues in the first *Planet of the Apes manga* adaptation in *Bessatsu Bôken'Ô* (Apr 1968).[6]

Although both of these follow the very basic template of the movie's storyline, they also toss in some bizarre digressions, such as an ape experiment in which a human male and female are sewn together vertically down the middle of their bodies, Stewart exiting her sleep chamber and having her own adventure while in flight, and Taylor and company (including a mysterious fifth

---

[6] Scan posted at https://groups.yahoo.com/neo/groups/PotaDG by Michael Whitty and Neil Foster.

crew member) encountering a dinosaur in the lake as they row away from their sinking ship. Like I said, bizarre. A third *Apes manga*, this time adapting *Battle for the Planet of the Apes*, appeared in *Weekly Shonen Champion*, written and drawn by Mitsuru Sugaya. Sadly, all three *mangas* have been all but forgotten.

The *Apes* franchise didn't make its stateside debut in comic form until 1970, however, when Gold Key Comics, the undisputed king of the hill when it came to licensed funnybooks, released a single-issue special adapting the first *Apes* sequel, *Beneath the Planet of the Apes*. Hitting stands mere months after the film's May 1970 release, Gold Key's take on *Beneath* featured some gorgeous old-school art by Italian illustrator Alberto Giolitti, who'd already spent quite a bit of time toiling in Gold Key's licensed comics salt mines via their long-running *Star Trek* and *Twilight Zone* books (among others).

While it may seem, at first glance, that the book's thirty-four pages are a bit scant to encompass the totality of the movie's ninety-plus minutes, Giolitti manages to showcase most of the film's highlights (and lowlights) with remarkable ease, which certainly speaks to his considerable artistic skills (or, conversely, to some of the deficiencies in Paul Dehn's script). In fact, Giolitti's ample use of reference photos and likenesses of the film's stars (well, James Franciscus, anyway – Charlton Heston is reduced to a sort of generic blond-haired beefcake in the *Flash Gordon* mold) help make this one of the most lushly illustrated *Apes* comics in the brand's long history.

Now, given that producer Arthur P. Jacobs and the other *Planet of the Apes* creatives concluded *Beneath* with very little intent to stay the course sequel-wise, it stands to reason that the folks at Gold Key had no designs on future visits to the *Planet of the Apes*. This, in turn, makes it a bit easier to understand why the one-shot *Beneath* adaptation is the one and only *Apes* product to emerge from their presses. As anyone other than Dehn would have said at the time, once you blow up the world, the story avenues sort of close down.

Of course, since you're reading this book, you're probably aware that the series had a few more flicks' worth of juice left.

But while the film series would continue to crank out new entries at a pace of one a year through 1973 – proving that even the end of the world was no impediment to the continued power of capitalism – it would take a little bit longer for *Planet of the Apes* to make its way back to the comic book page. In fact, it wasn't until after movie five, *Battle for the Planet of the Apes*, had closed out the run that the merchandising spigot truly began doing its thing. And in August 1974, with a live-action *Apes* series set to launch on CBS the following month, the brand's next big foray into comics began, this time via Marvel. As it happens, this coincided with a time of bold expansion by the publisher of the Fantastic Four and Spider-Man into a variety of new genres. Editor-in-chief Stan Lee had spent the better part of the 1960s doing his darnedest to establish Marvel Comics as the go-to purveyor for all manner of costumed cavorters, and then spent the next decade trying desperately to prove that wasn't *all* the company did.

It was this period of unprecedented expansion that helped spawn such groundbreaking, genre-busting titles as *Conan the Barbarian*, *Master of Kung Fu*, and *Tomb of Dracula*, all of which enjoyed long and healthy runs throughout the decade (and, in the case of *Conan*, far beyond). It's also what led the publisher to add *Planet of the Apes* – and, later, other science fiction titles, such as *Star Wars*, *Star Trek*, and *Battlestar Galactica* – to its lineup. Indeed, the franchise's continued cultural dominance made for a perfect fit with a company eager to align itself with a genuine mainstream phenomenon. Thus, rather than go the four-color route, *Planet of the Apes* debuted as part of Marvel's ambitious black-and-white magazine line. Each issue was packed to the gills with articles, interviews, original stories, and, most importantly for our particular discussion, comic adaptations of all five films in the *Apes* cycle.

The fact that the theatrical runs had long since concluded is a key factor in the comics' eventual effectiveness, as there were no marketing concerns preventing each adaptation from diving as deep as necessary to present each film's story as completely as possible. Now, bear in mind, for the sake of context, that these were published at a time when even VCRs were still a few years away from becoming a mainstay in most homes. If you wanted to relive the experience of watching a beloved movie, your options were either to wait for an eventual theatrical reissue or, as most folks likely did, to content yourself with a novelization or comic.

Luckily, the House of Ideas was more than up to the task of matching the theatrical experience, all while tossing in some of that inimitable Marvel flavor that readers had come to expect. In fact, of Marvel's five film adaptations, the publisher's take on the original 1968 film, featuring a script by Doug Moench and art by George Tuska and Mike Esposito, is the most readily apparent melding of the Marvel sensibility with *Planet of the Apes*. What becomes most apparent, right off the bat, is that Marvel failed to secure likeness rights for Heston (or, apparently, for any of the other actors not obscured under layers of John Chambers' patented foam rubber). Eschewing Heston's receding hairline and wiry frame, Tuska's George Taylor is a muscular he-man of a hero, with a mop of curly 1970s-style hair, to boot.

Still, while you kind of have to squint your eyes and turn your head slightly sideways to imagine that the astronaut whom Tuska has drawn is the same one Chuck Heston portrayed, we have no similar concerns from Moench's script, which is practically dripping with the same flavor of cynicism and borderline misanthropy that made Rod Serling and Michael Wilson's dialogue such a joy to listen to. If anything, Moench manages to dial it up a notch, making some of Taylor's haranguing of fellow astronaut Landon border on downright insufferable at times, without Heston's charismatic delivery to help make it go down smoother. ("You poor, stupid fool," he mutters in Landon's direction mere moments after seeing him get trampled by gorillas on horseback, which does seem sort of like kicking a guy when he's already down.)

The other thing that becomes apparent is the pains to which Moench has gone to make the comic translate not only the film's storyline, but also its unique pacing. With the ability to parcel out the movie's story in six chunks of roughly twenty-five pages each, the creative team had the luxury of playing to the film's strengths, allowing for the same slow-burn build-up that the movie's director, Franklin Schaffner, utilized in the lead-up to the famous ape reveal during the cornfield hunt. The same way that moment doesn't occur until almost a half-hour into the film, it doesn't happen in the comic until page 24 of a 26-page first chapter (with Taylor's exclamation of "Apes! Apes on horseback!" helpfully punctuating the moment, in case the artwork alone is too subtle for some readers).

The adaptation of the original film continues through issue six of *Planet of the Apes* magazine, and while it's an admirable effort overall, the conclusion is one area in which the limitations of trying to translate a cinematic experience to the printed page become apparent. The film's shocker of an ending (I'm assuming you're familiar with it) draws much of its power from a combination of Shaffner's framing, Heston's performance, and one heck of a phenomenal matte painting by William Creber. Without any of those to draw upon, Moench and Tuska do their best to emulate its impact, but the resultant double-spread of the Statue of Liberty's shattered visage simply lacks the comparable punch of its celluloid cousin.

Still, a few flaws notwithstanding, it's an altogether auspicious start to Marvel's lengthy jaunt through the catalog of cinematic *Apes* installments. In addition to anchoring the launch of the prestige *Planet of the Apes* mag, the

Moench-Tuska adaptation would also end up being re-purposed by the publisher for the first six issues of a colorized (and slightly re-edited) comic book titled *Adventures on the Planet of the Apes*, which would hit stands just over a year later, with a cover date of October 1975. It would also be reprinted nearly two decades later by then-*Planet of the Apes* license holders Malibu Graphics, in a 1990 trade paperback.[7]

Marvel's telling of the original *Apes* film is an impressive feat all by itself, but it's made all the more so when you compare it with other movie adaptations published before and since. With the breathing room that can only come from having more than 150 pages available with which to re-tell this tale, the creative team utilized the serialized format to its fullest. More to the point, they helped to set the tone for what audiences could come to expect from Marvel's *Apes* moving forward. And with the first film's adaptation completed, they were hardly going to rest on their laurels. Thus, Marvel's take on *Beneath the Planet of the Apes* began to unspool immediately the following month.

Moench remained onboard as writer (working off the script by Dehn), with Filipino artist Alfredo Alcala stepping into Tuska's shoes. And while Tuska's style fit in more comfortably with Marvel's general house style of that era, Alcala brought a refined, painterly style to the proceedings that made full use of the various line-weights, gradations, and greyscales for which the black-and-white format allowed. Also, unlike *Planet*, we actually have a point of comparison with *Beneath*, given the story's Gold Key go-round. This isn't so much about one being superior to the other (the necessities of serializing a story versus confining it to a one-shot are so different that a one-to-one comparison is both fruitless and unfair), but rather about how different writers end up choosing different parts of the same story to foreground.

Although Gold Key's Giolitti stayed relatively true to the general aesthetic of *Beneath*'s production and makeup design, it's clear that Alcala felt no similar constraints. In addition to flipping the appearances of our heroes by having a bearded Taylor and a clean-shaven Brent, Alcala also ups the "ick" factor of our favorite radiation-scarred mutants living in the remains of New York City. While the film's director, Ted Post, wanted the mutants to evoke the unnerving image of a human face with the dermis removed (he famously instructed Chambers to base them on images from *Gray's Anatomy* – the book, not the television

---

[7] This was the version I owned, by the way, with the binding just about wearing itself out from my constantly thumbing through it.

show), Alcala chose to dial things up considerably, with his face-melted horrors taking full advantage of the magazine format's slackened content restrictions.

Ah, yes. The stuff of which nightmares are made.

Also of note is how this particular telling of the story closes. Unlike the film and the Gold Key adaptation, both of which leave some degree of opacity regarding whether or not Heston's Taylor deliberately sets off the Alpha-Omega Bomb after being fatally shot, there's no such room for interpretation in the Moench-penned conclusion for *Beneath*, which appears in issue 11 of the Marvel magazine (August 1975), and which takes its cues from the shooting script. Here, Taylor has been shot several times and is clearly on his way out, but rather than slumping lifelessly onto the control panel and activating it post-mortem, he reaches out and actively presses the fatal button. Goodbye Taylor, goodbye Earth, and goodbye Marvel's *Beneath the Planet of the Apes*.

The sequel comic would also end up appearing a few months later in the color *Adventures on the Planet of the Apes* comic, beginning in issue six and filling the remainder of that title's brief eleven-issue run. And like its predecessor, it would be reissued as a Malibu Graphics trade paperback in 1990. For me, not having even seen the movie back then, and with VHS copies in exceedingly scarce supply, that Malibu trade was my one and only way to imbibe *Beneath* until many years later, when I was finally able to sneak a recording off one of those *"Planet of the Apes* Weekend" marathons that used to populate cable TV back then. (Needless to say, I was gratified to see that the mutants didn't look like the nightmare-sauce version Alcala had envisioned.)

With *Beneath the Planet of the Apes* safely under his belt, Moench was gripped by none of the creative panic with which the filmmakers had to deal when forced to invent another sequel out of a whole cloth following *Beneath*'s apocalyptic final moments. No, he was back at it the following month for part one of his serialized take on *Escape from the Planet of the Apes*, beginning in issue 12 (September 1975), this time with artist Rico Rival providing art honors. As before, Moench worked off the film's shooting script (which Dehn famously crafted after receiving a panicked "Apes exist. Sequel required." telegram from Jacobs) — and, as before, this allowed an interesting contrast with the *Escape* that audiences saw in theaters.

While most of the differences are subtle or inconsequential, the biggest divergence occurs right up-top. While the actual movie begins with the discovery of Taylor's repaired and re-launched spaceship off the coast of 1970s Los Angeles, the comic winds the clock back ever so slightly, showing us Zira,

Cornelius, and Milo launching the craft just in time to see the bomb's fatal detonation, and Earth's subsequent destruction, before being hurled into a time-warp and propelled back to the then-present. This scene was actually in the screenplay and was filmed, but was cut from the movie in order to preserve the audience's surprise at seeing the Ape-o-nauts unveiled. The sequence's inclusion in the comic highlights how the format allowed the story to expand its canvas in a way that the film series, which had a budget of about a dollar-fifty by the time *Escape* was in production, simply could not.

Another major distinction between screen and print – and this one is more a result of artistic interpretation than any particular divergence between the two scripts – is in the depiction of the film's primary antagonist, Doctor Otto Hasslein. As portrayed in the film by actor Eric Braeden, Hasslein is nuanced, conflicted, and driven to commit horrible actions because he has convinced himself that the survival of the human race is at stake. You certainly don't like the character by the time the credits roll, but Braeden imbues Hasslein with enough layers that he doesn't seem like a standard-issue, mustache-twirling baddie either. Indeed, one realizes just how *much* depth Braeden was able to imbue Hasslein with when one contrasts the movie version with Rival's.

Gaunt and wiry, with a long, thin nose and a receding hairline, he doesn't look altogether different from Thor's arch-nemesis Loki (specifically, the Jack Kirby model), and he practically screams "Comic book villain!" from his very first appearance. As it turns out, without Braeden's carefully modulated performance – the "Am I God's enemy or his instrument?" speech, for example – we lose the important effect of Hasslein gradually moving into the villain column, and with it our ability to sympathize with him. Nonetheless, the ship-bound climax, with chimpanzee fugitives Cornelius and Zira mercilessly gunned down by Hasslein, loses none of its emotional punch in the translation.

Escape from the Planet of the Apes spans five issues, concluding in issue 16 of the *Apes* magazine (January 1976). With the color comic book having folded a few months prior, it ended up not seeing print again stateside until the Malibu Graphics trade paperback in 1990 (which would, in turn, be the last such reprint from Malibu). By the time Marvel had wrapped up its retelling of *Escape*, both the live-action and animated *Apes* TV shows had finished their respective single-season runs, and much of the passion firing fandom had begun to fade. As such, the magazine was one of the few remaining places for *Apes* diehards to get their fix, and I'm sure at least a few fans had their fingers crossed that the series would stay afloat long enough to get through the remaining two films.

Right on schedule, the Moench-scripted comic for *Conquest of the Planet of the Apes* began unspooling the following month, this time with Alcala back on art duty. As with *Beneath* and *Escape*, the *Conquest* comic starts off quite differently from the film, and I'd argue that it's actually a more effective entrée to this story's particular status quo. While *Conquest* (the movie) plays its credits over hordes of extras in phony-looking monkey masks and colored jumpsuits to clue us in on how apes have become a servile class in the future world of "North America – 1991," it's ultimately undone by the cheapie nature of the whole thing. By now, the filmmakers were scraping every cent together to get these things made, and it showed. In contrast, *Conquest* (the comic) uses its unlimited budget to indulge us with a three-page sequence depicting one of the film's fascistic police officers tracking and gunning down a fugitive, ultimately revealed to be an ape.[8]

Also interesting is how the story's climactic final moments are staged in the comic, as opposed to in the film. As has become well-known in *Apes* lore, the original cut of *Conquest of the Planet of the Apes* was *far* darker than the one that actually ended up in theaters (which wasn't exactly a Sunday stroll either, by the way). Convinced that there can be no redemption for the human race, chimp revolutionary Caesar compels his followers to violently kill their human overseers as he looks on from above. This was hastily changed at the eleventh hour, however, to make our ostensible hero seem less bloodthirsty, and Roddy McDowall quickly recorded some "Kumbaya"-style dialogue about getting along, working together, etc., that was looped in over some wide shots and extreme close-ups. Family audience preserved? Yes, but at the cost of much of the ending's "oomph."[9]

When it came time to translate this pivotal moment, Moench had a decision to make, and he essentially split the difference. In the final chapter of *Conquest* (July 1976), he leaves in the fire-and-brimstone stuff, but has Caesar ominously intone, "That day is upon you now!" in the final panel. Fade to black. What follows, whether murder, bloody murder, or "Hey, just kidding, let's play

---

[8] Once again, this scene appeared in the screenplay and was filmed, but did not make the final cut. It also shows up in the movie's novelization, written by John Jakes.

[9] The original version, thankfully, has since been released on Blu-ray, as has the original cut of *Battle for the Planet of the Apes*, which adds a good deal of long-lost material involving the Alpha-Omega Bomb – also retained in the Marvel telling.

nice," is left entirely up to the audience. It's actually a masterful bit of scene construction that fully preserves the uneasy nature of where we're left at the end of the movie, while neatly sidestepping the feel-good stuff that only waters it down, all without explicitly overwriting it via the script's original coda (which has the ape mob brutally killing the villainous Governor Breck, portrayed in the film by Don Murray).

By issue 23 of the Marvel magazine, the *Planet of the Apes* franchise was starting to run on fumes. No new on-screen *Apes* projects were in the pipeline, which made it difficult to find much in the way of content for articles, but nonetheless, there was still one movie to go, and so began Marvel's take on the final feature, *Battle for the Planet of the Apes*. This time, Moench was joined by a different artist or team of artists for nearly every chapter of the story: Vicente Alcaraz, Sonny Trinidad, Alfredo Alcala, Yong Montano, Dino Castrillo, Michele Brand, and Virgilio Redondo. While this may have been a way to combat the Dreaded Deadline Doom, the rotating roster of illustrators can't help but give a disjointed feel to the proceedings, with quality varying wildly depending on who's handling which chapter.

A rather hideous Governor Breck (not Kolp) leads the fledgling mutant civilization in *Planet of the Apes* magazine #24 (Sep 1976).

That said, as with all of his previous adaptations, Moench deploys every trick of the format to add to the film's admittedly juvenile story (by Paul Dehn and John and Joyce Corrington) in a variety of clever ways. The biggest change here is the substitution of Governor Kolp (played on screen by Severn Darden) in favor of the previous film's Breck (I guess we know he made it out of *Conquest*'s conclusion alive after all), now scarred and psychotic thanks to ten-plus years spent living in the irradiated remains of a nuclear-bombed city, as the main (human) antagonist.

This was, of course, the filmmakers' intent all along, as reflected in the shooting script, before minor inconveniences like actor unavailability got in the way. On balance, the inclusion of Breck actually makes a whole lot more sense story-wise, imbuing the third act showdown with Caesar with a personal dimension that is sorely lacking in the finished film. Also of note is how this telling of *Battle* concludes. While the film closes on the crying statue of Caesar, leaving it to audiences to puzzle out whether they're tears of joy at humans and apes breaking the cycle of violence, or tears of sadness at the immutability of fate, the comic is far less subtle, implying quite strongly that in the end, it's always violence that wins out.

Battle for the Planet of the Apes concludes in issue #28, and it couldn't have wrapped up at a better time, as the magazine itself lasted for only one more issue before making like the rest of the franchise and quietly fading away. While the Marvel series had begun to run out of steam at the end, there's no denying that the publisher had an impressive run with its *Apes* book. By not being chained to a particular release date, the creators were able to go deep and wide in a way that we've rarely seen before or since with comics based on film properties, and could retell the stories with as free a hand as the license allowed, often making changes that actually improved the stories.

It's worth noting that *another* set of *Planet of the Apes* movie adaptations hit store shelves right in the middle of the Marvel run. These were the Power Records comics that came packed with a mini-LP to give kiddie audiences a visual and aural experience that was as close to the real thing as fans could get in those far-off days before the existence of iPhones and Netflix in your pocket. Credited to Arvid Knudsen & Associates, the Power Records stories breeze through four of the five films (they skipped over *Conquest*, presumably because of its darker story, though I'm not sure how *Beneath*, with the world literally blowing up at the end, passes muster by that measure) in twenty-one page chunks. Despite the relative brevity of these stories, they have some truly lovely artwork (still no likenesses, though, and the portrayal of Doctor Hasslein is even more wildly off the mark than Marvel's version).[10]

Ulysse Mérou, Nova, and their son Sirius escape to Earth, unaware it has become ape-controlled as well, in *A Majmok Bolygója*, which adapts Pierre Boulle's *Monkey Planet* (1981).

Following the cancellation of the animated *Return to the Planet of the Apes* in 1975, things would lie fallow for much of the next decade-and-change. In fact, the only comic to emerge during that span[11] was a Hungarian adaptation of Pierre Boulle's original novel, *Monkey Planet*, published in 1981 and featuring lush illustrations by Ernő Zórád.[12] This telling straddles the comic book and novel formats, alternating sequential art with long stretches of prose. Although this hybrid book makes for a neat little curiosity, it hardly filled the void for expectant fans who had, by that time, gone far too long without satisfying their *Apes* addiction (and who probably had no idea it existed outside of Hungary).

In fact, it wouldn't be until the late 1980s, when rumblings first began of a new flick in development at 20th Century Fox, that the license gained renewed

[10] A more in-depth look at the Power Records *Apes* run appears elsewhere in this volume.

[11] Other than a trio of British hardcover annuals, a set of children's filmstrips, and seven Spanish-language comics, discussed elsewhere in this book.

[12] Scans of Zórád's adaptation, including English translations, are available at Hunter's *Planet of the Apes* Archive (pota.goatley.com/hungarian.html).

currency. This was when the Malibu line launched, which was nice, but if you were following developments on the film front, the project's long journey through development hell – morphing from sequel to remake to reboot to, finally, "re-imagining" – was absolutely excruciating (a feeling that increased exponentially once fans actually got to see the finished product).

It's hard to encompass the feeling of soaring anticipation coupled with immediate, crushing disappointment that many viewers likely felt when they beheld the 2001 *Planet of the Apes*, directed by Tim Burton and starring Mark Wahlberg. And while the distance of time has made it more apparent what an obvious misstep the project ended up being for the franchise, that certainly wasn't the studio's hope at the time. Unlike the first *Apes* movie in 1968, which sold itself largely on the combined credibility of Pierre Boulle and Chuck Heston, *Apes* redux came loaded for bear with a vast coterie of tie-ins and merchandise.

On the forefront of these was a line of comic books from Dark Horse Comics, which had already built up a successful working relationship with Fox via its longtime stewardship of the *Aliens* and *Predator* licenses. While the Dark Horse line included several sequel stories, the centerpiece of its run was a 48-page adaptation of the film itself. Now, in the thirteen years since its theatrical run, *Apes* redux has been subjected to all manner of commentary and criticism. Whether one decries the failed attempts to evoke the original film or the failed attempts to differentiate from it – not to mention the total lack of character development, narrative logic, or explanation regarding that head-scratcher of an ending – there's no shortage of flaws to point out. But in the interests of brevity, I'll abstain from diving into that particular rabbit hole here.

Rather, I'll say simply that, given the hot mess that is the script by Wiliam Broyles, Lawrence Konner, and Mark Rosenthal, writer Scott Allie and artist Davide Fabbri probably deserve some kind of a prize for even attempting to tackle that source material. However, unlike the way in which Doug Moench finessed the medium to turn even mediocre *Apes* movies into worthwhile comic stories for Marvel, *Apes* 2001 is done no favors when its two-hour runtime is forced into a scant forty-eight pages, in the process helping the story lose what little semblance of cohesion it might have once had.

Indeed, some of the decisions that Allie (or, more likely, Twentieth Century Fox) made insofar as what to cut and what to keep are downright baffling. In the movie proper, we get a scant few minutes of exposition and character background about our leading man, USAF pilot Leo Davidson (Wahlberg), before his spacecraft falls through a time warp and lands him smack-dab in the middle of an ape-on-human hunt on an alien planet. The comic manages to chop out even that perfunctory bit of pipe-laying. Instead, in a pointed inversion of the methodical, slow-burn approach of the original film and its adaptations, our very first intro to Davidson and the ape world's status quo happens all at once, as the hunt begins.

Perhaps the most curious creative choice of all is in how the comic treats the remake's big twist ending, with Davidson returning to Earth only to find that it, too, has become a planet of apes in the interim. More specifically, the comic simply deletes that entire coda, instead coming to a close as Davidson's spacecraft takes off, leaving the monkey planet behind. Now, from a marketing standpoint, I can see how this makes a little bit of sense, given that the producers presumably wanted to preserve the timey-wimey twists (if you'll permit me to mix my sci-fi metaphors) of the ending for the theater (where audiences could *pay* before scratching their heads and swearing at the screen).

Including this scene in a comic book that was already on stands for a few weeks before the film's release would have tipped their hand – but leaving it out entirely makes the Burton film feel even more pointless an endeavor than it already was. A definite misfire, this. As it turns out, the world of the "re-imagined" *Planet of the Apes* was merely a brief interlude rather than a permanent transition. Dark Horse's ongoing series, following up on the film's events, didn't last very long despite its high quality, and once it became clear that no sequel was forthcoming, the licensing swung back in the direction of its classic configuration.

However, while the franchise itself has been revitalized of late, thanks to the box office success of *Rise of the Planet of the Apes* and *Dawn of the Planet of the Apes*, and while current licensee BOOM! Studios has put out various titles tying in with both the rebooted and classic movie series, neither of the new films has received a comic book adaptation (only prequels and sequels), nor do any appear to be on the horizon. On one level, this isn't altogether surprising. In an age when new films are available for digital streaming within weeks of their debuts, the need for a comic book substitute for a movie experience is a conceit that the medium may simply have evolved beyond. And, hey, if there's any series for which the notion of evolution is especially fitting, it's this one.

Madhouse of Ideas: Marvel Terrorizes the Planet of the Apes

by Sam Agro

Ape Fever

I had exhausted every option. My friend Daniel had a driver's license, but couldn't get the loan of his father's car. My mom was too exhausted from working at the family dry-cleaning business, and my dad looked at me like I'd completely lost my mind. I even tried groveling to my Uncle Ray, who was bunking at our house for the summer. (He wasn't my favorite relative, but a car is a car is a car.) His response was something like, "*Five* monkey flicks in a row? Are you crazy?"

My final prospect confounded, I slunk away to sob quietly to myself. I opened the latest edition of *The Tillsonburg News* and stared wistfully at the advertisement for the Skylark Drive-In Theatre. There was the ad, printed in stark black and white, mocking me... taunting me:

"20th Century Fox Wants *You* To... GO APE!"

A gorilla pointed out at me in the classic "Uncle Sam Wants You" pose. (I was certain if I pinned the ad to the wall, the ape's finger would follow me around the room.) Clearly, it was my sacred duty to attend this dusk-till-dawn ape extravaganza, yet there I was with no driver's license, no car, and no hope.

At this stage of my life – age fourteen, to be precise – I was in the grip of a very profound Ape Fever. The virus had been with me since *Planet of the Apes* first hit theatres in 1968, though at eight years old, I had been far too young to gain admission. I collected the Topps bubble-gum cards, however, which were bundled five to a pack along with a crumbly, paper-thin slab of bubble gum. I had no clue what the film was really about, but I imagined possible scenarios based on the vague clues afforded me in the captions on the backs of the cards. Since I had only collected about half of the 66 cards issued, I was way off.

My Ape Fever remained a low-grade infection until 1973, when CBS *finally* aired *Planet of the Apes* on network television. It was everything I'd hoped it would be and more. The mild infection bloomed into a livid, chimp-shaped rash, and I've been suffering from incurable primate mania ever since.

I didn't see all five *Apes* movies at the Skylark Drive-In that night, but other outlets for my simian addiction soon became available. One was the *Planet of the Apes* TV series.

The other was a comic book.

A comic magazine, actually, printed in black and white, and adorned with stunning, full-color cover paintings that would have compelled any *POTA* fanatic to trample an entire tea party of little old ladies underfoot to procure them. This magazine became as important to me as the movies themselves, and holds an honored place in my comic book collection.

Make Mine Marvel

By the time Marvel released its *Planet of the Apes* magazine, I was already a huge comics fan. I read a few DC books, like *Batman* and *Swamp Thing,* but I was, unquestionably, a "Marvel Guy."

The premiere issue of Marvel's *Planet of the Apes* magazine was loaded with features. There was an original *Apes* storyline under the name "Terror on the Planet of the Apes," as well as several articles about the movies, including an interview with screenwriter Rod Serling, and a backup comic series adapting the original movie. It was all wrapped in a stunning painting by pulp stalwart Bob Larkin. For someone in the grip of Ape Fever, this was manna from heaven. I had to forgo a couple of my usual comics purchases to manage the hefty $1.00 price tag, but it was worth the sacrifice.

I was already a big fan of artist Mike Ploog by then, as I'd been following his work on *Werewolf By Night*, *Ghost Rider*, and *Monster of Frankenstein*. Writer Doug Moench was a new addition to the Marvel bullpen, and though "Terror" was the first of his stories I had ever read, it wouldn't be the last. I became a huge fan of his long runs on *Master of Kung Fu* and *Batman*, to name just a few.

Their original storyline, "Terror on the Planet of the Apes," picked up some time after the events of *Battle for the Planet of the Apes* and its book-end sequences of the Lawgiver narrating the tale.

Inequality on the Planet of the Apes

Issue #1's story – broken up into two chapters, "The Lawgiver" and "Fugitives on the Planet of the Apes" – grabbed me immediately. It opened with a page featuring a human and an ape, Jason and Alexander, who were best friends. This was something entirely different from the original *Apes* film series, and it worked beautifully. The difference in social status between them was made immediately apparent by the contrast between Jason's animal-skin loincloth and Alex's simian-styled suit.

In the town square, the Lawgiver advocates peace and harmony amongst apes and humans, announcing that he is leaving on some matter of grave importance. He puts Brother Xavier, an incompetent member of his cabinet, in charge, leaving the community in a state of instability, and setting the stage for impending chaos.

The two friends part ways, and Alexander goes home to find that his father has been beaten for being too friendly with humans. Elsewhere, Jason's parents are brutally murdered by mysterious, hood-wearing gorillas, and their cabin is burned to the ground.

This skewed reflection of the inequalities between African-Americans and white people in North America was still relevant when "Terror" hit stands. The Civil Rights Act had been passed a decade prior, but real change was slow in coming. By making a human family the focus of the gorilla gang's violent attack, Moench ensured that a middle-class white kid like me could easily imagine a world in which I, too, could be treated as a second-class citizen.

In an evocative reference to the Ku Klux Klan, the Ape Supremacists hide behind hoods. All this was nicely in step with the themes of inter-species inequality explored in both *Conquest* and *Battle*.

Mike Ploog's depiction of the attack on Jason's parents is frightening. Rendering the scene in heavy inks and gray markers lends the scene a noirish quality. Jason discovers the destruction and chases impotently after the horse-riding gorilla culprits, falling farther and farther behind until collapsing from exhaustion.

I was moved, saddened, and worn out... and this was only the first chapter.

The inequality and intolerance depicted in this first storyline served as a thematic spine throughout the series, and I believe the book was at its best when it focused on those issues. An informal interview I conducted with Moench (which is referenced often throughout the rest of this essay) confirmed that Gerry Conway plotted the initial story arc. Working from Conway's outline, Moench effectively established these prevailing themes.

Few of the main characters are without some sort of prejudice, and Jason himself is quick to give in to hate. Alex is more even-tempered and thoughtful — but, then, his parents are still alive.

The dialogue is a little heavy-handed, but this is typical of 1970s Marvel. Still riding high on the success of Stan Lee's bombastic scripting style, the publisher had little reason to tinker with the formula. As the story progressed, however, Moench introduced several broad fantasy elements that were more in keeping with Marvel's house style than with *Planet of the Apes*. He also detoured into the psychedelic, which a few other Marvel titles were exploring, such as Steve Englehart's and Frank Brunner's trippy *Dr. Strange* stories, and Jim Starlin's *Warlock* series.

After the deaths of Jason's parents, things happen fast. We learn that the leader of the gorilla terrorists is none other than the city's "peace officer," Brutus. Alex and Jason track down the killers, but are quickly captured and bear witness as the gorilla murders his own wife, Zena, after she threatens to reveal Brutus's secret terrorist activities. The peace officer frames Jason for the crime, then throws him in jail.

Outraged by Zena's murder, the ape population protests and the weak-kneed Xavier sentences Jason to death. Luckily for Jason, Alex shows up at the jail to help him escape. The desperate duo become fugitives from justice, and their lives will never be the same.

Party in the Forbidden Zone

In issue #2 (again split into two chapters, "The Forbidden Zone of Forgotten Horrors" and "Lick the Sky Crimson"), Ploog's rich renderings instantly dragged me into the action. Jason and Alexander make good their escape from Ape City, but Alex convinces Jason to return. Brutus callously turns his wife's funeral into a soapbox for anti-human propaganda. Infuriated, Jason publicly accuses the gorilla of murder, and our heroes are on the run again. They flee into the

Forbidden Zone, in the hope of locating the wayward Lawgiver and clearing their names.

Here, Moench takes advantage of the Forbidden Zone's unknown nature to introduce some interesting new elements.

For a zone that's supposedly, you know, *forbidden*, the place is positively *teeming* with life. Alex and Jason encounter an indefinable species of peaceful, shaggy ape-men and, of course, mutants (which differ from those in *Beneath the Planet of the Apes*). They're diminutive, mush-faced cyborgs wielding laser pistols, and each are named after a different letter of the English alphabet. These mutant-drones, as they're known, emerge from their underground caverns and kidnap one of the shaggy ape-men. Jason and Alex follow them and discover an enormous smelting operation, wherein the scrap metal of Earth's past glory is melted down to construct shiny new war machines.

The classic *Apes* themes of subjugation and war are apparent here, but perhaps the most subversive element of this issue is the intimation that the shaggy ape-men might be the result of ape-human interbreeding. The closest any of the films came to interspecies hanky-panky were both the tentative kiss Taylor and Zira shared in the original film and the few additional chaste smooches in *Escape*. The idea that humans and apes mated borders on bestiality, which seems pretty ballsy for 1974.[13] At first, I wondered why Moench would depict this species as mute and dim-witted, but as the tale unfolded, I realized this was intended to give the ape-men a quality of unspoiled innocence. This choice would resonate meaningfully later on in the story.

At the end of the issue, the mutants discover Jason and Alex, then chase them from the underground caves until they run smack into a pack of gorillas.

Talk about your cliffhanger endings!

I spent the next two months in a state of perpetual suspense, hopelessly re-reading the second issue, praying that new pages would magically appear.

Brains of Unusual Size

After what seemed like an eternity, I was finally rewarded with a new issue.

---

[13] Early makeup tests were conducted to feature an ape-human hybrid child in *Beneath*, but that character never appeared on screen, likely because it was deemed too controversial.

While issue #3's story ("Spawn of the Mutant Pits" and "The Abomination Arena") was good, the artwork was a slight disappointment. Buckling under deadline pressures, Ploog handed over the inking chores to Marvel bullpen stalwart Frank Chiaramonte. Now, don't get me wrong, Chiaramonte was a solid inker who frequently inked Ploog's work on other titles. However, he had a much lighter touch with the gray tones, and this airier approach paled against Ploog's moody shadows.

My disappointment was fleeting, however, because the narrative soon whisked me away into the shattered wasteland of the Forbidden Zone.

Trapped between mutants and gorillas, Jason and Alexander retreat back into the underground tunnels and let the two gangs fight it out amongst themselves. The duo skirmishes with some mutant-drones before commandeering a mutant subway car.

One great thing about the book is the fact that Moench keeps things light during the action. Alex and Jason often banter back and forth, Hope and Crosby style, in the midst of mortal peril. The scene in the underground transport is quite funny, as they struggle with the unfamiliar controls and bypass a startled mutant waiting on a platform. Finally, the two are captured and hauled away for imminent execution.

Back at Ape City, Brutus intimidates Xavier into rubber-stamping permission to chase the fugitives into the Forbidden Zone (which seems increasingly less forbidden with each passing chapter).

In the caverns of the mutants, Alex and Jason are brought before the Inheritors, the brains of the outfit. And when I say "brains," I mean that *literally*: the Inheritors are *giant brains*, pulsing obscenely in huge glass tanks. They call themselves the Supreme Gestalt Commanders, and to the eyes of a fourteen-year-old comics fan like me, there was nothing in the world cooler than these enormous brains.[14]

The leader of the brains, Supreme Commander Be-One, has four grey-matter underlings. Among them are Be-Two, who sounds like a snarky '30s gangster, and Be-Three, an effete personality who speaks in rhyme. The

---

[14] In our interview, Doug Moench swore on a stack of Sacred Scrolls that he didn't get the idea for the Inheritors from *Star Trek*'s "The Gamesters of Triskelion" episode in which the titular gamesters are three living brains inside of a glass bubble. In fact, he claimed to have never seen an entire episode of the original *Trek* series. In truth, Marvel's jarred brains differ greatly from those in "Gamesters," in both size and personality.

Inheritors sentence Alexander and Jason to battle in an arena for the amusement of the mutant-drones. Our heroes begrudgingly team up with Warko, a captured gorilla soldier, and battle a trio of strange, mutated animals. Together, they break free of the arena and flee.

Jason and Alexander meet the Inheritors in "Terror on the Planet of the Apes" from Marvel's *Planet of the Apes* magazine #3 (Dec 1974).

As they rush through the maze of cave tunnels, the escapees finally locate the object of their search, the Lawgiver. The quartet jumps aboard a futuristic jump-jet and takes off.

Unfortunately, Warko pulls a gun on the elder orangutan and orders them to fly the machine to Brutus's encampment.

A Slow Boat to Ape City

Sadly, the art in issue #4 suffers further. Chiaramonte made a good start inking over Ploog's pencils, but deadline doom resulted in sketchier renderings in the final pages. The story, however – "A Riverboat Named *Simian*" and "Gunpowder Julius" – is a good one, heralding the arrival of two of the series' most beloved characters.

Inside the mutant flying machine from last issue, Warko threatens the Lawgiver, but Jason throws a control switch and they crash to the ground. Our heroes abandon the unconscious gorilla, but another mutant animal almost immediately attacks them. (You can't relax for a second in Moench's Forbidden Zone. The place is seething with malevolent life, and it all wants to kill you.)

Meanwhile, Brutus takes a meeting with the Gestalt Commanders, and we learn they are in cahoots. Brutus requests, and receives, an army of mutant-drones and war machines to bring back the Lawgiver.

Jason, Alex, and the Lawgiver come across some of the shaggy hybrid creatures drinking from a river, and deem it potable. When the Lawgiver is swept away in the undercurrent, Alexander, Jason, and even one of the shaggy bipeds jump into the river after him. All four are swept down into an underground cave, through a tunnel, and out over a waterfall.

Say what you will about the Marvel style of comics from the period. They may have been a little verbose and overblown, but they were never boring. Though a newcomer, Moench had the style down pat, and the action never let up for very long.

Having made it through the waterfall, the group floats downstream, right into the lives of Gunpowder Julius and Steely Dan. I immediately fell in love with these two irascible river men. According to Moench, both characters owe a debt to Ploog's gruff but loveable personality. As interpreted by Moench, this appears to be equal parts Daniel Boone and Yosemite Sam. The braggy Gunpowder Julius (named after a serendipitous Orange Julius stand) welcomes the refugees into his little riverside shantytown, where apes and humans appear to live in perfect harmony.

The backwoods *patois* is a little forced in places, but charming for all of that, and it supports Moench's appealing undertone of humor.

One of the most interesting aspects of Moench's take on the source material is the idea that myriad communities populate the world beyond Ape City. Many of these communities show the planet's four dominant species living in perfect harmony. Moench takes a quasi-anthropological approach to the world outside the confines of Ape City, and the result is fascinating.

There is also a nice reflection of Jason's friendship with Alexander in that of Gunpowder and Steely Dan. These grizzled riverboat companions, one human and one ape, may greet each other with homespun insults and punches to the face, but they're the best of friends. Luckily, they have none of the divisive baggage of injustice that looms between Jason and Alex.

At about this time, Brutus shows up with the mutant-drones and their war machines, but the gang has prepared for their arrival. Gunpowder Julius lives up to his name, igniting a trench full of explosive black powder under the encroaching mutant machines. Our heroes rush in for a hand-to-hand finale.

Brutus gets a bead on Jason, but accidentally shoots Shaggy instead. The gorilla then flees, and the somber defenders bury the shambling ape-man under a marker reading: "Shaggy: A part of both, he knew innocence best."

Dancing Girls and Giant Frogs

With an issue off and a little time to catch up, Mike Ploog comes back stronger than ever in issue #6, with "Malagueña Beyond a Forbidden Zone." He adopts a new style, drawing the final images in pencil. These tonal renderings allow the paper's texture to show through, highlighting the rustic quality of his work. This gives the story a gritty, almost dreamlike, atmosphere. While I feel the work Ploog did in the first two issues is amongst his best during this era, this soft, chiaroscuro approach is *even better*. Personally, I consider the drawing in issues six and eight the finest art of the entire "Terror" storyline.

After burying Shaggy, the somber comrades board the riverboat *Simian* and head upriver toward Ape City. In typical Moench fashion, it's not long before giant river-frogs try to make a meal of the crew. During the battle, Jason saves the Lawgiver from one of the slimy brutes.

Soaked and tired, the crew is drawn toward a fire burning on the shore, and sneak up on the scene. They discover another integrated community: a band of gypsy revelers, including Malagueña, a fetching young woman about Jason's age. Jason and his companions are discovered, and there's a tense standoff for a moment, until Mama Lena, the gypsy band's matriarch, invites them into the camp for a night of feasting.

The gypsies are one of Moench's more clichéd conventions, but it serves the purpose of introducing a love interest for Jason. This is a welcome respite to the testosterone-soaked adventure presented thus far.

Back in Ape City, tensions rise between apes and humans, and wishy-washy Xavier is floundering. At the same time, the giant brains receive an update regarding Brutus's failed attack on the riverboat town, and order the mutant-drones to keep an eye on the troublesome gorilla.

In the gypsy camp, Malagueña flirts with Jason, raising the ire of her simian suitor, Grimaldi (yet *another* example of interspecies dalliances). Grimaldi and Jason exchange blows until Mama Lena decrees they should settle the matter with a knife fight.

It's a knife fight *to the death*, of course.

Honestly, is there any other *kind*?

Though knife fights have been done *ad nauseum*, Ploog creates a very strong choreography for the sequence. The battle is nearly balletic in execution, yet maintains a fierce energy. Jason loses his blade, and Grimaldi gets the upper hand, but assistance comes from Malagueña, who offers Jason a new dagger.

Grimaldi risks it all on a single toss of his blade, but fails. He kneels in submission and awaits the death stroke, but Jason wavers, unable to kill in cold blood.

Suddenly, Grimaldi bursts into flame in front of the shocked ensemble. Brutus has fragged the poor ape with a mutant-drone laser, and our heroes are once again in his power.

The Bigger They Are

Ploog crafts more lovely pencil renderings for issue #8's installment, "The Planet Inheritors," and Moench obliges with a rousing tale worthy of the artwork.

Things look bad for Jason and his friends, as Brutus, Warko, and several mush-faced mutants have the drop on them. While the Lawgiver and Jason trade barbs with the former peace officer, Steely Dan sneaks up on the roof of a gypsy trailer and surprises the bad guys. Jason and Alex burst into action with their new friends Julius and Dan, as well as a midget gypsy chimp named Trippo and his knife-hurling human comrade, Saraband. In moments, the tide has turned. Jason points a mutant laser at Brutus's head, ready to take his revenge, but entreaties from the Lawgiver and Malagueña stay his hand.

What comes next is my second-favorite part of the story. Gunpowder Julius battles Brutus in a knock-down, drag-out fistfight, and it's a real beaut. There's none of the balletic feeling of the Jason-Grimaldi knife battle here, just brutal ape-on-ape combat. There's punching, ear gnawing, attempted head stomping, and you better believe that Brutus goes *down*.

Finally, the gang heads back out onto the river, Brutus in tow, toward Ape City, with Malagueña, Saraband, and little Trippo joining them for the adventure. Julius decides they should drop in on the Inheritors for a visit, and the gang sneaks in and locates a nice little ledge from which to spy. When the Inheritors reveal their intention to kill humans and apes alike, Brutus shouts his disapproval. Moments later, mutant-drones pour in from all sides.

Now comes my *favorite* part of the story. In the desperate battle that ensues, Saraband is fatally wounded. Not one to go down easily, the gypsy grabs a mutant in each arm, leaps off the ledge, and smashes into the glass sphere of one of the giant brains. The pulsing gray matter within slops out onto the floor, and several mutant-drones, psychically linked to their brainy masters, fall dormant. With half of the mutants incapacitated, the rebel band is able to make their escape from the Gestalt Commanders' cave labyrinth.

It seems that only the noble or innocent pay the ultimate price in "Terror on the Planet of the Apes." I was truly disappointed when Saraband died. The character had style, and giving us a little more time to get to know him would have made his sacrifice even more poignant. I have often speculated on what other adventures the knife-thrower might have had before that fateful day.

Little Trippo, too, is saddened at his companion's untimely demise, and the solemn crew once again must continue down the river without one of their friends.

Home Sweet Home

With issue #11, "When the Lawgiver Returns," the *Planet of the Apes* magazine was slightly altered. There were fewer pages, and the perfect binding was swapped out for the traditional saddle stitch. This change was adopted across Marvel's magazine line, including *Savage Sword of Conan*, and one presumes it was a move primarily intended to mitigate overhead costs. Whether sales were suffering at this point, I don't know.

Ploog is back to his ink and wash style in this issue, and it's great, but I really missed the lovely pencil renderings.

Unfortunately for the overwhelmed Xavier, the spreading violence of Ape City arrives on his doorstep, when Brutus's hooded gorillas attack and murder the orangutan. Later, two apes discover Xavier's body lashed to a pole in the town square and leap to the conclusion that humans have done the deed. After all, ape *never* kills ape... right?

The riverboat *Simian* deposits our heroes on the shore, and Jason, Alexander, Malagueña, and the Lawgiver begin their journey home. As they emerge from the Forbidden Zone, they encounter a makeshift wagon train of human refugees, who are getting out of Dodge while the getting is good. The Lawgiver coaxes the humans to return home, and they arrive just in time to interrupt a violent showdown. The Lawgiver chastises his wayward people, apes and humans alike, and sends them all to bed without any supper.

Elsewhere, Brutus gets wind of the Lawgiver's plan to give a speech and prepares for a showdown. He interrupts the sermon, calling for the Lawgiver's ouster. However, in a nicely played moment, Jason steps in to protect the elderly ape. When Alex joins him, so do several others from both species.

With an ape-human shield between him and the Lawgiver, Brutus plays his final card, ordering his gorilla guerillas to attack the square. The Lawgiver is wounded by a crossbow bolt, and Alex spirits him away from the scene. Jason doesn't join them. Instead, he attacks one of the gorilla horsemen and commandeers his mount.

In one of the most rousing sequences of the series, beautifully written and illustrated, Jason rides down Brutus, pulls him from his horse, and vents all of his festering rage. The youth hammers down the bigger, stronger Brutus with nothing but his fists and righteous fury, and is prepared to beat him to death. Once again, though, the Lawgiver steps in to stop him.

Instead of executing Brutus, or sentencing him to a trial for his crimes, the Lawgiver sees fit to settle for exile. Jason goes *ballistic,* and it's hard to disagree with his indignation. Brutus is a mad dog and a heartless killer. The crazy bastard should be eliminated with extreme prejudice, simian law be damned.

Jason renounces the Lawgiver and turns away. When Alex tries to stop him, he gets a good punch to the muzzle for his efforts. Jason stalks off into the forest, finished with Ape City and its denizens.

For me, this issue is the pinnacle of the series.

Even though it leaves some plot points dangling, this initial story arc is the most grounded in the lore of the first five films. The subsequent story arc seems to lose some of its *Apes* thematic focus, and becomes a more eccentric, fanciful affair.

During our brief interview, Moench described the atmosphere in the Marvel offices as quite *laissez-faire*. He said he would bump into Roy Thomas or Archie Goodwin in the bullpen, and they'd ask, "What do you have in mind for the next couple issues of *Planet of the Apes?*" He'd respond with a few ideas, and they'd answer, "Sounds good, go ahead." Apparently, 20th Century Fox also signed off on the stories.

However, I sometimes wonder if it might have been better if someone had intervened just a *little*. Perhaps some gentle editorial guidance here and there might have steered Moench's prolific idea machine a little closer to the spirit of the original films.

This isn't to say I don't love some of what comes next, though, because some of it is truly wonderful.

Progressing and Regressing

Accompanying this tonal change, the "Terror" saga underwent a slight name change as of issue #13. In "The Magick-Man's Last Gasp Purple Light Show," the first installment of the newly rechristened "Terror on the Planet of the Apes, Phase 2," Jason finds Brutus's treehouse encampment abandoned and heads off to find him. In Ape City, Alex and Malagueña confab with the Lawgiver and decide to go out in search of their friend.

At this point, Jason encounters one of the most interesting characters in the book, the cocky, eccentric – and deeply deluded – wayfarer, Lightning Smith ("Lightsmith" for short). Lightsmith is an archaeologist of sorts, sifting through the detritus of the past and humorously misinterpreting its uses. This idea is one of Moench's cleverest, and it affords him the opportunity for some light comedy and pointed satire.

Lightsmith and his mute companion, a gibbon named Gilbert, travel about in a steam-driven cabin called the Wonder Wagon, filled to the brim with 20th-century junk. Lightsmith's assertion that televisions were holy shrines, with which enlightened people would spend hours communicating with their god, electricity, is wonderfully ironic.

Alex and Malagueña, meanwhile, are beset by strange, shadowy figures in the forest.

Lightsmith tells Jason of his search for the fabled *Psychedrome*, which he believes holds all the knowledge of mankind. The wayfarer's ambition is to restore the planet to its former glory by bringing back "progress."

The next day, Jason, Lightsmith, and Gilbert cross paths with the Assisimians, a savage tribe of apes. By coincidence, these are the same creatures who kidnapped Alexander and Malagueña, whom they intend to burn at the stake. To effect their rescue, Lightsmith puts on a little show with some carefully staged fireworks. They free Alex and Malagueña from their stakes, but before they can make good their exit, the truculent Assisimian leader, Maguanus, sees through the deception. With the help of a machine gun, the group makes a slim getaway.

The reunion is not completely amicable, but a grudging truce is forged. By the end of the day, the party reaches Lightsmith's home.

And what a home it is!

In a stroke of genius that calls back to the final Statue of Liberty reveal in the first *Planet of the Apes* film, Lightsmith lives inside Mount Rushmore. The choice is, at once, in perfect keeping with the source material, and deliciously satirical.

The other presidents, like the Great Sphinx, have all lost their noses, but Lincoln's schnozzola is holding fast and concealing many secrets.

Lightsmith points the way to Abraham Lincoln's nose at Mount Rushmore. (*Planet of the Apes Magazine* #14, Nov 1975).

Up the Nose-Tube to Monkey-Junk

One of the few instances of editorial tinkering on the "Terror" strip appears in the title for issue #14. The original title, "Up the Nose-Tube to Monkey-Junk," was deemed unacceptable since the term "junk" had drug-culture associations. "Up the Nose-Tube to Monkey-Trash" thus became the published title of the piece, but Moench felt, and I agree, that the phrase "Monkey-Junk" has a certain charming assonance.

In this issue, Mike Ploog's usually outstanding work shows a few signs of strain. The layouts are more pedestrian compared to some of his earlier work, and the rendering lacks some of its usual verve. This is Ploog's last issue as the sole artist, and while his work is still solid, there are telltale signs of fatigue.

In spite of this, Ploog still comes through beautifully when presenting one of my favorite jokes of the series. As Lightsmith leads his new friends up into Lincoln's nose, a little dust gets in Alexander's face, causing him to sneeze. The action cuts outside Honest Abe's head, and the former president seems to sneeze along with him. Moench includes a lot of other comical little ironies in this issue as well. For instance, Lightsmith theorizes that the faces on Mt. Rushmore must represent terrible criminals, committed to stone as cautionary examples for future generations.

Lincoln's head contains some sort of presidential bunker[15] in which Lightsmith pontificates on his personal white whale, the mysterious *Psychedrome*. Simultaneously, Brutus infiltrates the caves of the Inheritors and blackmails the giant brains into lending him a platoon of war machines.

Back up Lincoln's nose, our heroes get drunk and listen to old tapes outlining how the *Psychedrome* is used for brainwashing. Lightsmith, of course, misinterprets "brainwashing" as a wonderful process by which his mind could be cleansed of all ignorance. While the group thinks, and drinks, Maguanus and his Assisimians sneak up on Gilbert in the Wonder Wagon. Gilbert slingshots a warning message up into Lincoln's head, and our heroes retaliate by dropping hand grenades out of the monument's eye-holes.

Finally, Jason and his friends parachute out of the giant sculpture and make good their escape in the Wonder Wagon, only to discover Brutus and his army headed in the same direction.

Shock the Monkey

Starting with issue #19, the strip changed quite dramatically, as Moench took the saga into some pretty unconventional places. I don't feel that the next three chapters ("Demons of the *Psychedrome*," "Society of the *Psychedrome*," and "Messiah of Monkey-Demons," in issues 19, 20, and 23, respectively) were

---

[15] This is one of the only aspects of Moench's *Apes* work ever referenced post-Marvel, as Mr. Comics's *Revolution on the Planet of the Apes* miniseries cited this very bunker years later.

of lower quality than those that came before. However, this particular arc *was* the least in keeping with the spirit of the original films.

It's a fun ride, but it just ain't *Apes.*

Moench tosses a lot of new stuff into the mix that seems out of place. He's got flying monkey-demons wielding swords... he's got multi-eyed aliens called "Keepers"... he's got a giant spaceship interior with no up or down (the *Psychedrome*) that looks like M.C. Escher's worst nightmare. It's more like something out of an Edgar Rice Burroughs acid dream than *Planet of the Apes.*

Now, all of that is forgivable, up to a point, if the story is interesting, and it is. Unfortunately, there's one thing for which I can't really let Moench off the hook.

He messes with the fundamental premise of the *Apes* mythos.

He suggests that it wasn't mankind who sent the bombs flying and destroyed the world, but rather these multi-ocular aliens, the Keepers.

Come again?

The entire run of the *Apes* movies hinges on the idea that mankind was the architect of its own destruction. That is the fulcrum upon which the premise turns. Refuting that one sad truth ruins the irony of Taylor's discovery that he's trapped in Earth's future. It reduces the anti-human sentiments of the Sacred Scrolls to mere inter-species racism, rather than justified vigilance. It steals away the significance of the mutants' worship of the doomsday bomb, and the zeal with which Hasslein pursues Cornelius's and Zira's intelligent offspring.

It's kind of a big deal.

I was surprised Moench wasn't called on this plot point, but he confirmed, in our interview, that he had almost zero tinkering from Marvel editorial or from 20th Century Fox. It seems Fox treated the comics adaptations with a sort of benign neglect. Perhaps they were too focused on the higher-profile television show to pay much attention.

So, there it is: my least favorite thing about the series. I stand by it, but I don't want to get bogged down by it.

The next big change on the strip was the artist. Though Mike Ploog was co-credited with Tom Sutton on the art for issue #19, it seems like Ploog's contribution took the form of breakdowns rather than full pencils. Though, perhaps, Sutton's bold, multi-media technique simply overpowered Ploog's pencils. In any case, the appearance on the page was much more Sutton than Ploog.

Sutton is a worthy successor. His gloomy finishes share some of the noir qualities that Ploog brought to the series, only more so. His rendering has an almost misanthropic quality that perfectly reflects the dark violence of this arc, and there are few artists from that time who could better represent the trippier tone. Does your story include flying monkey-demons? Bizarre, vertiginous cityscapes? Mind-controlling aliens with multiple, squirming eye-stalks? If so, Tom Sutton is, *unquestionably*, the right man for the job. In his hands, even the humdrum adobe of Ape City becomes a wild structure, like a mutant mushroom that sprang directly out of the earth in the form of a building to lure unsuspecting creatures inside for slow digestion.

In this arc, Moench makes one major concession to the *Apes* movies: the inclusion of *big-ass bombs*. While Jason and Alexander deal with flying monkey-demons and Lightsmith gets the thorough brainwashing he longed for, Brutus uncovers a huge stockpile of large, shiny, phallic-looking atomic bombs. The gorilla has no idea what kind of destructive power he's dealing with, but Mutant-Drone Bee does, and he reports Brutus's activities to the Inheritors. Bee is instructed to destroy the missiles before they can fly.

Back at Ape City, the Lawgiver has a heart attack and his doctors stand around conferring and being generally useless.

While Brutus deals with the implacable Maguanus, Jason and Alexander rescue the zombie-like, platitude-spouting Lightsmith, hook back up with Gilbert and Malagueña, and catch the 3:15 subway car out of town.

Finally, Drone Bee fires his blaster at the stockpile of bombs and explodes himself, the *Psychedrome*, and the mountain surrounding it all.

Whew! No one can ever say that Doug Moench scrimped on the action.

Bloody Vikings

With issue #26, "North Lands," Tom Sutton left the "Terror" strip and focused solely on Moench's "Future History Chronicles" seagoing storyline, in which the duo created some of the wildest comics ever created by man. As a result, journeyman Marvel penciler Herb Trimpe was parachuted in to continue the series. Now, it should be said that I am a *huge* fan of Herb's work on the Hulk and other Marvel characters. An issue of *The Incredible Hulk*, drawn by Herb, was what got me collecting comics in the first place.

That being said, his style isn't ideal for this property.

Herb's light-hearted, Kirby-esque approach is terrific on superhero stuff, but on the moodier *Apes* property, it feels a bit naïve, especially when compared to Ploog's lush, atmospheric renderings or Sutton's sinister, psychedelic illuminations.

Matching an artist to a property is like casting the right actor for the lead in a movie. Even great actors are sometimes wrong for certain roles. While Trimpe is a consummate pro, he is simply not the right actor for the part.

With the wild imagery of the *Psychedrome* behind him, Moench returns to his anthropological explorations. The hypnotized Lightsmith wanders off and, while searching for him, the gang encounters a clan of apey Vikings. Elsewhere, Lightsmith is whisked away to a nearby cave dwelling by the intimidating Snow-Shamblers, yet another hybrid species who, like the Shaggies, actually turn out to be rather gentle creatures.[16]

Moench was beginning to recycle some of his themes at this point, offering us another of his cultural variants and the senseless death of another innocent. Perhaps he was tiring of the strip, or was more engaged by the "Future History Chronicles" concept, but this final story arc (which included "Apes of Iron" in #27 and "Revolt of the Gorilloids" in #28) seemed a bit less sincere than the earlier ones.

Even with Maguanus and half of the Assisimians dead, the tribe keeps getting all up in everybody's grill. Brutus advances his war machines on Ape City, while the Inheritors lurk sullenly in their tunnels. Meanwhile, a new enemy – the mysterious Makers – send their ape-cyborg Gorrilloids out into the world to destroy everything, but Brutus makes them his allies. While the Lawgiver lingers at death's door, a gorilla named Moravius is appointed as the city's new peace officer, and Alex and Jason reunite with Gunpowder and Dan.

Ultimately, everybody converges at Ape City for a giant battle. Brutus pounds the city with his war machines, then sends in the Gorilloids to mop up. With victory at hand, the cyborg gorilla warriors go berserk and Brutus is forced to blast them. With his greatest allies now dead, Brutus's victory is short-lived, and by story's end, he finds himself arrested by his successor, Moravius.

I didn't have the presence of mind to ask Mr. Moench about this when we spoke, but I got the feeling the addition of the Gorrilloids was an attempt to give Trimpe something to draw that better suited his style. The half-gorilla, half-machine cyborgs fit Herb's superhero style quite nicely.

---

[16] Between the Shaggies, the Snow-Shamblers, and Malagueña's tryst with Grimaldi, as well as an ape-human named Mordecai in issue #5's "Evolution's Nightmare," the Marvel series sure seems to have fostered a bestiality fixation.

Brutus leads a Gorilloid attack on Ape City in *Planet of the Apes* magazine #28 (Jan 1977).

And that's where the story ends.

Or does it?

What Might Have Been

In an unpublished episode, "To Meet the Makers,"[17] Moench dreamed up a brilliant plot twist that could have been the series' most powerful moment.

Oh, there's an enormous, super-duper, albino Gorrilloid called Smashore, who has a grenade launcher in his metallic head, death-ray eyeballs, and laser-shooting fingertips. This would have been cool, no doubt, and it would have been right up Herb's alley.

However, even better than this would have been the deaths of Alexander's parents at the hands of hooded vigilantes. Not Brutus's gorilla KKK, as Jason first assumes, but *humans* adopting the same terrorist tactics. This sardonic twist would have brought the story full-circle, and even Alexander's tolerance may have broken under the strain.

But, alas, it was not to be.

The "Terror" storyline – and, shortly thereafter, Marvel's *Planet of the Apes* magazine – passed into oblivion. My Ape Fever subsided, percolating quietly in my bloodstream, and reemerging occasionally as some other comic, movie, or book triggered a flare-up.

Finally, in 2006, I actually had the opportunity to work on a *Planet of the Apes* comic. With an editorial assist from veteran comics artisan Ty Templeton, I wrote, penciled, and inked my own five-page back-up story for the above-noted *Revolution on the Planet of the Apes*, with colors by Bernie Mireault. That story, titled "Paternal Instinct," as well as an unpublished tale ("The Believer"), led me to connect with Rich Handley and *Simian Scrolls* co-editor John Roche, and eventually to my being included in this very book.

It's fate. It's destiny. It's the dad-blasted simian circle of life.

My Ape Fever has finally paid off.

---

[17] Archived online, with Moench's permission, at pota.goatley.com

Hope Springs Eternal: Tom and Doug's Marvelous Adventures

by John Roche

Part I: Freedom's Reaver – Tom Sutton's Voyage of Imagination Across the Planet of the Apes

Artist Tom Sutton's work on Marvel's *Planet of the Apes* series is nothing short of staggering. That is in no way meant to diminish the huge role that writer Doug Moench played in scripting the self-contained ape epic that is "Future History Chronicles," a saga for which Moench crafted sumptuous scripts that soared and swam, challenged and surprised, shocked and stirred. Doug, in fact, scripted every single one of the fifty-seven published chapters comprising Marvel's twenty-nine-issue *Apes* run. However, "Future History Chronicles" is, in purely artistic terms, Sutton's enduring legacy to *Apes* fans – and also, arguably, one of the best-kept secrets in comics.

Sutton drew two chapters of "Terror on the Planet of the Apes," as well as inking and finishing one Mike Ploog-pencilled chapter. But "Future History Chronicles" was his *Apes* opus, an astonishing explosion of art and imagination that gave wings to Moench's scripts and created an artistic masterpiece of the black-and-white genre. Indeed, many view "Future History Chronicles" as Sutton's artistic pinnacle. What, then, was this five- (very nearly six-) issue saga that gave Sutton full rein to cut loose and inhabit the Planet of the Apes?

The city-ship *Hydromeda* from "Future History Chronicles" in Marvel's *Planet of the Apes* magazine #12 (Sep 1975)

Making its debut in *POTA* issue 12 is "Future History Chronicles I," (the Roman numeral for each chapter denoting a series that is, indeed, a true chronicle). The first chapter, subtitled "City of Nomads," sets the storyline's tone, exploring the themes of ape-human antagonism and reconciliation in a violent, brutal world. Initially, our three main heroes are all human: the heroic, cerebral Alaric, a leader and warrior; his beautiful, tempestuous warrior wife, Reena; and Alaric's grizzled, bitter, ape-hating friend, Starkor. In chapter two, we meet Graymalkyn, a noble gorilla who is, in many ways, a simian analog to Alaric – an intellectual warrior equally exercised by the possibilities of peaceful co-existence between ape and man.

The interaction between these four characters becomes a lens through which we can observe the events unfolding around them. A wonderful narrative device that Moench utilized was to add the comments of an omnipresent thinker to the narrative. Ostensibly, these are Alaric's thoughts, though they feel, at times, to be the sad commentary of a higher power.

"City of Nomads" (the saga rejoiced in featuring mind-igniting titles for every chapter, each delineated in Sutton's keynote sensuous style) sees our human hero cast trapped on a huge ocean-traversing city-ship called the

Hydromeda, illustrated in a simply magnificent, incredibly detailed, two-page spread, the mere sight of which gives readers due notice that this will be a voyage like no other. The *Hydromeda* is powered by *Ben-Hur*-like human galley slaves, chained to their oars in desperate straits. Above decks, at some stage in the past, a civil war had waged between the ape species, with gorillas – the former slaves – dominating one half of the ship, and orangutans and chimpanzees occupying the other half from the opposite side of a devastated barrier area. Alaric, who had earlier escaped from the lower decks, prowls the ship as a crossbow-wielding assassin, fomenting a war between the rival ape species by dint of selected assassinations and sabotage.

Sutton, with his background in horror comics at both Charlton and Warren, was born to illustrate this series. From the early double-page spread of the *Hydromeda* in all of its grotesque, warped, majestic horror, the art leads us into a world created and given life by Sutton's pencil. Furniture, door fittings, clothing – all have a style and look unique to Sutton's approach to *Planet of the Apes*. The artist delivers a black-and-white masterwork that sears its way into the mind. Close inspection of the work reveals the consummate care he took with this art – there are panels that bear tell-tale signs of having been cut out and replaced, no doubt because Sutton strived for perfection.

The finale to chapter one sees our heroes escaping via one of *Hydromeda*'s boats, with the city-ship itself sinking in an orgy of devastation behind them. Had this been the only installment, it would have stood as a very satisfying one-shot. However, thankfully, Sutton and Moench were intent on creating a saga of epic proportions.

"Future History Chronicles II," published in issue 15, brings us "Dreamer in Emerald Silence." This story riffs on Jules Verne's *Twenty Thousand Leagues Under the Sea*, with the role of Captain Nemo being played by the ape named Ambrosia, who commands a living submarine called *Dwelleron*. The tale opens with another quite breathtaking double-page spread by Sutton, depicting the construction of a full-scale sailing ship by Alaric's human followers, who are marooned on an island. The work is being supervised by a group of likewise stranded gorilla ship-builders, who have designed the ship and have caused considerable resentment amongst the human workers, who despise taking orders from the apes.

The lead architect is Graymalkyn, a deep-thinking gorilla who is fiercely loyal to his species but is also fascinated by the possibilities of inter-species cooperation that Alaric has proposed. The counterpoint to both Alaric and

Graymalkyn is the human Starkor, who, despising apes and the tyranny they represent, cannot forget his past enslavement as a galley slave. Once the ship is launched, Starkor unfurls a flag depicting a shattered chain, naming the vessel *Freedom Reaver*, much to the protest of the gorilla contingent.

Sutton's draughtsmanship on this chapter is astonishing. The depiction of the *Freedom Reaver* in the opening double splash could have been lifted from a shipyard blueprint. The artistic style has a subtle difference, with a thinner, brighter line suiting the undersea vistas through which we are later taken. When our three male heroes come to be trapped on *Dwelleron*, he gives full vent to his imagination, illustrating all manner of exotic sea life and equipment.

As our trio escape the living habitat, Dwelleron and its master, Ambrosia, are destroyed in an explosion (a visit from Alaric rarely results in a happy ending for his hosts), and our heroes' voyage continues.

The next chapter, "Future History Chronicles III: Graveyard of Lost Cities," in issue 17, reveals yet another art style by Sutton, who seems to have rejoiced in the scope that the saga offered for experimentation and innovation. The artist had discovered that certain overlay art materials would "take ink" if an etching style was adopted to cut in, and this chapter, produced on oversized boards, is a riot of sharp, angular lines and shadows. The overall artistic style perfectly complements the gloomy, dank environment in which our three heroes (all male – Reena gets left behind again!) find themselves, having boarded a ship within a federation of combined city-ships. Their quest had been inspired by Graymalkyn's knowledge of a legendary place where apes and humans were said to live in peace and mutual cooperation. Inspired by this dream, Alaric had set out to find and explore such a place for himself.

Sutton's double-page splash, featuring a federation of rotting hulks that were once independent city-ships, is a macabre riot of faded glories and sad decay – a metaphor for the world our heroes inhabit. When an encounter with brigands leaves Starkor badly wounded, Alaric and Graymalkyn seek help in the form of Grimstark, an eccentric orangutan scientist living in isolation in a tower looming over the middle of the city-ship conglomeration. Grimstark has been dubbed "the Crazy One" by the less enlightened inhabitants below, who fear the "demon magic" powering his mechanical flying machines. The hermit's literally elevated knowledge and vision of a better future embodies Alaric's aspirations for the world – but, true to form, the denizens of that world end up attacking the dream, shooting Grimstark down with arrows as he attempts to fly to the coast aboard one of his machines.

Our trio make their escape, and Sutton casually throws in a final panel that is simply wonderful, depicting a ghostly image of Grimstark smiling down upon the *Freedom Reaver*, his face emerging from a cloud that gently blends into swirling seagulls, with no clear demarcation between the blend of cloud, birds, and orangutan. The overall effect is uplifting, encouraging us to heed Alaric's closing advice to follow dreams "wherever they may lead." Sutton clearly understood Alaric's worldview.

Issue 24's "Future History Chronicles IV: The Shadows of Haunted *Cathedraulus*" continues the trend of spine-tingling titles. Yet again, Reena is left behind as the males explore a mysterious, glowing hulk of a ship that they have encountered. However, she has had enough of such sexism by now and punches Alaric, receiving a slap back for her troubles and vowing that Alaric will never again touch her.

It is in this mood that Alaric boards *Cathedraulus*, with Starkor and Graymalkyn bickering beside him. Their continuing banter is a wonderful piece of writing by Moench, allowing us to steadily follow the development of a grudging mutual respect and, ultimately, the forging of a feisty friendship. For now, however, Graymalkyn and Starkor remain at odds, resulting in the trio splitting up to explore the cavernous ship. Alone, Graymalkyn discovers a terrified ape fugitive fleeing from evil humans, whilst Alaric and Starkor encounter an equally terrified human fugitive elsewhere aboard the vessel, attempting to escape from apes whom he fears will eat him.

Sutton arguably hits his peak during parallel sequences depicting two conflicting versions of history as related by the two fugitives. One account portrays humans as the victims of ape aggression, while the other shows simians as the object of human savagery. It transpires that *Cathedraulus* is run by a group of mutants – both ape and human – who rejoice in the title of "Missionaries of the Glorious New Order Born of Old Sin." The cult comprises survivors of a nuclear holocaust, who offer sacrifices of humans and apes alike to a monolith representing a nuclear missile.

Alaric and his cohorts discover that the next batch of sacrifices will be the recently captured *Freedom Reaver* crew. A savage battle liberates their comrades, after which a frosty reunion between Reena and Alaric is interrupted by the realization that a prolonged stay aboard *Cathedraulus* will leave them mutated as well. "Future History Chronicles IV" is the first in the saga, therefore, to end on a cliffhanger.

"The Shadows of Haunted *Cathedraulus*" is an incredibly dense and thoughtful installment that explores the entire history and philosophy of the simian world that Moench and Sutton have created. Sutton pulls out all the stops this time, from the floating cathedral's Gothic design to the frankly astonishing depictions of the differing versions of history as seen from the ape and human points of view. It is apparent that the illustrator was utterly enthused by the opportunities Moench was offering up with his wonderful scripts, and that boundaries were clearly being pushed – one panel depicts apes cooking and eating humans, and the original artwork for that page contains a margin note from Doug to editor Archie Goodwin, telling him that he will re-write the panel if it is deemed too graphic.

The panel stayed in, untouched.

Every panel is redolent of mood, shadow, horror, and shock – what, at first glance, seems simply to be an arch suddenly emerges, upon closer inspection, as a huge winged demon ape sculpture holding glowing globes in each claw. Sutton gives us a clinging, grabbing, scratching world of talons, tendrils, swords, and blood that is simultaneously claustrophobic and enervating. And yet, at the same time, one sequence contains a Lawgiver-esque figure, clearly anchoring this saga within the overall *Apes* mythology.

The fifth chapter appeared in issue 29, Marvel's final installment of *Planet of the Apes* magazine. "Future History Chronicles V: To Race the Death-Winds" (another amazing title!) opens where the previous chapter left off. Leaving behind a dubious crew, Alaric, Reena, Starkor, and Graymalkyn succeed in escaping *Cathedraulus* aboard an airship crewed by mutants seeking to flee the carnage inflicted by the *Freedom Reaver*'s crew (the *Reaver* itself having been sunk by the mutants). The airship (which has a balloon strangely reminiscent of the Campaign for Nuclear Disarmament's logo) takes our group up into dark, radioactive storm clouds, where they encounter a flotilla of massive, zeppelin-like airships that shoot our heroes down.

Much to the surprise of our heroes, however, they and their burning gondola land not in the sea, but on the springy undergrowth of a jungle. Unfortunately, the ensuing forest fire draws the attention of some of the jungle's inhabitants: namely, apes astride giant frogs, who identify themselves as Her Majesty's Cannibal Corps. These primitive simians are armed with spears, yet speak in impeccable Queen's English. Appalled by the destruction that the fire is causing to their jungle, they suspect our heroes are minions of a mysterious group known as the Industrialists.

A huge fight results in the capture of our intrepid four, with Graymalkyn, as an ape, eventually granted his liberty. The three humans, meanwhile, are slated for execution, but are spared that fate thanks to a last-minute save by Graymalkyn, giving Starkor cause to regret the abuse he had earlier heaped upon the gorilla. The group escapes deep into the jungle, where they stumble upon a huge walled city with a giant airship moored at each corner. Alaric ponders whether the occupants of the mysterious city might possibly be peaceful after all, but Graymalkyn doubts this, and a very mournful, powerful, final panel contains Alaric's closing thought: "Yes... I suppose I do, too...."

This typically thoughtful and downbeat *Apes* ending leaves just enough room for ambiguity. Is it just Alaric thinking this, alone? Or does the omnipresent voice speak for us all?

And there, for decades, the saga rested, leaving our quartet pondering the past and the future, a final-page splash depicting the protagonists framed by jungle, staring wistfully at a vaguely threatening edifice in the gloomy distance. Together, Sutton and Moench had chronicled a future history populated by vast city-ships, living submarines, mutants, vast airships, giant frogs, and sword-wielding heroes, giving us a whole new mythology occupying a unique corner of *Apes* and comics history.

But then, some wonderful detective work and perseverance from Rich Handley unearthed what none could have dared hope might exist – Doug Moench's script to an unpublished chapter, titled "Future History Chronicles VI: The Captive of the Canals." Handley obtained the script from Moench himself, who graciously provided this and two other tales lost to time once Marvel dropped the *Apes* license. The script[18] contains a note from Doug, saying "TOM: Hubris or not, I think this is the most imaginative one yet." The tragedy that Sutton never got the opportunity to illustrate this chapter is further heightened by Moench's note that whilst the script observes a "new policy" of page-by-page breakdowns, the "freedom is still there" for Sutton to "expand."

Chapter six would have revealed the city briefly viewed at the end of issue 29 to be called Sexxtann (a deliberate riff on oil company Exxon), home to the Industrialists, who occupy a six-sided, forty-two-level walled city filled with canals and surrounding an enclosed area of jungle. There, our four heroes encounter a giant mutated ape known as "Her Midgitsy," and learn that the

---

[18] Which can be read online at Hunter Goatley's *Planet of the Apes* Archive (pota.goatley.com/moench.html)

monstrous gorilla (in an homage to *King Kong*) was once the queen of the Cannibal Corps, before being captured and enduring evil experimentation at the hands of Sexxtann's malevolent occupants. The chapter ends with the city's partial destruction and Her Midgitsy's demise, with our heroes escaping to explore more of this strange, new land.

Sadly, Doug Moench's glorious descriptions of Sexxtann and its denizens will never see life in the shape of Tom Sutton's pencil. But perhaps that is being just a bit greedy, for the five chapters that Sutton and Moench gave us with "Future History Chronicles" are an astonishing example of just how great the comics medium can be when writer and artist are both enthused and inspire each other.

"Future History Chronicles" is a tremendous chapter of *Planet of the Apes* mythology, filled with hope for a better future for all species. However, the saga also deserves to be recognized as a major contribution to the legacy of comics. If Sutton needed a single signature series by which to be remembered, "Future History Chronicles" reveals the truly magnificent, innovative, experimental genius of one of the greatest exponents of the black-and-white comic craft that the industry has ever seen. That Sutton was given the freedom to express his genius on the *Planet of the Apes* was just the perfect creative storm.

Part II: Lost and Found – Doug Moench's Ephemera of the Apes

Of course, not all of Marvel's *Apes* stories were sweeping, ongoing sagas in the fashion of "Terror on the Planet of the Apes" or "Future History Chronicles." The nature of Marvel's *Planet of the Apes* magazine was such that one half was devoted to a movie adaptation, with the other half presenting an original tale. As such, there was ample opportunity for one-off, self-contained stories. Three tales were conceived as one-offs, though as we shall see, one went on to become more than that.

Issue 5 contained, as a lead feature, the story "Evolution's Nightmare." This Moench-penned tale was illustrated by a relative newcomer, Ed Hannigan, with inking by the legendary Jim Mooney. Whilst Hannigan went on to have a solid career in comics, this early story was, as editor Don McGregor explained in the opening editorial, the artist's "first full-length feature," and the aforementioned editorial noted that the art was created over-sized, on huge boards.

"Evolution's Nightmare" introduces us to a planet at war, with opposing armies of apes and humans facing each other across a barren wilderness, armed to the teeth with medieval-style armor and weapons.

A blood-drenched slaughter ensues, lasting until all but two of the participants are dead. The survivors are a human, Jovan, who has lost the use of his legs, and a gorilla, Solomon, whose arms no longer function. After the two enemies initially attempt to continue the battle, sense prevails and both grudgingly accept that they must cooperate to survive. By lashing Jovan to Solomon's back, the pair succeed – in Tony Curtis/Sidney Poitier style, à la *The Defiant Ones* – in crossing the wilderness.

The duo encounter a cave-dwelling hermit called Mordecai, who describes himself as "neither human nor ape... I am both..."[19] Mordecai nurses the two injured warriors back to health, only for Jovan and Solomon to immediately renew their battle.

Only after both fall exhausted does a glimmer of reason filter through to man and ape, and they accept Mordecai's injunction to visit an ancient city within the Forbidden Zone, so that they can truly appreciate where violence leads. Upon their arrival at the city, we see that it is a ruined San Francisco, populated by factions of warring mutant apes and mutant humans. Caught up in a battle between these two mutated forces, Jovan and Solomon are slain, with the battle continuing to rage around them.

"Evolution's Nightmare" is a modest success – the message that violence begets violence clearly defines the tale. The art, however, is patchy. It starts in fine, detailed graphic style, but slowly worsens until the final few pages are clearly rushed and not on par with what has come before (the editorial hints at deadline issues). As always, however, Moench delivers a crisp, thought-provoking script that stands as an interesting morality tale well in tune with the *Apes* saga's philosophical ethos. Still, it is perhaps telling that the deaths of our two main protagonists by story's end are not particularly jarring – nor, indeed, even upsetting. A downbeat ending to an *Apes* tale is by no means unusual!

The next new, original saga made its debut in issue 9. Originally conceived as a standalone, self-contained annual issue, "Kingdom on an Island of the Apes" was split into five chapters in the regular book (two in issue 9 and three in issue 10), as the move to a monthly schedule, necessitated by the magazine's popularity, created deadline issues. One interesting side effect of this splitting was that a new linking page to introduce the tenth issue was required, which

---

[19] Oddly, Moench includes a variety of ape-human hybrids throughout his tales, implying that despite all of the mutual hatred, a good deal of cross-species mating was taking place on the Planet of the Apes.

Planet of the Apes magazine #5 (Feb 1975) presents "Evolution's Nightmare," in which only by lashing Jovan to Solomon's back can the injured pair survive their trek across the wilderness.

was supplied by a young Walter Simonson (and which, in turn, became the cover to an Australian reprint).

"Kingdom on an Island of the Apes" introduces us to the wonderful Derek Zane, a talented scientist in the "present day" (1974) who believes he has discovered what happened to George Taylor's crew (oddly, he never makes mention of John Brent's follow-up mission… apparently, they don't matter to him as much), and has built a time machine prototype to rescue them. Rejected by NASA[20] and his girlfriend Michelle, Zane decides to put his theory to the test and launches himself into a future world dominated by talking apes.

Moench lets us get to know and like Zane – aided, no doubt, by the greater space available to him as a result of the originally planned book-length annual format. The tale begins with Michelle dumping Zane for being a dreamer, and his getting drunk to deal with the loss. After his brusque rejection by NASA, we are actually rooting for Zane and have a context to his life before we encounter a single ape. It's an important backstory that makes him one of the most "human" humans we ever encounter in any *Apes* story. Moench succeeds in creating a three-dimensional hero, and Zane immediately feels like a character we would like to meet again.

The art on this hidden gem of a story was provided by the wonderful Rico Rival, a superlative black-and-white artist, with faces full of expression and action driven by a tremendous kinetic energy. Whilst Rival would later illustrate the adaptation of *Escape from the Planet of the Apes*, as well as a single chapter of "Quest for the Planet of the Apes,"[21] "Kingdom" is arguably his finest *POTA* hour. Rival's unique style wonderfully serves the saga's mood and tone. Whilst Marvel's *Apes* run was truly blessed with a stable of great artists, such as Mike Ploog, George Tuska, Alfredo Alcala, and Herb Trimpe, Rico Rival is rarely mentioned – but absolutely deserves to be bracketed in such company.

Over the course of "Kingdom"'s five segments, ("The Trip" and "Arrival" in issue 9, followed by "The City," "The Island Out of Time," and "Battle" in issue 10), Zane escapes from Ape City, having made an enemy of Gorodon, a one-eyed, bloodthirsty gorilla who is aware that Zane witnessed his savage murder of a rival orangutan. Zane's escape takes him to an island called Avedon, where

---

[20] Although Zane meets with a NASA representative, Taylor's crew worked for another agency, ANSA, in the first film. The reason for the change is unknown, though it happens again in the television series.

[21] Discussed elsewhere in this volume

the mixed ape and human inhabitants affect Arthurian styles of speech and dress, including castles and jousts, and even an orangutan King Arthur.

The chimp known as Robin Hood must save Derek Zane from the clutches of General Gorodon (*Planet of the Apes* magazine #21, Jun 1976).

A climactic battle sees Gorodon and his army defeated in an assault upon the castle (named Camelot, naturally), with Zane slaying Gorodon and marrying the beautiful Lady Andrea (who is gorgeously depicted by Rival).

There is a hint, in the final panel, that Zane plans to "do a little exploring in the future," with a view toward finding Taylor and the others (Brent can apparently fend for himself). A year later, in issue 21, we finally get to revisit Zane's exploits. This follow-up, titled "Beast on the Planet of the Apes," sees a conscience-tormented Zane choosing to leave his comfortable life (and comfortable wife) on Avedon and renew his effort to locate the missing astronauts (a goal rendered somewhat problematic by the fact that Moench set the story in 3975, three years before Taylor's vessel would even arrive in that timeframe).

Teaming up with a chimpanzee called Robin Hood, Zane infiltrates Ape City and frees a female human who has the rudiments of speech, only for her to be shot during their escape from the gorilla General Zaynor. Giving her a proper burial, Derek posthumously christens her "Hope," etching that name (a metaphor for Zane's motivation) on her gravestone. Whilst Robin elects to return to Avedon, Zane resolves to keep looking for the lost spacemen, and we get a clear feeling that there is more to come from Derek Zane in future issues.

One joy of "Beast" is the debut of Herb Trimpe as an *Apes* artist. Trimpe's powerful graphic style is wonderfully suited to any action scene involving a gorilla, and his superior storytelling ability is nowhere better displayed than on the second page of this story, in which Trimpe, in only a single page, smoothly summarizes the entirety of the book-length earlier chapters. Trimpe would go on to illustrate three installments of "Terror" (providing two covers for the U.K. reprinting of that saga) and, in General Zaynor, give us another mean-eyed gorilla bad guy.

Sadly, Marvel's *Apes* run concluded with issue 29, apparently not due to sales but rather to political issues regarding licensing. Once again, Handley's efforts have produced a wondrous sequel in the form of Moench's unpublished script to "Journey to the Planet of the Apes" (renamed from its early title, "Return to the Planet of the Apes," to avoid confusion regarding the same-name animated TV series). Had the series continued, "Journey" would have been the opening chapter in a planned ongoing mega-saga featuring further Zane-y exploits.

The script was due to be illustrated by Val Mayerik (Moench gives directions to Val by name in the script, in fact) and possibly inked by Ernie Chan – issue 20 of Marvel's contemporary *Ka-zar* series was drawn and inked by Mayerik and Chan, respectively, and mentioned that the team of Moench and Mayerik would be moving on to an ongoing *Planet of the Apes* series. Issue 117 of Britain's *Planet of the Apes and Dracula Lives* features an out-of-context cover created by Mayerik and Chan, and might possibly have been a re-purposed splash from the planned "Journey" series, given that its action (two astronauts being restrained before a simian council) actually makes sense in light of this lost storyline's narrative.

"Journey" would have marked a major change of pace for Marvel's *Apes* efforts, and the foundations were to be laid for a lengthy run (Moench even refers to taking the cast into space at some later stage!), with subplots involving additional visitors from the past ("tempunauts" Mara Winston and Jackson Brock) utilizing Zane's so-called Temporal Displacement Module technology, which NASA, following Zane's disappearance, apparently decided could work after all. The story would have featured a domed "modern" city populated by apes, as well as a new chimp sidekick named Faron.

In the script's end notes, Moench sets out a plethora of future plot ideas and directions, and ambitiously even mentions an issue 60. With the *Planet of the Apes* movie adaptations completed, Marvel needed something to fill up those allotted pages, and it appears that the author had enough in mind to fill at least the next 31 chapters, astonishing though that may seem. Clearly, Marvel's cancelation of its *Apes* magazine was a sudden decision, as there were several stories in the pipeline, including not only "Journey" and "Future History Chronicles VI," but also another planned chapter of "Terror" ("To Meet the Makers," discussed elsewhere in this book) and a one-off tale, the curious "Forbidden Zone Prime."[22]

"Forbidden Zone Prime" is a teasing mystery of a story, because we have only fragments of finished art available, and no full script. We do have the opening few pages, which thankfully provide the title and suggest a very downbeat tone, in that all three main characters are said to be doomed to die – we are looking at "their lives in their final moments," Moench explains in an early caption. But since only ten pages in total have been unearthed to date,[23] readers are left to guess the overall plot. However, the pages that we do have open with a gorilla general, Zandor, exploring an area of the Forbidden Zone that appears to be a devastated Washington, D.C. Back at the simian settlement, we appear to be in an era set just after *Battle for the Planet of the Apes*, as the apes are constructing a ground-level Ape City of familiar style, whilst the humans are slaves still retaining the rudiments of speech.

The other pages that have been found are substantially taken up with a philosophical argument between husband and wife chimps, the whimsical poet Julius and his more grounded architect wife Viraga. In addition, we witness Julius's recuse and befriending of a beautiful human female, Steena, whom Zandor was about to attack for getting in the way of his horse.

---

[22] Also available at Goatley's *Planet of the Apes* site
[23] Thanks to private collector Edward Haber, who allowed Handley to photograph his original comic art pages and share them with other fans

It is reasonable to suppose that this story may have been a full book-length tale spanning forty pages or more, as the final page we have is number 16, and yet the plot is far from being resolved within another few pages. At present, we can only surmise that Julius, Steena, and Zandor somehow end up in Forbidden Zone Prime, where they apparently trigger some sort of device or encounter some form of danger that claims them all, as predicted in the opening captions. Hopefully, additional pages will one day surface to fill in these gaps.

Another mystery is the identity of the strip's artist. We don't have credit details since that page is among those still missing. One page of original art has the name Sonny Trinidad written on it, but Trinidad (via his children, Norman and Cherry Trinidad) denied having drawn the tale when Handley asked them about it, and whilst it is in no way a definitive attribution, certain art elements are similar to Dino Castrillo's earlier *Apes* work on the *Battle* adaptation. The Filipino school of artists could sometimes confuse matters by having various illustrators help out and chip in, à la the "Crusty Bunkers" style.[24] Without more evidence, though, a definite identification of the artist remains elusive.

One glorious postscript to "Forbidden Zone Prime" is that the Bob Larkin cover intended for that issue, depicting a magnificent gorilla general in front of a ruined U.S. capitol, has also surfaced – and it's a beauty. The fact that the art for "Forbidden Zone Prime" is finished, washed and lettered, coupled with the fact that a finished cover seems to have been ready strongly suggests that, despite the pain of the magazine's cancellation all those decades ago, we now at least have the rudiments, cover and all, of what may well have been issue 30, containing a book-length original tale.

Alas, we may never know what other tales might have sprung from the fertile imagination of Doug Moench in continuing his one-man scribing of Marvel's *Planet of the Apes*. What he has already given us is a wonderful bounty indeed. However, hope springs eternal, and it may be that additional "Prime" pages will appear, or even that the Moench Vault will creak open again one day to reveal more wonders. Inspired by the likes of Alaric, Zane, Mordecai, and Julius, we can but dream.

---

[24] The "Crusty Bunkers" was a collective pseudonym used by a group of inkers associated with Continuity Studios (the New York City-based art and design agency of Dick Giordano and Neal Adams) from 1972 to 1977.

Quest for the Apeslayer: Embracing the Best and Worst in Media Tie-in Fiction

by Joe Bongiorno

Only a few decades past, media tie-ins were derided as low-quality hack work, commissioned by big media properties or their licensees to cash in on the popularity of a film, television series, or novel. The fantasy and science fiction genres were still struggling to be perceived as meriting serious literary consideration, and the comic book medium was altogether dismissed as the fodder of kids and overgrown adolescent males. Suffice it to say that science fiction and fantasy media tie-ins told in the comic-book medium were essentially the lowest of the low. Even highly regarded franchises, such as *Planet of the Apes*, were typically overlooked in the four-color realm, despite the laudable efforts of Marvel Comics.

Today, not only are science fiction and fantasy widely recognized as legitimate artistic endeavors, but the once-lowly comic book has become a welcome member of the literary and cinematic community. According to sci-fi author and commentator Charlie Jane Anders, "they're a growing slice of the publishing world – and at this point, you can't claim it's impossible to create meaningful, groundbreaking work in the tie-in novel world."[1] Even fan fiction has begun to ascend the summit of acceptability, maintains writer Aja Romano.[2]

Media tie-in fiction is now proudly written by prominent authors – some Pulitzer-prize-winning ones – many of whom confess that they view their freelance writing for an established universe as having just as much weight and significance as their original material, even acknowledging that more fans will likely read the former than the latter. Karen Traviss, author of the renowned *Star Wars: Republic Commando* series, noted that writing media tie-in fiction for the *Star Wars* universe was the best thing that ever happened to her because it liberated her as a writer: "The restrictions of media tie-ins force you to grow. Ironically, the freedom lies in having to think outside your *own* creative box. Canon and continuity make you work harder to find work-rounds: necessity really is the mother of invention."[3] This sea-change in the attitude of authors, publishers, and editors toward media tie-in fiction comes on the heels of the reading fan-base who have long regarded it as meaningful, entertaining, and artistically satisfying as the initial work that spawned it – and sometimes even better. More than one reviewer has noted, for instance, that both Mr. Comics' *Revolution on the Planet of the Apes* and BOOM! Studios' recent *POTA* efforts equal – or even surpass – the quality of the film sequels themselves.

That is not to say that every new media tie-in novel and comic book is award-worthy, nor that works from decades past were of lower quality. But with the once-broad excoriation of the field by and large now faded, one can better analyze each work based on its own merits, or lack thereof, to determine whether it functions as a work of art, as a successful continuation of the elements developed in the original work, or even as kitsch.

Media tie-ins predominantly comprise sequels, prequels, and spinoffs, usually involving the main cast of characters and environments first encountered in the original works. Some are set in the universe of the original,

---

[1] "Untold Adventures: The Complete History of Tie-In Novels":
http://io9.com/5411331/untold-adventures-the-complete-history-of-tie-in-novels
[2] "I'm done explaining why fanfic is okay":
http://bookshop.livejournal.com/1044495.html
[3] *Star Wars on Trial*, by David Brin and Matthew Woodring Stover; Dallas, TX: Benbella Books, 2006.

but otherwise do not involve the main cast, setting, and/or time-period.[4] *Planet of the Apes* tie-in comics have encompassed both types of stories.

It is a considerable challenge to write in an established universe, and is often a more difficult task than writing an original story. Traviss noted that "it takes a new level of discipline to fit canon and remain true to the shared universe while keeping the original style and approach that the publisher signed you for in the first place. And writing characters who've been known and loved by fans… is genuinely challenging. I know. I've just done it, and it's hard. When I want a rest, I go back to my own series. It's far easier in skill terms."[5]

Aside from having to meet the factors that go into any well-crafted literary work, an effective story set in an established universe must generally meet four additional criteria:

1. If utilizing the same characters as the original work or works, it must capture the personalities and voices of those characters. And that, in itself, is not enough. As people in the real world are not static entities, neither are realistic fictional characters, and the author must find ways to extrapolate from what is known of each character being utilized, in order to plumb deeper, as well as to explore other facets of their personalities that may not have yet been revealed – and he or she must do so within the boundaries established by the property holder, which keeps the author from going too far beyond the larger context of the story without prior approval. This usually, though not always, precludes death, disfigurement, and other major changes to the characters.

2. It must adhere to the thematic elements of the original work, exploring and deepening those themes that are organic to the story being told, and, where relevant, adding new ancillary themes. For this to function effectively, the overall story must, of course, be well-written, or else the themes will fail to resonate, either on account of their presentation in a heavy-handed manner, or because they get lost in a sloppy, ineffectual narrative.

3. It must be faithful to the history of what came before, yet accessible to new readers who have never read anything in the series. The former is often sacrificed by those authors and editors who don't care to research the world of the series, but more often than not, it is abandoned by corporate franchise holders who undervalue the loyal readership, deeming it more profitable to use funding to market to newer, younger readers

---

[4] Additionally, other media tie-ins comprise parodies, alternate universes, and re-imaginings, but for the purpose of this essay, I am focusing strictly on fiction set in the same universe as that of the original work.

[5] *Star Wars On Trial*, by David Brin and Matthew Woodring Stover. Dallas, TX: Benbella Books, 2006.

than to maintain a long-running continuity that requires experienced editors to oversee. This almost always damages the series and franchise, as it alienates and embitters long-time readers. Rebooting continuity is anti-literary, in effect keeping the world and its characters in stasis, as it reinvents the wheel time and again.

4.   It must be tonally consistent with the original work and yet adventurous enough to step outside of it. This is the most flexible of the four criteria, but still requires a delicate balance, as new readers will want and expect more of what they liked in the original work. Catering too much to that produces a work that is derivative, as stories need to progress and expand, not merely ape (pun intended) what came before. And yet, if the work strays too far beyond the scope of the original, it risks becoming something alien and unrelated. Generally, a long-running series with a large universe and broad scope is better at allowing for new and different styles, concepts, and approaches than a smaller and narrowly focused world.

Contrary to the popular belief that authors must eliminate restrictions to achieve what they deem maximum creative freedom, constraints generate creativity, and authors who set out to meet the above criteria, overcome the challenges, and operate within boundaries often produce works of astonishing artistic merit. In examining the merits of two very different *Planet of the Apes* media tie-ins published by Marvel Comics in the 1970s, "Apeslayer"[6] and "Quest for the Planet of the Apes," it's of interest to consider whether either succeeds in meeting these criteria.

Although the *Planet of the Apes* mythos is derived from *La Planète des Singes,* the 1963 French literary work by Pierre Boulle, most *Apes* media tie-in fiction has been based around the 1968 film and its four sequels. *Planet of the Apes* is, in essence, a beast fable told in a science fiction milieu (this is particularly true of the film iterations). Examples of this genre include Aesop's Fables and the Reynard the Fox stories from antiquity, and, in modern times, Richard Adams's *Watership Down* and George Orwell's *Animal Farm*. The beast fable is largely allegorical, satirical, and/or socially critical, in that it utilizes talking animals to represent and reflect human foibles, flaws, and hypocrisies, as well as the traits that reflect our better nature. Fantasy and science fiction have long borrowed this technique, as its fantastic characters and alien species are little more than revamped talking animals. In the case of *Planet of the Apes*, Boulle merely returned the genre to its origins.

---

[6] Since Marvel never gave this saga an official title, I shall refer to it as "Apeslayer" for the purposes of this essay.

In Boulle's novel, as well as in the films and Marvel's comic book spinoff, several multifaceted themes play upon the idea of human hubris, including sharp criticisms of militarization, imperialism, cultural conditioning, slavery, the hegemony of religious and scientific dogma, and the deeming of one's inherent superiority based on a "might makes right" ideology. Humans are not only at the lower end of the social spectrum, inhabiting the place animals currently do, but are treated with the same brutality and oppression with which vast numbers of animals are currently treated in our world. This makes for a series that not only speaks to the animal-rights issue, but also looks seriously at human-rights abuses, such as racism, subjugation, and exploitation. As in our world, there exist a ruling elite who know the truth, but who choose to suppress it, along with any dissent, in order to maintain the status quo of those at the top of the hierarchy.

Somewhat competing with the series' more heady philosophical and socially conscious merits is the fact that, as film reviewer Craig J. Koban noted, *Planet of the Apes* "was one of the first films that exploited a previously untamed territory – multi-million-dollar merchandising tie-ins and targeting certain demographics – to help develop the film into a proto-blockbuster that are a dime-a-dozen during our current summer months."[7] While many credit *Star Wars* – which exploited the same demographic and created what is arguably the most successful blockbuster series to date – it is arguably the *Planet of the Apes* series that started the trend. And as noxious as film purists may find this, an unbiased analysis of its media tie-in materials reveals that two very different types of stories emerge: the oft-castigated, seemingly thoughtless knock-off done with little to no consideration for the artistic merits of the source material that preceded it, and the thoughtful, philosophically cogent work that expands on the story, characters, and themes established in the original works with perspicacity. This seemingly incongruous mixture of highbrow art and lowbrow entertainment can also be found in *Star Wars* and *Star Trek*, and in much of the media tie-ins that exist down to this day, and is the cause of the not-unreasonable claim of fans who contend that it's worth wading through the latter to arrive at the former.

---

[7] *"Planet of the Apes*: 40th Anniversary Retrospective Review":
http://www.craigerscinemacorner.com/Reviews/planet_of_the_apes.htm

Jonathan "Apeslayer" Dozer, as envisioned by Herb Trimpe and Frank Giacoia in Marvel UK's *Planet of the Apes* magazine #27 (Apr 1975).

The latter, in this case, is represented by "Apeslayer," which has been widely criticized as being among the worst *Planet of the Apes* stories ever written, with not a few making the argument that it falls into the category of being "so bad it's good," and thus worthy of kitschy amusement. In fairness to the story's authors, Gerry Conway and Roy Thomas,[8] "Apeslayer" had not been conceived or intended as a *Planet of the Apes* story at all, but rather as a Killraven tale, and was originally published as such in comic anthology *Amazing Adventures* volume 2 #18 (May 1973).

Killraven was itself a Marvel spinoff character created as a *War of the Worlds* media tie-in. How he ended up as Jonathan "Apeslayer" Dozer has much to do with the early economics of Marvel, which ran a monthly *Planet of the Apes* magazine in the United States and a weekly reprint title in the United Kingdom. Because the British *Apes* weeklies repackaged material from their U.S. counterpart, it wasn't long before Marvel UK caught up to the American series and found itself in the dilemma of having run out of existing stories to reprint. Marvel could have commissioned new stories to appear exclusively in the United Kingdom (and several years later, it did just that for its *Star Wars* weeklies, resulting in the publication of some of the great early work of Alan Moore). Or it could do what the *TV Comic* editors chose to do with their *Doctor Who* strips a few years earlier: simply take a story they'd published before, change the names, and replace a few heads. Short-lived editor Mark Hanerfield chose this approach for the *Planet of the Apes* dilemma, and thus Martians became apes and Killraven got a hair dye and became Apeslayer.

The story itself was likely deemed workable for *Planet of the Apes* due to the fact that it deals with a character overcoming the oppression of overlords in a ruined New York City sometime in the distant future. All the editor had to do, besides the cosmetic changes, was edit the text – which he did, albeit without paying enough attention to detail. The name "Killraven" was overlooked in two places, while the extraterrestrial elements of the original story were left intact in three other instances, creating a bit of confusion across the eight issues in which the saga ran (Marvel UK's *Planet of the Apes* #23-30).

Apeslayer's story begins with Jonathan Dozer as a young child escaping the predation of apes who have advanced technologically to the point at which they

---

[8] And, in later issues, Marv Wolfman and Don McGregor. Artists on the story included Neal Adams, Howard Chaykin, Frank Chiaramonte, Frank McLaughlin, Herb Trimpe, Frank Giacoia, and Yolande Pijcke.

have built tripod war machines, created mutants, and genetically engineered a species of sirens (women with the power to hypnotize men). Several human scientists have gone over to the side of the apes, aiding them in their plans to exterminate the human race and capture some for sport in gladiatorial arenas. When the boy's mother and baby brother are killed, he is captured and trained as a gladiator, at which he excels until he grows into adulthood and escapes. Finding a band of resistance fighters called the Freemen, he soon becomes their leader and gains renown fighting against their human and ape oppressors.

Dozer's exploits bring him to the attention of the so-called Generals and Ape Masters, who view him as a threat. A plan is put in motion to capture him, led by the Warlord, whom Dozer had literally disarmed years earlier. Vengeful for having had to endure a prosthetic limb, Warlord succeeds in capturing Apeslayer, and begins to experiment on him. But a female scientist, the rather coincidentally named Sandra Simian, takes a liking to the courageous man and, with the help of her mutant pet (alternately called "Grok" and "Zom," depending on the editing quality of a given panel), frees him, leading to a confrontation in the former Yankee Stadium, where Apeslayer and his Freemen prove victorious.

Putting aside the story's origins and editorial mistakes in order to examine the "Apeslayer" saga according to the four criteria listed above, we can immediately rule out the first criterion as inapplicable, since the story utilizes new characters in a different time period. Of the characters presented, they are mostly two-dimensional and bereft of verisimilitude and development.

The thematic requirements noted in the second criterion are present, touching on oppression and rebellion. Yet, because the writing is so ham-fisted and clumsy, these themes soon vanish within the tale's single-minded sphere of nonstop action and violence, which has more to do with juvenile male wish-fulfilment than it does with exploring human or social issues. This, of course, is one of the early, valid, and still-prevalent critiques of comic-book tropes.

The third criterion requires that a new work maintain a measure of continuity with what has come before in prior stories, and that proves problematic in several areas, for obvious reasons: a) the "Apeslayer" miniseries establishes an ape society that is far more advanced than those shown in the films and on television,[9] b) the presence of various mutated animals and ape-

---

[9] Though this could indicate a setting long after the events of the television series but before the first movie.

created mutants seems incongruent with the world shown on screen,[10] and c) Dozer's dialogue notes that mankind had created a self-sustaining ecology before the apes attacked. The latter appears to contradict the authoritarian regime depicted in *Conquest of the Planet of the Apes*, though it could be understood as the protagonist having attained false or incomplete information. As a result, it is unclear whether or not "Apeslayer" meets this criterion, since there is a poor connection to continuity that requires explanations not provided.

The fourth criterion involves tonality with the original works. Given its alien tripods, mutant animals, and mind-controlling sirens, "Apeslayer" would clearly appear to be atonal. Yet, the miniseries does feature talking apes, the ruins of New York City, and a bellicose, bare-chested man running around, not to mention that mind-controlling mutants feature prominently in the film *Beneath the Planet of the Apes*. In many respects, these elements could have worked in a better-written story, as Marvel's "Terror on the Planet of the Apes," Malibu Graphics' *Ape Nation* miniseries (which crosses over with the television series *Alien Nation*), and BOOM! Studios' recent *Star Trek/Planet of the Apes: The Primate Directive* crossover all deal with invading aliens. On the other hand, there are not a few fans who find the giant brain jars of "Terror," *Ape Nation*'s Tenctonese, and *Primate Directive*'s Klingons to be egregious examples of having crossed the line.

Of the four criteria, "Apeslayer" by and large fails to meet the first and third, passably meets the second, and only barely meets the fourth. Even in its original form, the story would have elevated itself had it been presented in a better-written narrative with a protagonist who wasn't a Conan clone, set in a world that didn't feel like the John Carter of Mars novels and about a dozen other comic books of the day, rather than *Planet of the Apes*. In all, it demonstrates that the experiment of redoing another story with new names and heads was a well-intentioned, desperate, and ultimately poorly realized failure. While it can be said to have kitsch value, it remains an indicator of how low Marvel regarded its own material, as well as how the industry viewed consumers. While some may point to these issues as being typical of the era, many of the problems exhibited in "Apeslayer" can be traced back to as early as 1930s pulp magazines, which – although violent, misogynistic, and targeted to prepubescent male wish-fulfilment – also included examples of great literary

---

[10] Of course, this is true of several other Marvel *Planet of the Apes* stories as well.

works. So, too, there are excellent stories that emerged from the same era that produced the "Apeslayer" saga.

The cybernetically enhanced Warlord fights for the simian Masters in *Planet of the Apes* magazine #28 (Marvel UK, May 1975).

A valid argument can be made that in the modern day of the hyper-critical fan and autocratic corporation, there is less "cheese" and chicanery, but also less abandon and experimentation. Art and entertainment, when owned by large companies, has a tendency toward homogeny, pre-determined by the strategy of marketing firms seeking to replicate what has proved successful amongst designated target groups. And yet, despite this, numerous examples within media tie-ins bear evidence of having overcome that pattern.

One example of the high quality of storytelling that emerged from the comic-book medium in the 1970s, and standing on the opposite end of the spectrum from "Apeslayer," is "Quest for the Planet of the Apes," written by Doug Moench and illustrated by Rico Rival and Alfredo Alcala. Published in issue 22 of Marvel's U.S. magazine, the story was broken down into two chapters, subtitled "Seeds of Future Deaths" and "The Keeper of Future Death."

The story begins two years after Caesar overthrew Governor Breck and his minions in *Conquest of the Planet of the Apes*, as the ape civilization led by Caesar begins to prosper on the outskirts of the former city in the aftermath of nuclear war. But beneath this hard-won peace grow the seeds of evil, as humans – including the former governor and his assistant, MacDonald – have become imprisoned and mistreated slaves, and a warmongering gorilla named Aldo threatens to usurp Caesar's power. When Caesar prevents Aldo from beating a slave, the gorilla challenges his authority, proposing that the pair go into the Forbidden City and procure something of value. Whoever brings back the "best thing," Aldo proposes, will become ruler of the apes.

Caesar agrees to the proposition, though MacDonald warns him that the city has been destroyed by a nuclear explosion, and that the resultant radiation is deadly. Caesar, however, is determined to see the quest through, and leaves with Aldo at dawn. The death and destruction he witnesses there give him a new insight that he deems more valuable than any physical item, but Aldo discovers a cache of guns, and attempts to kill Caesar with one. He fails, enabling the chimp to return and deliver his message of warning. Aldo follows with an arsenal of firearms and attempts to rally support for his cause, but in the ensuing confusion, Breck leads some of the slaves to revolt. MacDonald runs off to warn Caesar, but too late, as Breck and the slaves take possession of Aldo's guns and hold Caesar's wife Lisa hostage.

The elderly orangutan Mandemus attacks Breck from behind, but the slaves begin firing. The gorillas fight back, leaving dead apes and humans everywhere.

Aldo develops a passion for firearms in "Quest for the Planet of the Apes," from *Planet of the Apes* magazine #22 (Jul 1976).

When the conflict passes, Caesar points to the guns as the cause of destruction, but the apes are yet unsure and many are afraid of the gorilla force under Aldo. The gorilla again challenges Caesar, this time to a one-on-one fight to the death, and Caesar accepts once more. Using his wits, Caesar manages to trick Aldo onto a tree and into a rope, humiliating him. Caesar is thus reaffirmed as Ape City's leader, and his first act is to free the humans. He changes his mind about destroying the guns, however, much to the frustration of Mandemus, whom Caesar assigns as guardian of the armory, ordering that the weapons be released only to him and in the direst of need.

"Quest for the Planet of the Apes" bridges the fourth and final films in ways that are logical and thought-provoking. Analyzing "Quest" from the perspective of the four above-noted criteria, it's evident that it meets the first, authentically capturing the voices of the known characters, particularly Caesar and Aldo, bringing those characters along a physical and psychological journey. Caesar's relationship with Lisa, the concern that haunts him at her discovery that she's pregnant, and the intelligent ways in which he proves he's a leader worth following are how Moench develops the characters to the point at which audiences will meet them again in the film *Battle for the Planet of the Apes*.

The second criterion is that of thematic harmony. "Quest" follows on the tenets of the beast fable in examining ways in which humans and talking apes are, in fact, no different, contrasting the violent Breck with Aldo, and the clear-thinking MacDonald with Caesar. This becomes overtly apparent to Caesar when he sets out to take revenge on the fallen governor but comes to realize that turning to violence will only diminish him.

Yet, despite his horror at having seen the result of man's capacity for destruction in the Forbidden Zone, Ape City's savior doesn't entirely embrace the pacifist ethos either, as he makes a last-minute decision to keep the guns Aldo brought, albeit under lock and key. This leads to a debate about gun control, in which Mandemus argues that guns are of themselves an evil, while Caesar – thinking of the security of his wife and unborn child – counters that they're a necessary one. The story doesn't resolve this debate, content to merely raise the question and allow the reader to decide for herself, but in light of the fate of Caesar's son Cornelius in the fifth film, it may paint a tragic picture of policies made in fear.

The third criterion that good spinoff fiction must meet is that of adherence to prior stories' continuity, and in this regard, "Quest" is in good stead, serving as a direct prequel to *Battle* without duplicating that film's plot devices. Significant bits of continuity also fill in many of the blanks left by the preceding and succeeding movies: What happened to the world? How was the Forbidden Zone created, and how did it come to be forbidden? How did Ape City attain firearms, and how did Mandemus end up the keeper of Caesar's conscience? How did the humans end up in the situation in which we find them in *Battle*? And what became of Breck and the first MacDonald brother after *Conquest*? (One has to wonder, though, why Aldo would still be in a position of authority in *Battle*, given his traitorous, murderous actions in "Quest." Caesar is apparently very forgiving – and this trait eventually costs him his son's life.)

"Quest" also meets the fourth criterion, that of maintaining a relatively consistent tone with the source material. Unlike Moench's longest-running *Apes* story, "Terror on the Planet of the Apes," which sometimes strayed too far into strange territory, the author this time achieves the proper balance of adherence and expansion. For all its satirical elements, the *Apes* series took itself and its metaphysical elements seriously. So, too, does "Quest," which deepens the debate amongst fans regarding whether the series represents a circular timeline, in which events continue repeating themselves in a loop, or an altered timeline, in which the cycle of events that began with the first and second films is thwarted by Cornelius and Zira when they go back in time in *Escape from the Planet of the Apes*. "Quest for the Planet of the Apes" appears to favor the latter, implying that Caesar's more compassionate choices, his refusal to allow vengeance to dictate how simian society will function, and his realization that violence will only continue the cycle of slavery and domination, all serve to thwart the dark dystopian future of the first film, breaking the cycle once and for all.

"Apeslayer" and "Quest for the Planet of the Apes" represent the broad spectrum that is commonly found in media tie-ins, from the mediocre to the magnificent, from the inchoate, silly, and amusing to the intelligent, philosophical, and oftentimes grim. The presence of both in the Marvel run can be seen as a source of irritation, with the aficionado having to endure one to get to the other, but it can also be viewed in a different light, as presenting a kind of balance between what is light, fun, and diverting with what is darker, deeper, and more sober – low art and high art, enhancing and enriching the world of the original films, while playing with and provoking readers, pushing the boundaries of stories, and experimenting to see what does and doesn't work.

What readers and critics may come to appreciate, in time, is that it is impossible to have one without the other, that only in the allowance of creative freedom and experimentation can great stories emerge, but so, too, will many more that fall short. So celebrate them both, for out of the same fertile but imperfect soil they grow, some to fame and others to infamy – and, not unlike the apes for which this saga is fashioned, they represent man at his best and worst.

The Simian Records: Giving Children the Power to Go Ape

by Dan Greenfield

For a child of the 1970s, it goes without saying that entertainment options in those days were limited compared with what we have today. But it's what options we did have that speak so much about that era.

For me, *Planet of the Apes* was a television phenomenon. And by that, I don't mean the TV show. Other than the Topps trading cards, I pretty much bypassed the CBS version of *Apes* because I thought of it as ersatz, outside the realm of Taylor, Cornelius, and Zira.

No, *Planet of the Apes* came to my home via Apes Week, when the first four movies were shown as part of *The 4:30 Movie* on New York's Channel 7[1]. (The fifth film, *Battle for the Planet of the Apes*, aired during the channel's Sci-Fi Week, since the 1968 movie was split into two parts and shown during Apes Week's Monday and Tuesday slots.)

This was a special event for me, and for many others. Every day, after school: *Apes*. There was also the occasional prime-time network showing, and even late-night airings on Channel 2.

But you see, the recurrent theme here is that all of these options were decided for us. If I wanted to see *Planet of the Apes*, I had to wait for it to come

---

[1] For the uninitiated: en.wikipedia.org/wiki/The_4:30_Movie

around, or imagine it in my mind while playing with my Mego Cornelius and Zaius action figures.

Believe me, that was still pretty great. But it's not like today, when I can pop in a Blu-ray if I feel like watching *Beneath the Planet of the Apes* while lazing on the couch. Or I can stream the first film because, for whatever reason, I enjoy going to sleep with it playing in the background.

So what other options were there? How could I sate my "ape-tite" when *The 4:30 Movie* was feeding us Gidget Week?

Apes on the Turntable

Power Records tried its damnedest to help. Without using the word "damned," of course.

A New Jersey-based offshoot of Peter Pan Records, Power Records produced a broad range of storybook recordings, from Batman to Spider-Man to *Star Trek* and, of course, *Planet of the Apes*. There was an array of packaging options, ranging from LP anthologies to simple 45 RPM records. But the backbone was the company's "Book & Record" set – which promised, on the cover, "The Action COMES ALIVE As You Read!!"

On the indispensable website Hunter's *Planet of the Apes* Archive,[2] there's a clipping from the February 1975 issue of *Playthings* magazine, which reads as follows:

> **Peter Pan Records debuts 4 *Planet of the Ape* [sic] titles**
>
> NEWARK, N.J. – Peter Pan Industries announced the release of four *Planet of the Apes* titles on its Super Adventure Series. This series is on the Power label and retails for $1.49.
>
> The four available book and record sets include: *Planet of the Apes*; *Escape from the Planet of the Apes*; *Battle for Planet of the Apes* [sic]; and *Beneath the Planet of the Apes*.
>
> Each set consists of a 7" record and a 7" 20 page book in full color. Vivid dramatizations and accompanying music follow the text of the book faithfully, so that the youngster can listen to the record and read along in the book simultaneously. The artwork of the series is graphic and exciting for children of all ages.
>
> Since *Planet of the Apes* motion pictures and television programs are a current hot category, great demand is now anticipated for this item.
>
> Attractive counter and floor displays are available; each with a complete assortment of merchandise and full-color headers.

[2] pota.goatley.com/powerrecords.html, presented by Hunter Goatley

Pull out the *Planet of the Apes* 45 record, set it on the player, put the needle down, and there you were, thousands of years in the future... any time you wanted.

The books themselves were produced by a publishing house called Arvid Knudsen and Associates, an agency whose history has been largely swept away by the sands of time. (I like to think that Arvid Knudsen was actually a contemporary of Otto Hasslein, but maybe that's just me.) Knudsen himself authored at least seven children's books between 1981 and 1986, as part of Prentice Hall's Sports Basics Books (*Wrestling Basics*, *Boating Basics*, *Aerobics Basics*, and *Football Basics*) and High-Tech Basics (*Computer Software Basics*, *Home Computer Basics*, and *Photography Basics*) lines, and he also edited Robert Southey's *Goldilocks and the Three Bears* for Peter Pan Records. Otherwise, little is known about the man or his "associates."

Bending the parameters of space-time – and eagle-eyed readers of the *Playthings* press clipping above will also notice this – if you look at Power Records' *Planet of the Apes* output, you will immediately see that one chapter of the story is missing: *Conquest of the Planet of the Apes*.

Viewed from an adult standpoint, *Conquest* is a series high point. It's low on the cheese factor and much higher on the fear scale.[3] While it's not at all subtle, the movie articulates well the series' metaphors for race and class conflict, acting as a distorted vision of the real-world riots that were plaguing urban America in the late 1960s and early '70s. It stands with the first movie as a cautionary tale about the direction in which our society is heading, and it doesn't take a social anthropologist to point out how frightening much of the imagery remains today. For all of its advances, this is still a country riven along class and racial lines.

I note this because it makes me think that Power Records left *Conquest* out of its Book & Record lineup due to its heavier, more complicated themes. I do recall, as a child, being unnerved by the film whenever it was on television, so perhaps it wasn't an entirely unwise decision.

What's striking is just how many of those sociological themes have been wiped from the Power Records *Planet of the Apes* catalogue.

The first film's adaptation opens with a space capsule hurtling through purple-blue space, its mission gone awry. The narrator intones: "Three

---

[3] This is particularly true of the extended Blu-ray version, with its original, bloodier revolt and ending restored.

astronauts, traveling in a state of suspended animation, approach their destination after eighteen months in a space craft flying at the speed of light..."

Gone is Charlton Heston's soliloquy from the film, which, though heavy-handed ("I feel lonely") sets the stage for what's to come. Here, Knudsen's team gets right to it – it's all about the adventure and the unknowing.

Fair enough. This is a project geared toward children, after all, whereas the films aimed much higher. That the movies worked on multiple levels is emblematic of their considerable cultural success.

But even within the confines of the Power Records version, the producers make some very specific, if sometimes subtle, alterations. Putting aside that Landon looks more like Charlton Heston than Robert Gunner, and that Taylor resembles Steve Rogers,[4] I can't help but raise an eye at what happens at the bottom of the second story page.

In the film, one classic Taylor character moment is when he breaks out in an ugly, mirthless laughing roar upon watching Landon plant a tiny U.S. flag in the soil of this "new" planet. It's a scene that says so much about a time when a large portion of the American public was growing increasingly divided about the nation's sense of exceptionalism. Mind you, the film was released in 1968, an awful and turbulent year.

But that's only part of it. It's a scene that tells you so much about Taylor, who has already articulated his disenchantment. Taylor is mocking Landon's optimistic belief that the United States still matters in their newly found time, as well as the bizarre notion that anyone who might be alive back home would even know what he'd done.

In the comic, the complete opposite is the case. Landon is cast as the pessimist against a classically heroic, never-say-die Taylor. When Landon plants the flag, his skipper congratulates him, remarking, "Ha! And I thought you were ready to give up!"

No antiheroes for the kids. And certainly no scoffing at the flag.

On the other hand, casual sexism is still A-OK!

As the astronauts encounter the primitive humans, Dodge notes, "Maybe you guys didn't notice, but that pretty one looked very human!" To which Taylor, good-naturedly smacking him in the shoulder, replies, "Hey! Not bad for a 2,000-year-old man!"

---

[4] The alter ego of Marvel Comics' Captain America

I mean, it's one thing to water down themes – but to add a bit that's not even in the movie, just for the sake of an easy "Hey, baby!" line?

Are these small things? Yes and no. Power Records could be expected to make certain changes – in any adaptation, you can't expect a word-for-word recreation of the film and all that's in it. But by making these choices, the company made some political decisions of its own.

All that being said, I don't want to take the joy out of these books, nor do I wish to take them all that seriously... because they are incredibly fun. The story pretty much follows most of the film's major beats (though the apes learn of Taylor's ability to speak in a much less iconic way – no "damned dirty apes" here). This includes, somewhat surprisingly, the discovery of Landon's frontal lobotomy.

Finally, we make our way to the Forbidden Zone and the confrontation that takes place there. Taylor is allowed to escape, and he comes upon the ruins of the Statue of Liberty.

It was never going to happen, of course, but I would have loved to hear the voice actor bark "Damn you!! God-DAMN you ALL to HELLLL!" Instead, we get, "Oh, no! No! Nova... now all the pieces come together. This is my planet Earth, 2,000 years in the future, and my civilization destroyed itself. Oh, Nova, Nova – *you* are what is left of the human race!"

Doesn't exactly have the same ring to it, does it?

Oh, well.

Does *Beneath the Planet of the Apes* (Power Records, 1974) show the mutants of New York City... or the Walking Dead?

Beneath the Planet of the Apes carries on in much the same way. Some tightening here, some liberties – no pun intended – taken there. The art, as with the other installments, is alternately appealing and awkward, soaked in lurid colors. The voice acting is wooden and perfunctory, except for Brent, who sounds more like Heston than Taylor... who sounds like Dudley Do-Right.

Taylor disappears, Brent finds Nova, and Ursus rallies the troops – sadly without the money line, "The only *good* human is a *dead* human!" Just as in the movie, the story of *Beneath* really kicks in once the two humans find themselves in Queens (or, more specifically, under what was once the borough).

They make their way to the mutants' headquarters (presumably under Manhattan – unlike the movie, the comic doesn't make it clear enough) and here's where, again, we get to see the loaded choices Power Records made. The mutants don't try to force Brent to kiss or kill Nova – but we do get to see under-dwellers praying to an atomic bomb and taking off their faces so we can view their ravaged "inner selves."

Everything goes south, just as it does on screen – the apes invade, the Alpha-Omega Bomb is armed... and this is where things take a hard turn off the road. Nova isn't killed, Brent isn't shot – and a grieving Taylor doesn't set off the missile with ambiguous intentions.

Nope, it's a mutant who clutches his chest as he hits the doomsday button.

The Earth still blows up, though. (With a postscript: "And now we too have seen the future. Must it be our future? Now that we know... can we make sure it will not be?")

Bedtime, kids!

We move on to *Escape from the Planet of the Apes*. This comic is actually the only one I owned when it was first released in stores. And it's how I learned what the word "detest" means, as in Zira's "I detest bananas, young man!" (In the movie, she merely "loathes" them.)

One of the coolest parts of the comic, though, is the first panel, showing the world being destroyed in the future. It's a great shot, all reds and browns and blues and yellows.

And one of the most noteworthy parts involves Hasslein himself. Instead of him being a tall, handsome, sinister, dark-haired man with a mild German accent, as portrayed by actor Eric Braeden, he's a totally over-the-top white-haired guy in full Colonel Klink mode: "Theece talking apez will be confined for liiife. I em senting 'em to Camp Elevun. Und zeir offzpring vill be tekken awey..."

He might as well have said, "Ve hef vays of mekking you talk." Of course, there's no "escaping" the grim finale – which is, in its way, the darkest moment of all the films. Zira (carrying a baby chimpanzee) and Cornelius are both gunned down (though we don't actually see the baby die in this version). Then we revert to Armando's circus, where the voice actor does his best Ricardo Montalbán and asks the chimp couple's real child, "How are you doing, little fellow?" before extolling the wonders of rich, Corinthian leather.

And, yes, little Caesar calls out "Pizza! Pizza!" Oops, I mean "Mama! Mama! Mama!"

So then we skip over *Conquest* entirely and move on to the execrable *Battle for the Planet of the Apes*, the nadir of Apedom, both on film and in comics. Caesar chases Aldo up a tree and the gorilla falls to his death, though we don't get the one cool part of the movie, the chanting of "Ape has killed ape" during the chase. Oh, and Caesar's statue cries.

So there's that.

If you want to relive any of these adaptations, or check them out for the first time, I highly recommend the aforementioned Hunter's *Planet of the Apes* Archive. All four comics and recordings are available there, including cover art.[5] And you can download all of it.

Apes of a Different Color

There was another kid-friendly bit of comic-bookish entertainment that was popular at the time: Colorforms. The apes got into the game with the *Planet of the Apes* Colorforms Adventure Set.

These were those flat, rubbery-plastic, die-cut figures that would stick to a play surface depicting a particular setting – in this case, Ape City. The vinyl Colorforms pieces could be repositioned in order to create new scenarios of sequential art, sort of like paper dolls. The wholly unnecessary instruction booklet included examples of how to have the characters interact with each other, in comic-strip form.

For example, one panel showed Taylor leading Nova by the hand and thinking, "Lots of monkey business here! Must keep background surface clean

---

[5] Also archived at the site are a quartet of audio-only recordings – *Mountain of the Delphi*, *Battle of Two Worlds*, *Dawn of the Tree People*, and *Volcano* – that Power Records released based on the 1974 *Planet of the Apes* television series. These, however, were produced without accompanying comics.

with a damp cloth from time to time... the plastic pieces will stick better!" I so much would have rather they had him saying, "Take your stinkin' paws off me, you damn, dirty ape!"

But I guess that would have been too much to hope for.

The instruction booklet to the *Planet of the Apes* Colorforms Adventure Set.

In addition, there was a third option if you wanted to relive the first film: namely, coloring books. And I collected them obsessively.

Artcraft published a series of coloring and activity books of varying lengths and content, each featuring sequential artwork. Some contained short adaptations of the movie, while others were somewhat longer. The activity books featured puzzles and games, utilizing much of the same artwork from one volume to the next. And while the interiors focused mostly on the first film, the beautifully painted covers drew from the sequels as well.

From a storytelling standpoint, the books are understandably rudimentary and toned down, since they were, of course, aimed at young children – though they are, in their own way, more accurate than the Power Records version of the story. According to Goatley's website – where you can find a selection of the coloring books – they were illustrated by Nan Pollard. The artist, who died in 2012, worked on more than 2,000 children's books, coloring books, and paper doll cut-out books during her career, covering such franchises as Disney, Curious George, the Berenstain Bears – and *Planet of the Apes*.

With a necessary economy of linework, the characters look more like the actors than they do in Peter Pan's kinetic stylings. And they leave more of the story elements intact: Kids even get to color in Taylor shooting up his sleep serum in the spacecraft!

As a seven-year-old, I could not get enough of these coloring books.

As a 47-year-old, I admit to enjoying living in the future, where we have all sorts of instant-gratification devices that allow us to be entertained at any time, whether on television, on a desktop, on a laptop, or on a tablet. But 40 years ago, if you were a young child, it was Power Records, Colorforms, and coloring books, or it was nothing.

Were they good enough? I'm not going to get all nostalgic and say yes. They weren't. But there were what we had, and I loved them just the same.

"You will come with us. You are our prisoners!"

A gorilla guard apprehends prisoners while apparently ballroom dancing in the *Planet of the Apes* coloring book (1974).

Apes Abroad: No Love at Home, Alan and Pete Roam

by Jim Beard

By 1974, people had begun to lose interest in apes.

Those sensational simians had a good run; you couldn't fault them that. But by the time of the 1974 television series, the ardent love affair afforded to the *Planet of the Apes* concept through five feature films throughout six years had dwindled to a low back-burner flame. The TV series arrived with good intentions (make more money!), and a fine pedigree (bible by Rod Serling!), but the audience just wasn't hungry for it anymore, not like they used to be.

The *Apes* spinoff merchandise kept chugging along, though, snaring a few kids who maybe didn't know enough to move on to the next big thing. The TV series' astronauts, Alan Virdon and Peter Burke, and their chimpanzee friend, Galen, ended up as Mego action figures, but for some reason weren't deemed worthy to take their place in U.S. comic books of the time, unlike their film progenitors. Oh, there were the Power Records original stories, but while the Marvel Comics black-and-white magazines were just getting cranked up and running in 1974, Burke, Virdon, and Galen must have been looked upon as second-class citizens, not good enough to grace American comics.

So, when there's no love at home, the only recourse is to roam. And two other countries welcomed the wayward astronauts and their ape buddy with open arms.

After the short life and even quicker demise of the *Apes* TV series, everyone involved (and a few who weren't) had their own theory about why it didn't work. Some felt the show dumbed down the overall concept. Some claimed the episodes were too repetitive. Others cited the more intelligent humans in the series taking the spotlight away from the fascination of an ape society. Still others said that airing it opposite *Sanford and Son* was a death-wish.

Did the *Planet of the Apes* TV series comics published in the United Kingdom and, of all places, Argentina from 1974 to 1977 address and correct those purported problems?

Yes – and no.

Annuals of the Apes

For students of pop culture, the translation of a successful concept by a foreign culture from the culture of its origin can be a fascinating thing. Often, the translators forget key elements of a concept and make ham-fisted mistakes, while in other instances, such alterations are made on purpose, so as to ease the transition by adding comfortable cultural tropes and excising the "offending" bits. For the most part, the *Apes* TV series made the leap across the pond to British comics intact, with only a few minor flags indicating its new English masters.

British comic annuals are a mainstay of the country's publishing traditions. Big books filled to overflowing with not only comic stories, but also prose fiction, puzzles, and games, the annuals are beloved for all they offer readers.

Three *Apes* annuals – hardcover books, each titled *Planet of the Apes (Authorised Edition)* – were published by Brown & Watson from 1975 to 1977, extending the show's artificial life past its fourteen-episode offering, both in the United States and in the United Kingdom. Each book contained the aforementioned comics, prose, and puzzles, much of it by anonymous creators, unlike American comics and their credited writers and artists. In all, the art and writing of the *Apes* annuals are competent, even good at times, though their standard of coloring leaves much to be desired in comparison to their U.S. counterparts (which isn't saying much in the 1970s).

All but one of the original stories in the annuals maintain the North American setting of the TV series, as well as the core concept of astronauts

Virdon and Burke stranded in the far-flung future world of ape domination, and on the run from gorilla soldiers while aided and abetted by the friendly chimpanzee Galen.

Under a full-color photo cover of the show's gorilla antagonist, Security Chief Urko, 1975's *Planet of the Apes* #1 boasted two complete comic stories, as well as four prose tales.

The first of the comic stories, "Journey Into Terror," has our heroes searching for an advanced human civilization, but running afoul of an ape dragnet for two fellow humans named Stern and Lang. Mistaken for them, the two time travelers are captured, but are later freed by Lang and Stern, who blow up an ape armory, terrorist-style — something the British would know about all too well. Some Briticisms creep into the proceedings, such as the phrase "catch you up," and the art approximates the actors' likenesses, but never truly captures the unique simian styling of the TV series makeup.

The annual's second comic tale, "When the Earth Shakes!" introduces ape culture to the Beatles (in the form of LPs) and a vintage fighter airplane (humorously known as *Jefferson's Aarpan*, most likely an in-joke reference to American psychedelic rock band Jefferson Airplane), which a group of humans worship, and which Virdon and Burke covet for what the artifact might offer them as a potential flight to freedom. Giving credit where it's due, ape Koro acknowledges that the human art of winemaking is fully theirs.

After an initial prose adaptation of the 1968 *Apes* feature film, the annual rolls out an interesting prose tale focusing on Galen, wherein the chimp chances a meeting with his former mentor, orangutan Councilor Zaius. Somewhat out of character, Zaius allows Galen and his human friends to go free, though he offers them no help in dealing with Urko. "The Scavengers" offers yet another conclave of humans, this time populated by runaways from ape tyranny. Finally, in "Swamped," the pursuing Urko stumbles into quicksand, prompting a rescue by the two astronauts. The story is practically a play-by-play guide on how to write not only an *Apes* TV episode, but also a cliché-ridden entry for any TV series throughout the 1950s, '60s, and '70s.

One stand-out feature of the first British annual is the beautiful art by John Bolton, who later went on to make a name for himself at DC Comics and with other prominent comic gigs.

A year later, Brown & Watson produced a second *Apes* annual, doubling the number of prose stories from the 1975 book. By that time, text stories in comic books, once existing purely to gain a better postage mailing rate, were a thing of the past in the United States. In the U.K., they were still standard operating procedure in 1976, and the second annual offered six such stories under its photo cover of our three protagonists. Sadly, none of the tales rise above the by-then tired on-the-run theme of the TV series.

"Galen's Guerillas" opens with the three fugitives striking out for the Rocky Mountains, only to be captured and held against their will, this time by humans instead of apes. Virdon educates the pacifist Galen in the art of guerilla warfare (as opposed to gorilla warfare, with which he's already well acquainted), again perhaps a nod to the long unrest in Britain. The story winds up a treatise on bows and arrows versus guns, a theme that surely resonates with many downtrodden peoples, including Ewoks and emerald-clad billionaires. In "From Out of the Past," our heroes find yet another cache of pre-Armageddon computer equipment (as they did in the TV series' "The Legacy"), which is lost in an earthquake (à la the episode "The Trap").

Existing as merely filler material, "The Captive" tells of Urko capturing Galen and Virdon rescuing him – yes, that's really the entirety of the story – while "Raiding Party" turns the capture around yet again, with the human astronauts being seized in another village, but able to slip away when Zaius makes a rare appearance to quell violence. "When the Ghost Walks" revisits the old chestnut of a wacky human inventor "haunting" a building to chase people off (though this time without any meddling kids and their pesky dog), while in "The Marksman," the 1976 annual finally imparts a mote of interest in its prose offerings, with a plot by Urko to use a human sniper to assassinate Zaius (he doesn't succeed).

Artist John Bolton returns to *Planet of the Apes* in the first of the annual's comic stories, "Pit of Doom." In this tale, Virdon, Burke, and Galen fall – literally – into an ancient germ warfare store, wherein they find explosives and the means to allow their gorilla pursuers to do themselves in by their own hubris. It's a trope often used by classic pulp tales, such as in the adventures of Doc Savage, when instead of the heroes sullying their hands to kill their enemies, their enemies slit their own throats with the knife of stupidity.

The second comic tale, "Ship of Fools," features the fine artwork of Oliver Frey, who (along with Bolton) elevates the illustration level of the 1976 annual above that of its predecessor, with lush lines and rich detail. Our heroes come upon the Pacific Ocean in their wanderings, as well as a group of humans led by a man named Werner, who are building a sea-going ship to "escape... to a better land in the west." Predictably, though, gorilla soldiers threaten to gum up the works, and Burke and Virdon use themselves as a distraction so that the would-be human mariners can make their escape across the waves.

If British children (or whoever was reading the annuals) were itching for something more from their *Planet of the Apes* fiction – and if they were still paying attention at this point – they were rewarded in 1977 with an *Apes* annual a cut above the first two years' releases. The art was still competent, but the writing took an upswing that, while not exactly dramatic, signaled that someone behind the scenes was at least trying to break out of the TV series' mold.

Urko once again graces the cover, holding court over an annual that begins with a comic story titled "Blow for Blow." A young gorilla officer named Jehan plans to mount a military coup against Urko and grab the security chief's title for himself. Ape kills ape[1] as the coup blossoms into violence, and we learn that Zaius had expected such a scheme to unfold. Urko chases Jehan into the desert and they fight *mano a mano* (paw a paw? *pata a pata?*) until Zaius intervenes, giving Jehan a choice: exile or death. The young officer chooses exile, and the tale ends on an uneasy note: Zaius can better use Jehan alive, a pawn should the orangutan ever decide Urko has outlived his usefulness.

Beyond the fascinating study of the apes' politics, two other features make this story stand out: black-and-white art that is reminiscent of Mike Ploog's illustrative style in the American *Apes* comics, and the complete lack of Virdon, Burke, and Galen. Their absence makes for a refreshing change of pace, one that will continue later in the annual.

A prose story titled "The Prophet" follows, involving an old human man named John who delivers sermons about human dominance pre-holocaust. Virdon and Burke uncover John's secret (that he's not a prophet at all, but has simply gained advanced knowledge from ancient library tapes, which he is using to offer humanity hope), and the prophet leads a group of villagers away to found a new, better civilization.

The second comic tale, "Breakout," reveals a prison camp for human renegades, and our heroes attempt to fashion a gas-filled balloon to use as a distraction against the camp's gorilla guards. It ends pretty much how you

---

[1] The films' sacred law, "Ape shall not kill ape," is never mentioned in the TV series and doesn't seem to be in effect among West Coast apes, given how frequently gorillas try to shoot or otherwise execute Galen. This trend continues throughout the British and, later, Argentian comics based on the show.

might expect – that is to say, by the numbers, and far too reminiscent of the 1975 annual's "Journey into Terror," as well as more than one TV episode.

The prose story "The Arsenal" uncovers yet one more set of ruins for the fugitives to stumble into, this time hiding a stockpile of weapons that Urko has hoarded. The astronauts blow up a building and engage in a gun battle during the course of the narrative, finally running off with some of the weapons before the curtain call. This treasure trove of theirs is curiously forgotten in subsequent stories.

If anyone was falling asleep by that point in the annual, the next prose story might have awakened them from their boredom. Titled "Power Play," it acts as a kind of spiritual sequel to "Blow for Blow," but turns the tables on Zaius to Urko's benefit. The orangutan leader plans to present legislature to the council to grant freedom to a portion of humans in the city, but when his documents end up missing, he follows their trail to the ape warden of yet another prison, who arrests Zaius. An unlikely savior, Urko comes to Zaius's rescue, waving the missing documents under his nose, complete with forged wording granting freedom to *all* humans. Chagrined at being routed in his plans, Zaius curtails any future endeavors to benefit humans (which is just as well, since he never seemed inclined to help mankind in the televised adventures anyway).

At this point, our imaginary reader might have taken notice that once again, the annual presented a tale unsullied by Virdon, Burke, and Galen. It would not be the last time before the final page was reached.

The remaining two stories in the book stand not only as the last of the British entries in the *Planet of the Apes* fiction parade, but also as two examples of an attempt to think outside the box. "From Out of the Sky," a comic tale, opens with an event that is something of a standard in the *Apes* universe: a crashed spaceship. The difference here is that unlike George Taylor's ill-fated crew, a female astronaut survives the crash this time. Virdon and Burke rescue the woman from (what else?) gorilla soldiers, and Burke recognizes her as Verina Bolton,[2] someone he knew from his past. "We're on Earth, baby," he tells her flippantly, then continues to operate as a condescending jerk throughout the rest of the story. The fugitives find a fuel leak in Bolton's ship and, when they decide it is still space-worthy, realize it could only take one

---

[2] A patch on Verina's uniform provides her last name, Bolton, a strong indicator that this particular story was illustrated by John Bolton.

person back through the space-warp (not unlike, at least thematically, every other episode of *Gilligan's Island*).

Verina Bolton is captured by gorilla soldiers in "From Out of the Sky," from the Brown Watson Books 1977 annual.

Bolton is nominated as the flight candidate, due to her lesser weight (and the fact that she's not a series regular), but the plan is that she'll tell her superiors about our heroes' plight and they'll mount a rescue. Before she leaves, Burke cooes in her ear, "I'll buy you dinner in 1990..." The gorilla soldiers are drawn away from the ship, it launches successfully, and when Virdon expresses some doubt about how things might work in their favor, Burke, smug bastard as he is in this story, smirks, "No girl's ever stood *me* up for dinner!"

Cue the Gleek Laugh (so named for the propensity to have a roundtable chuckle over the alien monkey's antics at the end of many *Super Friends* episodes). Galen is completely useless in the story, but that's okay, because it's purely a window into the lives of the human fugitives and their brief brush with someone from their own era.

In the prose story "Flight from Terror" (interesting how the 1975 annual began with "Journey into Terror"), a trio of chimpanzees, fed up with Urko's and Zaius's ongoing treatment of both humans and apes, desert Central City to see what they can see in the larger world. They sail a boat down the coast and end up in, of all places, Peru, where they discover advanced humans living in their own advanced world, far from the ape dominance of North America. These humans, though, turn out to be as cruel as the gorillas when they grab the chimps and reveal their wish to take back the entire planet for *Homo sapiens*. The trio escapes, of course, and wanders off to continue their exploration.

The 1977 annual raised the bar for what could be done with new stories set in the universe of the TV series, but it ended far too soon, and the so-called *Authorised Editions* never returned. Someone at the helm had a glimmer of ingenuity and creativity there at the end, but toiling away at it two years out from the demise of the show (and, presumably, poor sales figures) took its toll and the experiment died. The Western world shut the door on any more such tomes, with our fugitives still on the run at home and abroad.

Furry Filmstrips

The United Kingdom had one more thing to say, in terms of original *Planet of the Apes* comic-style stories, and that came in the form of a children's toy.

In 1975, the makers of the Chad Valley Picture Show added the apes to their popular Sliderama Projector series,[3] and as with the annuals, they fashioned the entry around the TV show. The box in which the actual toy projector was packaged heralded "224 Slide Pictures," by counting each panel of every comic strip on each slide. There were sixteen slides in all, though the box claimed there were only fourteen, and each slide seemed to contain two "stories," each with its own title, but in reality, some slides continued on to the next.

For the most part, the Chad Valley strips cover several episodes of the TV series, albeit in a kind of *Reader's Digest* version. In slides masterfully labeled "Crashland," "The Capture," and "The Escape," Virdon's and Burke's trials and tribulations on the Planet of the Apes begin, more or less following the events

---

[3] A British toy similar to the Give-a-Show Projector sets sold in the United States

A melodramatic Peter Burke reenacts Taylor's trial in "The Trial," from Chad Valley Picture Show Sliderama Projector, filmstrip #539.

of "Escape From Tomorrow" and segueing into episodes such as "The Trap," "Tomorrow's Tide," and "The Cure." British children must have thrilled to read an adventure concerning malaria on their bright, colorful filmstrips.

Interestingly enough, a scene from the 1968 feature film is inserted into the proceedings. When Burke is captured by the apes, he is put on trial, à la Taylor's hearing, presided over by an orangutan council, complete with the movie's famous "See No Evil, Hear No Evil, Speak No Evil" pantomime.

The dialogue, delivered in squarish, ugly word balloons, too often simply repeats what is already being shown, similar to Silver Age comic books, and is about as ham-fisted as you might expect. When the council accuses Burke of falling from the sky, he screeches back at them in fine, bombastic Shakespearean fashion, "Not *fell*, you fool! FLEW!"

The art on the slides is roughly at the level of a coloring book, heavily outlined with no real attempt at shading. There's a certain quality to it, though, that evokes the work of American comic book artist Hank Fletcher, an obscure early-1940s creator who produced some of the strangest comic illustrations ever. The Chad Valley strips, cramped in their tiny panels, offer oddly proportioned figures, much like Fletcher's work, and solid blocks of primary colors, no doubt to make an impact once projected onto a wall.

While not truly original in the sense of creating a new adventure for our intrepid astronauts and their chimp friend, the filmstrips at least attempt to craft something unique by weaving together disparate elements from the TV series and the first film. But it would be far from the oddest *Planet of the Apes* TV tie-in comic-style project. For that, we must fly down to South America.

Simian Samba

While the *Planet of the Apes* license drew its last raggedy breath in Britain in 1977, over in the next hemisphere and a few continents away, an enterprising Argentinian publisher named José Alegre Asmar worked quietly to continue the apes' existence. Why quietly? That might be because his company, Editorial Mo.Pas.Sa., also worked illegally, with neither permission nor approvals from Twentieth Century Fox or its affiliates.

Over the course of seven issues of *El Planeta de los Simios*, Editorial Mo.Pas.Sa. produced a series of *Apes* stories based on the TV show concept that, while illicit, actually hewed closely to the original formula *and* broke some new ground, perhaps even moreso than its U.K. counterpart, Brown & Watson.

Maybe the apes thrived in the warmer environment, away from the chillier air of the British Isles.

Writer Jorge Claudio Morhain wrote all but one of the seven issues (in Spanish), working in a fairly straightforward manner laced with attempts at poignancy. Issue #5 was scripted by Ricardo Barreio, aping Morhain's style. Like Morhain, artist Sergio Alejandro Mulko illustrated six of the seven issues; his art often looked crude and rushed, and he took liberties with the familiar design of the apes, but there's a certain something to the overall visuals that lend an exotic feel to the stories. By comparison, T. Toledo's art on the fifth issue comes off even cruder.

In 2004, a group of *Planet of the Apes* fans took on the challenge of translating and reformatting all seven issues of *El Planeta de los Simios*, so that they might be read and enjoyed by an entirely new generation of non-Spanish-speaking *Apes* aficionados.[4]

In so doing, the translators corrected a bizarre error in the original Spanish-language versions involving the characters' names. Jarringly, the astronauts were sometimes called Adam Dircon and Jhon (not John) Burton, while their chimp friend was named Golden! But in other tales, they retained their on-screen names. Morhain, in an interview published in *Simian Scrolls* magazine,[5] explained that Alegre had changed the names from the writers' original scripts (though apparently in only some issues, which probably gives a good indication of why Editorial Mo.Pas.Sa. eventually folded) to avoid facing a Fox lawsuit, under the rather dubious guise of their being "an alternate history."

El Planeta de los Simios #1 sports a colorful cover illustration, but its insides are entirely in black-and-white. Its sole story, "The Wandering Jew," waxes philosophically as it opens, asking the tough questions of the core *Apes* concept: Who is to blame for the state of the world? And why did it happen? Strangely, the setting of the tale (and all subsequent issues) is on the East Coast, in direct opposition to the TV series' evident West Coast status quo. There seems to be no rhyme or reason to that, save for perhaps Editorial Mo.Pas.Sa.'s desire to capture the feel of the first two feature films. Or it could be that the writers simply did not realize – or care – that the television series had been set

---

[4] These English translations are archived for downloading at Kassidy Rae's *Planet of the Apes*: The Television Series Website (potatv.kassidyrae.com/simios.html).
[5] Handley, Rich. "Discovery, Fandom and Restoration on the Planet of the Apes." *Simian Scrolls* #10, January 2005 (pota.goatley.com/scrolls/simianscrolls_10.pdf).

in and around California, possibly due to how the show was translated for Hispanic audiences.

Virdon and Burke are attracted to the sound of music emanating from a lonely building, but Galen calls it "noise" and "irritating." The fugitives find a hermit, Ahasuerus, behind the Glenn Miller tunes (yes, you read that right), and meet a sympathetic female ape veterinarian, à la the films' Doctor Zira. It all turns out to be a ploy by the gorillas to lure humans in for capture, and after postulating that Ahasuerus might be the Wandering Jew of Christian mythology, they start up a James Bond film in a decrepit movie theater as a loud, boisterous distraction to escape the soldiers. The hermit is revealed to be a cyborg, by the way, created during a pre-holocaust experiment to prolong life.

The fugitives are ecstatic to hear the sounds of Glenn Miller music in "The Wandering Jew," from *El Planeta de los Simios* #1 (1977).

Issue #2 featurs two stories, one short and nonsensical, the other offering a bit more depth. In fact, the latter seems more like something one might find in Marvel's *Planet of the Apes* magazine.

"New Life... on the Old Planet" sees our heroes passing the Statue of Liberty (since the TV series was set long before the films, circa 3085, that predates Taylor's discovery of the monument by nearly a millennium), and, inexplicably, operating out of their ruined spaceship[6], despite the vessel having thoroughly exploded in the TV show's pilot episode. They are captured, naturally, and escape, but not without a lot of physical fighting, the introduction of a half-naked human female, and a reaffirmation of Galen's friendship with his human compatriots.

"Depth" pulls back the curtain on a "taboo" tower that survived the atomic bombs and a group of humans who now worship it. Virdon and Burke become holed up in the structure to hide from gorilla soldiers who are also forbidden to enter the tower. When Tormo, the apes' leader, states, "There is no taboo that can resist a good gun," and then rushes in to capture our heroes, the fugitives discover a world of intelligent rats (known, believe it or not, as Monstrous Rodents) living on a pile of bones underneath the tower. A lot of running here and there and teeth-gnashing follow, but in the end, Tormo has a change of heart and helps the humans fight the rats. The weirdness of the giant rodents and their blind, albino human subjects makes this tale stand out, as does the odd moment when Virdon and Burke question Galen's loyalties.

The theme of taboos continues in *El Planeta de los Simios* #3's single story. In "Beach of Time," the fugitives come across a girl named Nebia, about to be executed... by shark. It all involves apes forcing humans to gather up ancient relics from a beach, and another taboo preventing anyone from taking them. Burke begins to romance Nebia, while Virdon looks into gathering copper wire and transistors for a goniometric radiometer (these guys can build *anything*, thus drawing even more thematic parallels to the seven stranded castaways on an uncharted desert isle) to zero in on the East Coast Scientific Center, which is transmitting radio signals using thermal energy. This is yet another case of a writer stretching the limits of credulity to use human technology from the past in the time of ape domination, and the "shock" of our heroes stumbling across something from their era while in a more primitive year. And, of course, Nebia is forgotten in subsequent stories, as are all such walk-on, walk-off characters.

Note: humans tend to be more primitive in the Argentinean comic books than they are in the TV series, which, in a way, harkens back to the first two

---

[6] Which, for the trivia-minded, is called *Probe Six*, according to *"Planet of the Apes Initial Concept Pages,"* a document produced during the show's development

feature films. While able to talk, these humans fall somewhere between the TV show and the movies in terms of their mode of dress, use of tools, etc.

Apparently obsessed with the ruins of New York City, writer Morhain tells of collapsing buildings among the old devastation in issue #4's story, "Ultra-Sonic." An elderly orangutan named Harimon, described as a "sorcerer," exhibits a dangerous interest in ancient human technology and a specialization in sound equipment. Urko wants to destroy the sprawling city once and for all, and Harimon's "pure magic" of ultrasonic sound waves provides a means to that end. The story features some effective moments, such as Virdon breaking down emotionally when he thinks that Burke has been killed, Burke fighting Urko, and the normally pacifistic Galen striking Urko to help his friend.

The Argentinean comics focus several times on tension between Virdon and Burke and their supposed friend Galen; after our human heroes congratulate themselves on their actions, "Ultra-Sonic" ends with a rare full-page portrait of a disgusted Galen remarking, "Humans... all they know how to do is boast! Bah!"

It's back to two stories with *El Planeta de los Simios* #5, and a new writer-artist team. In "The Star Gods," Virdon and Burke follow the trail of another crashed spaceship that Galen has somehow heard about, to a remote ape village in the mountains. There, they run afoul of Arpo, a priest-tyrant who rules the village with a combination of iron fist and mystic mumbo-jumbo. The ship turns out to be the *Bluestar*, launched two months before the fugitives' own space mission, but containing no survivors. Recognizing it as a human-made craft, Arpo forces our heroes to repair the ship (in two weeks!) for his use in a bid to take control of the ape capital. As one might expect, it all ends in tragedy for the apes and the loss of another means out of Crazyland for the fugitives. One of the most noteworthy aspects of the tale comes in the humans' grousing over Galen's over-zealousness in posing as their "master," and in their threat to "kick his ass."

The second story in the issue, "The Master of the Forests," concerns the astronauts' travels "increasingly north" and their encounter with the ape Tromh, the titular "master," and the region of forest into which the fugitives stumble. Basically, it's a "let the games begin" trope, when the spelling-contorted Tromh forces the fugitives to fend for themselves during a manhunt, and our heroes look for ways to beat the hunters at their own game.

There is little to credit in issue #6's single offering, the intriguingly named "The Zombies." Another natural disaster, this time an avalanche, separates the fugitives from the pursuing Urko, and they wind up in yet another village, one with the "it must mean something different in Argentina" name of Fandomville. The zombie-like inhabitants fail to recognize Galen, but Virdon and Burke set about building them a mill anyway, and Virdon romances a female villager called Maia (despite his having a wife and child back home, and his single-minded on-screen determination to get back to them). A plot concerning gorillas hooking the villagers on opium-laced wine develops, but as always, our heroes turn over the apes' apple cart and the humans pack up to leave for the mountains.

One presumes that the publishers were optimistic about their growing audience at the time of this issue; during a lull in the story, the writer re-caps the *Planet of the Apes* concept "for new readers." The series would last for exactly one more issue.

"The Circus," in *El Planeta de los Simios'* final issue (which, despite being the seventh installment, was numbered as issue #1 due to Alegre changing his company's name to Editorial Tynset s.A), boasts color, though only crude blocks of it here and there throughout the black-and-white line art. Burke, once more captured by apes (it was his turn, presumably), is taken to a so-called "palace," which turns out to be the ruins of the Metropolitan Opera House, where he is subjected to gladiator-style battles. In an interesting turnabout of the old trope, the human winners are executed and the losers mated with each other, in order to drive out any "spirit of rebellion" that might lurk in the species.

In this issue's – and the series' – final tale, "Rockets," the fugitives discover one more village, this one built over a hidden laboratory, and coveted by an ape scientist who seeks to learn the power of flight. Burke and Virdon find a dozen or so rockets, and – well, you could probably write the rest of the story by now.

The illicit Argentinean *Planet of the Apes* comics came to a truncated end after seven issues, most likely due to both sales and the publisher's fears of being found out by the American license holders (which could very well explain the abrupt company name change). It can be said that *El Planeta de los Simios* contained more experimentation than its British counterpart, though that, in itself, isn't saying much. In all, the book clung to the TV series' concepts and clichés more than it strayed, but its glimmers of originality were at least interesting for the time it took to read them.

TV's *Planet of the Apes* lasted for just fourteen episodes. Some might say it was undeserving of tie-in projects and merchandise, a footnote in the history of the apes that failed to make any significant mark on the property, and one that

American publishers were wise to ignore. But Burke, Virdon, and Galen trudged on through, seeking other shores to continue their story – and for better or for worse, what they found made for an interesting footnote of its own.

Marshall Arts: Malibu's Adventures on the Planet of the Apes

by Rich Handley

When fans reminisce about the *Planet of the Apes* franchise's best comic books, Marvel's 1970s magazines and the current run from BOOM! Studios are frequently praised for their detailed artwork, imaginative storylines, and memorable characters. Mr. Comics' *Revolution on the Planet of the Apes* also gets its due praise. But another publisher's efforts are often unfairly overlooked.

Following Marvel's cancellation of its magazine in 1977, *Apes* lore remained nearly extinct for the next thirteen years, aside from the Power Records film adaptations and a handful of British annuals and Spanish-language comics based on the television series. In 1990, Adventure Comics (a Malibu Graphics imprint) breathed new life into the *Planet of the Apes* saga, launching a monthly comic that ran from April 1990 to July 1992. In addition, Malibu supplemented the ongoing title with a variety of one-shots and miniseries that continued to hit stores until the release of its final issue (*Forbidden Zone* part 4) in March 1993.

Quality varied, with a few clunky moments along the way, but most stories hit their mark. At times humorous, tragic, action-packed, whimsical, poignant, and topical, the Malibu line was a worthy successor to the *Apes* mantle, expanding on the films' concepts, characters, and settings, while covering a lot of new ground. Yet, despite its creative diversity of stories, the company's efforts have sometimes been dismissed by critics as weakly written or inferiorly drawn. Too often, the series is forgotten, lost among the dim glut of glitz-and-glitter, form-over-substance titles that dominated the early 1990s comics boom.

Frankly, the series deserves more notice than it tends to receive.

Launched in 1986 by Tom K. Mason and Dave Olbrich, Malibu Graphics operated as an independent comic publisher for eight years until being purchased by its *Planet of the Apes* predecessor, Marvel Comics, in 1994. The company drew acclaim for its Ultraverse lineup, introduced the world to *Men in Black*, and made a name for itself as a publisher of licensed comics, including *Alien Nation, Mortal Kombat, Puppet Master, Robotech, Star Trek: Deep Space Nine, Street Fighter*, and more.

At 51 issues, *Planet of the Apes* tied with *Deep Space Nine* as Malibu's second-most prolific licensed comic (surpassed only by *Robotech*). With Gary Chaloner, Roland Mann, *Men in Black* creator Lowell Cunningham, and the late Mike Valerio penning miniseries and one-shots, writer Charles Marshall scripted all 24 issues of the monthly title, as well as two minis (*Ape City* and *Ape Nation*) and a *Planet of the Apes* annual, for a total of 34 of those 51 issues. Marshall landed the *Apes* gig after Mason, Malibu's creative director, asked him to submit a proposal.

Promotional materials for the black-and-white monthly placed the first issue 100 years after Caesar's death, during the leadership of his grandson, Alexander. An *Apes* timeline published in Marvel's eleventh issue[1] placed Caesar's death in 2040. If that dating can be accepted as applicable within the Malibu framework, that would set the opening arc of Malibu's monthly series in approximately 2140.

Marshall had originally proposed a four-issue miniseries, but this was expanded into an ongoing title. The writer set out to establish a core group of characters around whom he could build evolving storylines and conflicts. This enabled him to explore Ape City and its surrounding areas from the viewpoints of multiple protagonists and antagonists.

---

[1] "Outlines of Tomorrow – A Chronology of the Planet of the Apes," by Jim Whitmore.

"The establishing movies – the first two – are both set in and around the New York City area," Mason said when interviewed for this essay.[2] "Sure, Taylor, Landon, and Dodge walk around a lot in the first one, but how far is that really, and is that indicative of the whole planet? So I envision a much bigger *POTA* universe – what's it like in Mexico or Japan or Russia? I think it's silly to assume that the Ape City of the movies is all that's left."

In fact, Mason added, Ape City seems connected to the rest of the world. "In the movies, the apes all have guns, all of the same type, so they're not just leftovers from human society," he noted. "And they show no concern over their use of bullets. Clearly, they can get more guns and more ammunition, so there's manufacturing, technology, factories of some type that can make uniforms and weapons. Making that leap opens up a world of possibilities to explore. How they make guns isn't as important as the idea that the world of apes is much, much bigger than just what's in the movies."

Among the main cast are Alexander (who, despite being Caesar's descendant, is drawn rather orangutan-like); Coure, a widow who becomes Alex's mate and co-leader; the orangutan elder Jacob, son of *Battle*'s Virgil; traitorous gorilla General Ollo; his mute, pacifistic, gentle-giant son, Grunt; a human named Simon who resents his people's place in simian society; unethical chimp scientist Doctor Moto; and gorilla special officer Heston (named, of course, after actor Charlton "George Taylor" Heston).

Providing much of the humor are dimwitted gorilla guards Jojo and Frito – *Planet of the Apes*' own Laurel and Hardy, with a little Jar Jar Binks thrown in for good measure – who spend their time goofing off, brawling, sleeping, and eating any food they can get their stinkin' paws on. "Charles is a funny guy," Mason said. "He likes to put humor into his work when appropriate. And we'd talked about this, too – it's too easy to assume that all gorillas are mean, all chimpanzees are scientists, and all orangutans are wise leaders. You can't create interesting characters that way. So making the guards funny and giving them personality helps the story. I don't recall any negative feedback."

In fact, Mason added, he received very few complaints about any aspect of the series. "We'd get maybe four or five letters on each issue, mostly from the same people, all of them mostly positive because the feedback culture was very different" than today's online world, he explained. "People might nitpick details, or want to see certain things, but there was never anything close to

---

[2] Other quotes from Mason are culled from that same interview.

negative feedback that would make us reconsider our choices. I'm sure that would be very different now, with the role that the Internet plays in fan reaction, and now that *Apes* is back in the pop-culture spotlight as a success story."

The Monkey Planet

Malibu's debut storyline, collected in trade paperback as *The Monkey Planet*, appeared in the first four issues, titled "Beneath," "Escape," "Conquest," and "Battle" (paying homage to the classic sequel films). This story kicked off an eleven-issue run penciled by Kent Burles and inked by Barb Kaalberg, who designed their own aesthetic closer in style to the physiques of actual apes than to the iconic facial appliances created by makeup artist John Chambers.

"When we got the license," Mason recalled, "Kent was available and looking for work, and *POTA* was the only thing we had that was remotely suitable to his style. The change from the classic Chambers designs was made by Kent, because that's his style and because we weren't going to be copying the movies."

Those accustomed to Marvel's reverential approach may have been put off by seeing apes drawn non-reminiscent of their on-screen counterparts, with elongated, exaggerated features. It's a definite departure from what came before, and it's sometimes difficult to tell the gorillas from the orangutans and chimpanzees, but once readers adjust, there is much to enjoy about the detailed artwork, from the outfits, architecture, and landscapes to the characters' highly expressive faces.

Marshall wastes no time getting into the story, opening with a full-page close-up of General Ollo's fearsome, spittle-dripping maw as he orders two human slaves to fight to the death for his amusement. When that ends too quickly, he ups the ante by forcing two apes into the arena. He and his Aldonite followers later steal the armory's weapons cache, imprison all humans and non-gorillas alike, and seize control of Ape City, which they rechristen Gorilla City. There is no doubt, from page one, who the main villain will be. One of the vilest, most hateful gorillas in *Apes* lore, Ollo displays an unstoppable thirst for power and dominance. When called on his flagrant disregard for the sacred law that ape shall not kill ape, Ollo reveals why this is so: he follows not the teachings of Caesar, but rather of *Beneath*'s General Aldo.

The author makes good use of irony in his introduction of Simon. While reading an encyclopedia from a hidden cache of books, describing gorillas as shy and friendly creatures, the teen hears his mother being murdered upstairs by Ollo's gorillas. Cradling her dead body, Simon grabs a handful of books and heads out alone, setting the stage for his future development as an ally-turned-enemy-turned-ally with whom readers can empathize.

Alexander meets the Grinch-like Children of the Forgotten Apes in *Planet of the Apes* #2 (Jun 1990).

This premiere issue sets up not only Ollo's treachery and Simon's grief-fueled fury, but Alexander's self-doubt as the inheritor of Caesar's legacy, as well as his close friendship with Jacob. The elder orangutan joins him as he sets out on a quest of self-discovery to relive Caesar's journey from *Battle* and thus become a better leader. In the Forbidden City, they meet a very pregnant Coure as she and her human dwarf protector, Max, search for Coure's missing mate, Joshua. Joining together, they enter the ruins of the former Ape Management Complex.

Marshall introduces an array of fascinating new elements to *POTA* lore. These include the Children of the Forgotten Apes, who have remained trapped in an Ape Management basement since their ancestors were cut off from Caesar's rebellion in 1991. The human mutants locked them in cages with little food or water, and after 150 years of living in radiation, they developed the ability to foresee the future. Though this may seem far-fetched, the concept is certainly no less implausible than *Beneath*'s telepathic bomb worshippers.

Alex frees the "Funky Monkeys," as their captors had mocked them, and forges an alliance with their leader, Dunzell. Oddly enough, the Forgotten Apes are eight feet tall and have unusually elongated heads, giving them the appearance of Doctor Seuss's Grinch if he'd been an ape drawn by *MAD* magazine's Don Martin. This, unfortunately, makes their introduction a bit more comical than was presumably intended.

A friendship develops between Simon and Grunt, each an outsider with no family to offer support (Ollo despises his son and even tries to have him killed... father of the year, he is not). After the illiterate gorilla saves the boy's life, Simon repays his kindness by reading to him from J.R.R. Tolkien's *The Hobbit*, and also teaches the mute how to communicate via sign language.

Unlikely friendships are common during Marshall's tenure (Heston and an extraterrestrial in *Ape Nation*, Coure and her human protector, and so forth), but there's something especially charming and innocent about the bond between the small human and his larger, childlike friend – perhaps a callback to John Steinbeck's *Of Mice and Men*. (*Of Apes and Men*?) A clever bit of subtle irony occurs in the second issue: after Simon begins reading *The Hobbit* to Grunt, the scene cuts back to the crazed mutants, one of whom looks and speaks like that novel's Gollum character.

In the final two chapters of *The Monkey Planet*, Ollo orders all resistant apes shot, while Coure finds Joshua's body, buries him near the Statue of Liberty[3], and names their newborn child after him. Jacob encounters Joshua's

---

[3] Some fans view *Conquest* and *Battle* as occurring in California, given that *Escape* takes place in that state, and that the *Conquest* novelization identifies Breck as California's governor. Others consider the Ape City of *Battle* to be the same East

Aldonite murderers, who torment him until Simon and Grunt save his life. Meanwhile, Moto begins torturing humans at Ollo's behest, to determine whether the effects of a plague that has rendered them mute[4] are permanent.

Alex returns to Ape City, where Simon helps him quell Ollo's coup, and Grunt, after a vicious brawl with his traitorous father, throws the fallen tyrant into a lake. Alex then challenges the general to a knife-staff duel, slicing Ollo's face and banishing him from Ape City. But despite Simon's role in defeating the Aldonites, Jacob's distrust of humans compels him to burn the boy's books. This drastic action, mirroring Zaius's efforts to suppress knowledge of mankind's past in the first two films, puts both Jacob and Simon on a darker path.

Rebuilding and Regrowth

Issue 5, "Loss," opens with Alexander and the recently widowed Coure sharing a night of passion. He later grants her a seat on the council (showing that even in ape society, sex and power often go paw in paw), and names Jacob his Defender of the Faith. Alex also invites Grunt to lead the army in his father's place – a dubious offer that doesn't bear close scrutiny, for despite Grunt's bravery, honor, and sheer physical strength, he lacks a military background, so it's doubtful that other gorillas would follow him, especially those still loyal to Ollo – but the pacifistic mute declines.

Alex instructs Jacob to make Simon a council member, but the orangutan disobeys, unwilling to grant a human such authority. Unaware of this, Simon blames Alex for being pushed aside despite having helped defend Ape City against the Aldonites. Furious about the book-burning, the teen twice tries to murder Alex, then flees into the night. Simon's expectation of being asked to help lead Ape City is rather unrealistic (Alex actually doing so is even more surprising), but the assassination attempt is nonetheless a powerful moment, as Simon had been positioned as a series protagonist. That he would betray Alex and Grunt in so brutal a manner is shocking.

Out on the road, Simon encounters an Aldonite soldier, who convinces him to join forces with the exiled Ollo, claiming their common enemy makes them allies. The gorilla has marked his own face with a deep scar across one eye, in

---

Coast town depicted in *Planet* and *Beneath*. Apparently, Marshall fell into the latter camp.

[4] Prescient foreshadowing, perhaps, of an as-yet-unrevealed effect of Will Rodman's virus from *Rise of the Planet of the Apes* and *Dawn of the Planet of the Apes*?

solidarity with the similarly injured Ollo. Tragically, the youth accepts the offer, cementing his role as a villain. Meanwhile, Jacob opens the Sacred Scrolls and adds a passage to the 29th Scroll, 6th Verse:

> Beware the beast "man," for he is the Devil's pawn. Alone among God's primates, he kills for sport or lust or greed. Yea, he will murder his brother to possess his brother's land. Let him not breed in great numbers, for he will make a desert of his home and yours. Shun him, drive him back into his jungle lair, for he is the harbinger of death.

This, of course, is the same verse that Zaius tells Cornelius to read at the end of the 1968 film. The revelation that Jacob is the passage's author[5] is effective, providing a strong tie-in to the movies and helping to explain how mankind fell so low in society's estimation, given Caesar's vow to treat humans as equals.

In the sixth issue, "Welcome to Ape City," Marshall does something unusual in an effort to drum up new sales – he drops the comic's fourth wall (and not for the last time), welcoming newcomers to the title in the form of an ape character named Reador ("reader"... nudge, nudge), whose face is never shown, and whose gender and species are unspecified. The issue is drawn from Reador's viewpoint (think first-person shooter video games), with only the character's furry hands indicating he or she is non-human.

Although a filler issue, "Welcome to Ape City" offers a glimpse of simian societal structure, in which all citizens are provided with free homes, and goods are available via a barter system. We learn about the Lightfeet, an ape tribe modeled after Native American cultures, who will play a vital role later in the series. We get to know Vonar, Ape City's self-described "bohemian simian." And we discover that Grunt has agreed to lead the new army after all.

Members of the cast give Ape City's latest citizen a tour of the area (thereby bringing new readers up to speed on previous issues), with Coure/Marshall telling Reador/reader, "I hope you'll stay around for a good long time." A clever tactic, to be sure. As a storytelling experiment, it's a charming issue that is unlike any other *Planet of the Apes* comic to date. Frito

---

[5] Several different scribes and dates have been attributed to this verse. According to an early script outline of *Battle*, it was written by Lawgiver Zeno during Caesar's lifetime. Malibu's Jacob is said to have penned the passage a century after Caesar's death, while *Revolution on the Planet of the Apes* claims Lawgiver Augustus wrote it three centuries after *Conquest*, and BOOM!'s monthly *Apes* title attributes it to Alaya, circa 2680. Ty Templeton's original concept for *Revolution* would have had General Thade, from Tim Burton's remake, writing the verse in question.

and Jojo exchange some cringe-worthy dialogue, however, such as Frito threatening to "murderize" his friend in *Loony Toons* fashion, underscoring just how cartoonish the two oafs tend to be.

The main storyline resumes in issue 7, "Survival of the Fittest," in which Moto kidnaps and dissects Max for scientific research. As he stores the dwarf's head in a freezer, Moto begins to feel uncharacteristic remorse about his work. Moto is an intriguing character, but his guilt pangs come out of nowhere. Why is he suddenly developing a conscience about dissecting humans, given his impassioned speech endorsing humanity's complete extermination just one issue prior? A change of heart can make for wonderful character growth, but in Moto's case, that growth is not entirely an organic one, and would have benefitted from developing over time.

At one point, Alexander gives Jacob several scrolls to copy, including a record of Caesar's revolution, but Jacob, in proto-Zaius fashion, buries the knowledge so future generations will never know the world was once ruled by humans (which actually contradicts Cornelius's account of history in *Escape from the Planet of the Apes*). The orangutan is one of Marshall's standout characters. Although a good ape who cares deeply for his people, Jacob is ruled by fear, and thus makes bad decisions that will adversely shape Ape City's history for nearly two millennia.

Alexander and Coure venture into the wilderness and are robbed by bandits, who are killed by a lava spray following an earthquake. Ape City scouts later locate the thieves' corpses and Coure's jewels, and mistakenly assume the couple to be dead. Jacob convenes Ape City's council to read Alex's last orders, which name him as Alex's successor to lead the city.

Meanwhile, an ornery orangutan named Roto enters the picture and starts picking fights about town. He narrates the issue, calling himself "the meanest, dirtiest ape in the city." Grunt challenges Roto to a brawl, which lasts for two full days (comic books aren't reality, kids) with no clear winner. But when a quake-damaged building leaves children in peril, the two behemoths work together to rescue them – and, in so doing, predictably bond in friendship. As with Moto's enlightenment, the message is a bit ham-fisted. But it's a fun issue, and Roto is a hoot.

Typical of Marshall's *Apes* work, the issue tells stories on several simultaneous fronts, with mirrored dialogue providing effective transitions from one to the next. After Roto thinks "Don't you ever get tired, Grunt?" the next panel sees Alex announcing, "I'm tired, Coure." A bandit, upon stranding Alex and Coure in the wilderness, remarks "If they make it out alive, they *deserve* to live," which cuts to Roto fighting a group of apes and deciding, "I let them live, though they *don't* deserve it."

He also wrote a Christmas issue.

"Here Comes Travellin' Jack," in issue 8, introduces a simian Santa Claus. The jolly orangutan, known as Travellin' Jack, rides around in a horse-drawn cart decorated in jingle-bells, collecting items of interest so he can return each year to share them with the citizens of Ape City. Much like his human counterpart, Jack departs after delivering his gifts, bellowing a hearty "Ho! Ho! Ho!" Exactly what one expects from *Planet of the Apes*, no?

The city rejoices as Travellin' Jack benevolently bestows his gifts. This leads to much merry mirth, as Jack gives Jojo two fruitcakes to share with Frito, which the rascally scoundrel eats, telling his friend that Jack left him nothing. Finally, the visitor finishes his gift-giving and rides out into the wilderness. There, he drops a box of coats, food, and first-aid materials for Alex and Coure, who have fallen ill in the desert, as depicted in a particularly effective two-page spread showing Alex experiencing a terrified fever dream. Like Santa Claus, Travellin' Jack apparently sees you when you're sleeping and knows if you're awake – or dying – and he's come to help.

But Jack's actions raise a question about his benevolence – or, at the very least, his intelligence – for if he knows his friends are stranded and sick, why doesn't he tell someone their whereabouts? Wouldn't it be more helpful to give them a ride back to Ape City, rather than tossing supplies out the side of his sleigh and riding off with them still marooned, yelling "Ho! Ho! Ho!"? Even more astounding, Alex and Coure seem satisfied with their customer service. Cue The Waitresses: "That Christmas magic's brought this tale to a very happy ending."

The concept of a simian Saint Nick is the point at which Malibu comes closest to jumping the proverbial ape-shark. What saves this issue from being completely goofy is a scene showing what has become of Simon and his Aldonite companion. The gorilla has been training Simon to fight, but abuses him like a slave. The mistreated youth clearly regrets the choices he's made, but is too scared to attack or escape before reaching Ollo's camp.

Mason points out that there was a conscious decision to take the *Apes* comic in unexpected directions. "What Charles and I had talked about, when setting up the series, was this: we weren't going to set it in the same city as Zira and Cornelius, and we weren't going to try to fit stories into the existing timeline of the movies," he says. "That just felt like a recipe for disaster. There was a rumor – later proved false – from 20th Century Fox that they were developing a new movie. I thought if we ran the material along those lines, we'd crash into the supposed continuity of whatever Fox was doing and it would create problems getting the book out."

Recent events come to a head in issue 9, "Changes," in which Jacob, tired of seeing mankind make trouble for Ape City, pronounces a death sentence for a human petty thief. Under Jacob's leadership, the city takes its first big leap toward becoming the human-hostile society of 3978. Other apes react in shock at the decision, which readers might find incongruous with the apes' on-screen attitude, unless one considers that this is still only a century after Caesar granted mankind their freedom and equality in *Battle*. The plague may have rendered man mute, but most apes would still be aware that humans are not merely animals. Heston, in fact, makes that very case to Jacob, but the orangutan delivers an impassioned speech about the evils of man:

> The human world was once filled with terrible and dangerous knowledge. The balance of power has changed, but I am afraid that there is much we still have to fear from their kind. Should the humans regain their capacities for thought and speech, it would bring on a millennium of chaos and death for our people. It would bring an end to glorious Ape City.

Zaius's condemnation of mankind in the 1968 film is echoed strongly in Jacob's sentiment. It's no wonder that, by the time of the first film, the elderly orangutan would be so determined to hide all knowledge of humanity's history – that mindset had been established nearly 2,000 years prior. We need look no further than Virgil's son in laying the groundwork for future dogma.

Meanwhile, a feverish Alexander wanders off, hallucinating about Ollo coming back to taunt him. A simian child named Xanda offers him food, and he dubs her Echo since she repeats everything he says. The two save an ape named Narobi from an alligator attack, and Narobi brings them to the village of the Swamp-Apes, who embrace Alex as their savior, believing he was sent to protect the tribe from invaders. It turns out that the invaders are the Children of the Forgotten Apes... and Alex no longer remembers that they're his friends.

Alex's amnesia is a distraction that knocks readers out of an otherwise smoothly flowing narrative, since it's obvious he'll regain his memories just when he needs them most. Characters always do in fiction (*The Bionic Woman* notwithstanding), and it's an overused cliché. Rarely does amnesia work as a plot device, as fans of *Miami Vice*, *24*, *Angel*, *Castle*, and countless other television programs would attest to. Thankfully, it doesn't last long in this case.

Countdown to Countdown

Issue 9 also contains a one-page chapter, mysteriously titled "Countdown Five," which sets up a scenario that will play out to great effect five issues hence. For now, no context is provided, and the sudden appearance of three space-suited astronauts is effectively jarring. Captain James Norvell discovers that his vessel is in peril, and orders his crew, August Anne Burrows and Lieutenant Ken Flip, to strap in and prepare for "a world of trouble." End of story.

What the heck is going on?

Such tantalizing teases continue for the next four issues. In issue 10's "Countdown Four," the rocket's stabilizers give out and the ship begins to lose altitude. "Countdown Three," in issue 11, sees the vessel crash into the Mississippi River; Norvell tries to contact Control, but gets no answer. In "Countdown Two," from issue 12, the crew swims to the surface, boards an inflatable raft, and finds the lifeless, bombed-out ruins of what was once St. Louis, Missouri. Finally, in issue 13's "Countdown One," they row to shore, and Burrows marks the spot in case they need supplies, berating Flip for jokingly tossing his prosthetic limb at her.

The set-up is intriguing, the Burrows-Flip dynamic makes for wonderful foreshadowing of what's to come, and the payoff will be well worth the five-month wait. But first...

Back in the main storyline, issue 10's "Return to the Forbidden City" has Alex leading a squad of Swamp-Apes to the city in question (which more resembles Middle-earth than the irradiated buildings of *Beneath* and *Battle*). He spots Dunzell strategizing with Ollo – who is manipulating the Forgotten Apes as their new military advisor – but does not remember either of them.

Dunzell's forces surround Alex and bring him to the deposed gorilla, who delights at having his nemesis handed over to him. Though this moment certainly provides tension, Ollo's return seems shoehorned, his alliance with the Forgotten Apes out of character for both sides. Regrettably, this marks a change in Ollo's effectiveness as a villain. In the opening story arc, he is a menacing, imposing force – a bullying bigot with deadly delusions of gorilla grandeur and the military might to back him up – analogous to Marvel's Peace Officer Brutus. But after leaving the city, he becomes more cartoonish. If gorillas had mustaches, Ollo would be twirling his so fast at this point that he'd look like the Tasmanian Devil was dancing on his upper lip.

Out in the dessert, Grunt rescues Coure and leads her back to Ape City, where she has a score to settle with Doctor Moto. One particular scene, in which the two stand on a bluff overlooking Ape City, is worth noting. Just as their depictions of the Forbidden City differed greatly from what was shown on-screen, Burles and Kaalberg also forged their own version of Ape City. On their canvas, the city is huge, sprawling across hills and valleys, continuing off-page into the distance, and filled with adobe huts of all shapes and sizes. In this case, the divergence works quite well.

Coure makes a beeline for Moto's laboratory (a cross between the labs from *Alien: Resurrection* and the 1931 *Frankenstein*) to accuse him of murder, but before she can present her evidence, the scientist hypnotizes her into forgetting it. Yes, that's *two* amnesia plot devices for the price of one, with hypnosis thrown in as an extra twist – the clichés are flying fast and furious. But on a positive note, we get to see Simon grow tired of being ordered around and beat his Aldonite trainer senseless with a tree branch.

Issue 11, "Warriors," introduces a supernatural element and arguably violates on-screen canon in the process. Years prior, Aldo's spirit had appeared to Ollo, calling the latter his "instrument" and reminding him that the weak do not deserve to live. Inspired, Ollo killed his entire tribe, traveled to Ape City, worked his way up to head of the military, and recruited others to the Aldonite cause. But surprisingly, Marshall also claims that Aldo was banished from Ape City after surviving his fight with Caesar in *Battle for the Planet of the Apes*.

Cue Zaius: "Heresy!"

Granted, the movie never outright *says* that Aldo died falling from the tree, but it doesn't have to. Caesar heavily implies as much when he asks, "Should one murder be avenged by another?" If he had merely exiled Aldo, why would he need to ask such a question? It can be more than reasonably inferred that Aldo is dead by film's end. He's no more. He has ceased to be. He's expired and gone to meet his Lawgiver. He's a stiff. Bereft of life, he rests in peace. He's run down the curtain and joined the choir invisible. This is an ex-Aldo.

Putting that aside, though, "Warriors" is an enjoyable tale that provides a compelling background for the fallen general. And while it's difficult to accept Aldo's ghost appearing to his followers, the scene is sufficiently creepy, and may merely be a delusion on Ollo's part. The gorilla's spiritual awakening is depicted as a lightning strike that terrifies his soon-to-die comrades, but Ollo faces it bravely, newly empowered and quite possibly insane.

Ollo beats Alex to the point of death, but Dunzell – who has a healing touch thanks to radiation exposure (and, really, is that any more ridiculous than telepathy?) – saves his life. With Alex's health and memory restored, he and Dunzell are able to prevent a battle between the Swamp-Apes and the Forgotten Apes, by appealing to their mutual love of peace. Ollo's plans are thwarted, and the apes stop warring like a bunch of trigger-happy humans. It's a typical and expected ending. But what's *not* expected is Alex's next move: he pardons Ollo for his crimes and invites him to return to Ape City – and, amazingly, the gorilla accepts his hand in friendship.

A new art team, M.C. Wyman and Terry Pallot, replace Burles and Kaalberg as of issue 12, bringing the look of the series more in line with the films' aesthetic. Distinguishing between gorillas, chimps, and orangutans becomes a good deal easier than it was under the prior artists, though some characters, such as Roto, Dunzell, and Grunt, are drawn radically differently than before, requiring that dialogue include their names so readers can identify them.

The story, aptly titled "Bells," depicts the buildup to the wedding of Alex and Coure. The city celebrates news of their engagement, Dunzell and Echo travel in for the affair, and Simon apologizes to Grunt for betraying everyone. Frito and Jojo have some zany antics as they trade belongings with half of Ape City's citizens in an effort to come up with the perfect wedding gift. Ollo attends the ceremony, then attacks Joshua's caretaker and departs the city, leaving the infant on Coure's doorstep with a note warning that he will someday return as a conqueror. It's an effective moment, unexpected given the lighthearted tale in which it occurs, and reminds readers that despite Alex's naïve offer of peace, a scorpion ever remains a scorpion (even when he's a gorilla).

Issue 13 apparently occurs around a decade later (circa 2150), as it takes place following *Ape Nation*, a crossover miniseries between the *Planet of the Apes* and *Alien Nation* franchises, and reflects that story's noticeable age jump for Simon, as well as for Alex's and Coure's children.

The issue features three mini-stories. The first, "Frito & Jojo's X-cellent Adventure," sees the two goofy gorilla guards trading most of their belongings to acquire a fake treasure map, which leads them 50 miles outside Ape City. There, the friends discover several cases of Hostess fruit pies, still fresh after a century. The guards gorge themselves on hundreds of pies, then pack up the remaining snacks and head home the next morning. Jojo and Frito, like Hostess fruit pies, tend to fall into the "you either love 'em or hate 'em" category. For those in the "love 'em" camp, this story is actually quite a funny romp. But fans who find their slapstick silliness out of place in the *Apes* universe will likely not see this issue as an exception.

The second tale, "Honey, I Shrunk the Apes" (yes, after paying homage to *Bill & Ted's Excellent Adventure*, Marshall also riffs on *Honey, I Shrunk the Kids*... it's just that kind of issue, and it's amusing), ties in with Malibu's *Ape City* miniseries, and is as weird as you'd expect it to be. In France, a scientist ape named Benday tries to help a giant gorilla called (what else?) Cong, whose massive size is endangering his health. Benday attempts a mass-reduction procedure, but instead shrinks Cong so small that he must also shrink an ape named Mongo to find him. Cong and Mongo are nearly eaten by weasels, and when Benday's assistant, Flannagan, tries to shrink the animals (instead of, say, putting them in a cage), he inadvertently grows them to enormous height. In the end, the overheated lab equipment explodes, leaving Cong an inch tall.

As absurd as the above synopsis may sound... well, actually, there's no conclusion to that statement. It *is* as absurd as it sounds. And yet, it's undeniably entertaining. Say what you will about Marshall's approach to *Planet of the Apes* – he brings the funny.

Story number three, "Drunken Interlude," provides a tie-in to *Ape Nation*. A bit jarringly, the author drops the fourth wall again in the opening panel, with the following humorous narration:

> There's really not enough room here for a proper recap of all that's gone on in what was once called Western Europe. So go out right now and buy all four issues of the recent *Ape City* miniseries, available at fine comic shops everywhere. This will get you up to speed on what's happening, plus give the creators of that book a little extra spending money. I happen to know that said creators are having a little cash flow problem at the moment and would appreciate the additional income.

Several pages depict a bloody battle from that miniseries (which would make sense only to those who'd read it – cross-marketing at its finest). Heston, meanwhile, finds a rare moment to relax with a Tenctonese woman named Elysa, and opens up to her about the deaths of his life-mate, Keysha, and their unborn child. It's a touching scene in an admittedly lackluster issue (and, in fact, probably would have worked better if included in *Ape Nation* itself). The real highlight of the issue, though, is the fifth and final one-page chapter of the "Countdown Zero" prequel.

Countdown Zero

Issues 14 to 17 bring their A(pe)-game, as Marshall crafts what is arguably Malibu's second finest monthly storyline, the four-part "Countdown Zero." In part one, the astronauts (who'd lost contact with Earth during a mission to Mars) know nothing of Caesar's rebellion and the subsequent nuclear war. Dismayed by the devastation they find, they head east and are stunned to see apes walking upright, wearing clothes, and conversing – in Spanish, no less! The travelers eventually meet a tribe led by a deadly, white-eyed gorilla called Zar.

August Burrows awaits the birth of her daughter, accompanied by a certain talking doll [*Planet of the Apes* #17, Oct 1991].

The apes abduct Norvell in part two, but Burrows rams them with a pickup truck and rescues him, and they drive 200 miles before resting. Flip shows signs of snapping from stress (you might say he's flipping out), so Burrows eases his mind by having sex with him, inspiring male readers everywhere to act crazy whenever in the presence of a woman. This decision proves short-sighted, for when she spurns Flip's later advances, his mental state worsens. They find a library, where a magazine article about apes replacing cats and dogs as mankind's pets offers insight into what happened in their absence. Moments later, Zar's gang drops in from a skylight.

The astronauts fight their way back to the truck in part three and make their escape, but Flip senses an attraction budding between his comrades, and broods jealously for days. He attempts intimacy once more, growing violent when Burrows again refuses, compelling Norvell to slug him. Later, as the two men scout out an old grocery store, Flip fractures his commander's skull with a shovel, leaving him for dead.

The story concludes in part four, in which Zar captures Burrows and treats her with surprising respect, offering tea and claiming he wants only to learn how evolution turned upside down. But once she tells him all she knows, he orders her killed. Norvell suddenly shoots Zar, then dies in her arms. Mourning his loss, Burrows journeys east with Flip but ignores him, having figured out what he did to her lover. Realizing she's pregnant, she raids a store for supplies, including a doll that says "Mama." After she confronts Flip, he commits suicide out of shame. Finally, she travels alone to the Long Island shore, seeks shelter in a cave, and waits to give birth.

"Countdown Zero" works on several levels. It's intensely paced, featuring an original take on the usual *Apes* formula, with the astronauts arriving not in the far future, but soon after Caesar's revolt. It's well-illustrated, making strong use of Wyman's and Pallot's particular talents (with all due respect to Burles and Kaalberg, this story would likely not have been as effective if drawn in their style). It features three fully realized human characters with whom readers can relate – even the traitorous Ken Flip – playing out a love triangle that never seems forced. And it's remarkably different in tone than the first thirteen issues, breathing new vitality into the comic.

After Flip tries to kill Norvell, a reflective narration from Burrows reminds us that *Planet of the Apes* is, among other things, a *Twilight Zone*-esque vehicle for social commentary: "Our worst enemy wasn't Zar or his followers. Our worst enemy wasn't contaminated water or spoiled food. We... *we* were our worst enemy. We always have been."

Most significantly, "Countdown Zero" concludes on an unexpected note, showing that this isn't just a filler tale unconnected to the greater storyline – it's *very* connected. Marshall reveals, in a twist no one could have seen coming much before the final pages, the back story of the talking doll found by Cornelius in the 1968 film. Brilliant.

Beginning of the End

"Gorillas in the Mist," in issue 18, brings the action back to the time of Alexander, with Coure finally realizing that Moto must have killed Max. By odd coincidence, a strangely guilt-ridden Moto has, for seven nights, been dreaming of the dwarf exposing his evils — and being capable of speech, to boot. The scientist tries to bury himself in his work, but fails to assuage his anxiety, and the vision of Max ultimately convinces him to create a noose and hang himself in his lab.

It's a well-crafted end to the character, his interactions with ghost-Max effectively moody and somber... and yet, something about it seems a bit off, mostly due to timing. Moto's hidden guilt at having harmed humans was hinted at in issue 7, but his actually killing himself over it occurs without much foreshadowing. Some prior evidence of his depression might have gone a long way toward making his fate more organic. Plus, the writer seems to have forgotten the ten-year time jump in the interim. Still, it's a very good issue, and the fact that no one ever mentions Moto or his death in later issues shows how isolated he'd become.

A side story features frivolous Frito accidentally blowing up Vonar's statue of Alexander, and then falling to his near-death from a high cliff. The scene, played for campy laughs, is juxtaposed with Moto's fatal curtain call, and there's a certain sweetness to Jojo's panicked concern for his friend, even if it's all a bit over the top.

"Countdown Zero" may come close to being the best storyline of Malibu's monthly *Apes* comic, but issue 19, "Quitting Time," tops the chart — and, once again, it takes place near the time of Caesar's 1991 rebellion. Just as "Countdown" is built around the identity of a character hinted at but never shown in the first *Apes* film, "Quitting Time" stars a person who actually appears, albeit very briefly, in *Conquest of the Planet of the Apes*.

The protagonist, Carson McCormick, works for Ape Management Publications, writing instructional pamphlets at Governor Breck's behest, such as *Breeding Your Ape* and *Punishing Your Ape*, explaining how human owners should handle their simian servants. McCormick's wife wants him to purchase an additional ape for their domestic use, but he has grown uncomfortable with ape enslavement, which he fears (rightly so) will someday backfire on humanity.

Throughout the issue, McCormick walks in and out of *Conquest*'s events, accepting a circus flier from Armando and Caesar in one scene, and receiving a simian shoe-shine in another — the very shoe-shine shown on screen, in fact.

McCormick, it turns out, is the businessman who, in *Conquest*, finds his socks splashed with shoe polish by an ape inspired by Caesar to rebel. As the film and comic progress, the copy writer learns of Armando's death, then is ordered to craft a new pamphlet, *How to Terminate Your Ape*, once Ape Management stops accepting apes for reconditioning. To the man's credit, this makes him particularly uneasy, enabling the audience to empathize with him despite his complicity with Breck's fascist regime. Make no mistake, though – he may be sympathetic, but he's no MacDonald. He's a company man to the end.

Fans can easily determine (thanks to announcements made over the city's public-address system) when in the movie each page and panel takes place, as McCormick experiences the lead-up to Caesar's revolt. One memorable scene involves him dreaming of a circus in which ape clowns taunt a human audience. The next day, his office ape uses a letter-opener to murder both McCormick and his secretary, while his family simultaneously dies at the hands of their house ape. As his life fades away, McCormick's final thoughts are of simpler times, and of the circus.

Powerful stuff.

"I think those kinds of stories always resonate," Mason mused, "because they are both within and outside of the ongoing continuity. It happens everywhere – Batman will fight the Joker for only so long before there's a special story where he just has to deliver a package to a lonely girl across town, or Jimmy Olsen takes a day without Superman. They reveal a lot more about the character and/or the world. Anytime you can tell a good side story within the existing world, it gives you a bigger piece of that world – and, in doing so, it becomes a story that you remember."

And then there's issue 20, "Cowboys and Simians," featuring the return of the Lightfeet tribe. This issue could be one reason the Malibu run is sometimes panned. Back when Marvel had the *Apes* license, the result was pretty trippy: ape Vikings, ape Gypsies, ape cyborgs, frontier apes. With that in mind, are ape cowboys and ape Native Americans really any more absurd? Maybe.

Mentioned briefly in monthly issue 6, and also showcased in *Ape Nation* and the *Planet of the Apes* annual, the Lightfeet live in the mountains outside Ape City, seeking enlightenment and transcendence. The concept has the potential for good storytelling if handled properly – but it could also come off as groan-worthy, like the Tibetan-inspired Mountain Apes of the animated series. Unfortunately, this farcical issue has more of the latter and less of the former.

Carson McCormick learns a karmic lesson from Stella the ape in *Planet of the Apes* #19 (Dec 1991).

The annual also introduced readers to the Ape Riders, a quartet of simian bounty hunters who travel the former Western United States, rounding up outlaws. In this issue, the Riders are hired to track down a rogue Lightfoot called (wait for it) Dirty Hairy, who has abducted the daughter of King Louie, the orangutan leader of New Dodge. As if that weren't already goofy enough, Hairy employs four doofus hench-apes who look and act like a certain 1960s television rock-and-roll band. Hint: the thugs' names are Dolenz, Tork, Nesmith, and Jones, and people say they monkey around.

In his effort to be clever, Marshall shreds credibility by opting for entirely non-subtle references to pop singers, Clint Eastwood films, and Disney jungle cartoons, rather than delivering a believable pastiche on the classic Western genre. It's a shame, too, for what could have been an offbeat but fun tale is instead one of Malibu's most eye-rolling chapters.

But not *the* most eye-rolling. That comes next.

Ollo, Gov'nor

Back in issue 11, Ollo claimed that the spirit of Battle's Aldo had appeared to him, urging him to be strong – or perhaps it was just a hallucination of Ollo's deranged mind. But Aldo would not be the last film character to come back from the dead in the Malibu run. No, the four-part series finale, presented in issues 21-24 (illustrated in parts one to three by M.C. Wyman and Peter Murphy, and in part four by Craig Taillefer), features the reanimated ghosts of both Governor Breck and Caesar. And this time, there's no ambiguity – they're real, and they're all-powerful.

In his introduction to issue 21, "The Terror Beneath, 6" Marshall explains that this final storyline is designed "to bring everything back in order, so that this planet of the apes will be the same planet of the apes that Taylor and his crew land on down the road." As such, the author cleans adobe house, destroying much of what he built up during his two years as series writer.

To accomplish this goal, Marshall has a group of human mutants hold a séance to resurrect Breck's spirit, in the hope that he'll restore mankind to the top of the evolutionary chain. The ghost (or possibly a demon, given the fiery power he displays) has his own plans, however. Disgusted at the mutated state of his city's descendants, he kills them all. The former governor then goes on a murder spree, wiping out one group of Malibu apes after another – the Forgotten Apes, the Swamp-Apes (including Narobi and Echo), and even Ollo's

---

[6] As with the first four issues of the series, the last four also take their titles from the classic film sequels.

Aldonites. Only Dunzell survives long enough to mutter an enigmatic warning to Heston: "Seize her."

In "The Terror Beneath," Governor Breck's spirit goes all Bane on General Ollo (*Planet of the Apes* #21, Feb 1992).

Marshall takes time to show what happened to Simon (who, now an adult, has made a home within the ruins of the Statue of Liberty[7]), and to introduce

---

[7] See the discussion of issues 3 and 4.

Anne Burrows, the granddaughter of August Anne Burrows, from the "Countdown Zero" arc. A question arises regarding the astronaut's longevity, however. In issue 17 (set circa 1992), the elder Burrows was in her 20s or 30s. But according to this issue, she's still alive – Anne lives with her – even though it's 160 years later. This means Grandma Burrows is around 180 years old. Must be the radiation!

In issue 22's "The Land of No Escape," the wholesale slaughter of Marshall's creations continues, with Breck smiting a bazooka-toting Travellin' Jack, followed by the Ape Riders. The governor-ghost then meets a scavenging, non-mutated human tribe and promises to help them regain dominance, and they embrace him as their god and savior. Back in Ape City, Simon offers Alex and Coure his assistance in the coming war. Out in the wilderness, meanwhile, the Lightfeet prepare to battle the evil entity, knowing it will mean their deaths as well.

How will they do this? Why, by calling upon the spirit of Caesar, of course.

In issue 23, "Final Conquest," Lightfoot leader Zakula "hears" Dunzell's final words in Heston's mind, realizes he'd actually said "Caesar," and instructs his tribe to summon Alexander so they can revitalize Ape City's founder from the afterworld. In the final issue's "Last Battle," Caesar fights specter-Breck as others battle on the physical plane. Breck gains the upper hand, until great Caesar's ghost engulfs his old enemy. The Lightfeet then join minds to lend their power to Caesar, sacrificing themselves to close the door to the spirit world.

With normalcy restored, Simon and Anne (who, naturally, seem destined for future romance) urge the council to at last bridge the species divide and welcome humans back into Ape City. Jacob agrees to give it a try, and Alex decrees that the future lies not on the path of fear and racism, but in making the world a better place, mirroring Caesar's actions at the end of *Battle*. Finally, the issue (and series) ends on an amusing note, with Frito and Jojo reading a scroll of fourth-wall-less thanks from Marshall, and wondering if they'll ever get their own miniseries.

All in all, it's a happy ending for Ape City... but not for the thousands of apes and mutants whom Breck murdered along the way. It's an unsatisfying and rather gratuitous conclusion to an admirable, ambitious run, with the senseless slaughter seemingly designed purely for shock value (the deaths of young Echo, Dunzell, and the simian Santa) or to provide a hasty closure (Ollo dying helplessly at the hands of a supernatural power, and not due to Alex besting him).

What's more, there's a degree of illogic at play here. If Jacob never trusted humans in the past, why would he begin doing so after an evil, reanimated human kills thousands of apes within a single day? It's kind of like Padmé Amidala refusing all of Anakin Skywalker's advances in the *Star Wars* prequels until after he admits he has committed genocide against a Sand People tribe. Oh, *now* you think he's okay to hang out with?

It's not a terrible four-parter, per se, and there are enjoyable elements to it, but it all comes across as rushed, as though Marshall knew the series was coming to an end but didn't have sufficient time to wrap it all up before the final panel. Plus, the séance and ghost aspect is a bit out of place in the *Apes* mythos, making this storyline the most difficult one to swallow.

Mason sees it differently. "I'm very much okay with that [ghost] stuff," he said. "It was an easy way to tap into existing continuity without causing problems. Every society has supernatural elements of some kind and of various kinds, so why should ape society be any different?" Admittedly, that's a fair point.

Reading Order

Reading the Malibu Graphics *Planet of the Apes* comics can be tricky, as the various miniseries and one-shots[8] occur between the monthly issues, which are not always told chronologically, and refer to each other's events. As such, reading the monthly title first, followed by the one-shots and minis – or vice versa – might leave first-timers confused by the cross-references and storytelling gaps. The best way to read the series is thus according to story order.

Listed below is a suggested reading order, including the year or era in which each tale takes place (based on the assumption that the monthly title begins in 2140), in order to help fans maximize their reading experience.

- Monthly series #19 (1991, during *Conquest of the Planet of the Apes*)
- Monthly series #9-13 – backup story (1992)
- Monthly series #14-17 (1992)
- *Terror on the Planet of the Apes* #1-4 (2070, Marvel Comics reprint)
- Monthly series #1-4 (2140, collected as *The Monkey Planet*)
- Monthly series #5 (2140)
- *Ape City* #1-4 (2140)

---

[8] Discussed at length in the next essay

- Monthly series #13 – *Ape City* tie-in (2140)
- Monthly series #6-8 (2140)
- Monthly series #9-13 – main story (2140)
- *A Day on the Planet of the Apes* annual (2141)
- *Urchak's Folly* #1-4 (2142)
- *Blood of the Apes* #1-4 (2142)
- *Ape Nation* Limited Edition (before 2150)
- *Ape Nation* #1-3 (2150)
- Monthly series #13 – *Ape Nation* tie-in (2150)
- *Ape Nation* #4 (2150)
- Monthly series #18 (2150)
- Monthly series #20-24 (2150)
- *The Forbidden Zone* #1-4 (circa 2300s)
- *The Sins of the Father* one-shot (3948)

Offering a mixture of comedy, tragedy, romance, and social commentary, Malibu's *Planet of the Apes* line – particularly Marshall's monthly title – provided a welcome respite during the long, lonely gap between Marvel's comic magazines and Dark Horse's Tim Burton spinoff. "We knew it was going to end, simply because the contract was up and we weren't going to renew," Mason recalled. "It wasn't an issue of sales or creativity. And there wasn't a panic about it. Two years is about as long as we stayed with anything up to that point. We'd figure out the end date of the contract, and then work backwards to figure out what would be published during the last six months, to maximize the value of the deal."

Despite a few misfires along the way, the publisher produced numerous memorable tales that helped to keep the fires of *Apes* fandom alight during the dark times. Adventure's simian saga may have ended after a mere three years, but the saga of simian adventure endures to this day – and Malibu Graphics played an undeniable role in that longevity.

Simians, Savages, and Simpletons: Mini-Adventures on a Monkey Planet

by Joseph F. Berenato

Adventure Comics gets a bad rap.

For three short years in the 1990s, Adventure – an imprint of Malibu Graphics – was the keeper of the *Planet of the* Apes comics flame. During that time, they produced a monthly series that ran for 24 issues, as well as two one-shots, five four-part mini-series, a "Limited Collector's Edition" issue, and a four-issue reprint of Marvel's "Terror on the Planet of the Apes" storyline.

Fifty-one issues in three years. That's an awful lot of *Apes* output for such a short amount of time. And most of it was quality work.

Most, but not all. With an average of one new *Apes* comic every 23 days, there's bound to be a misstep or two. But are the occasional dips in quality deserving of some of the ridicule and ire directed toward Adventure's run?

Yes, it was the 1990s. Yes, much of the artwork is black-and-white, a tad roughhewn, and some of it looks like it was drawn on a used cocktail napkin by Rob Liefeld.[1] Yes, many of the apes bear little to no resemblance to the makeup

---

[1] Liefeld is generally associated with the "extreme" style of 1990s comic-book artwork. For a better understanding of his style, Google "Liefeld Captain America."

style created by John Chambers for the films and subsequent television incarnations. And yes, some of the storylines spread the suspension of disbelief to the breaking point, even in a fictional future universe about a world full of civilized simians.

But now, 25 years later, we have the benefit of the distance of time to give us a better perspective on the merits of Adventure's run. And it ain't so bad, really.

The previous essay does a marvelous job of covering the humble beginnings of Malibu Graphics and its Adventure Comics imprint, so there's no need to rehash them here. It also quite adeptly takes an in-depth look at the monthly *Apes* series, so – again – no need to cover that well-trodden ground. What it does *not* do is cover the rest of Adventure's *Apes* offerings – the aforementioned mini-series and one-shots – though it foretells the coming of an essay that would do so.

This is that essay.

The previous entry in this book offers a suggested reading order for the minis and one-shots, based not on publication dates but on the chronological order in which the events of those storylines occur. While this is useful for understanding the placement of each story within the larger framework of the franchise as a whole, this essay will look at each of Adventure's smaller stories in the order in which they were released.

And so, without further ado...

Ape City

The series opens with a chimpanzee wearing a fedora and sunglasses and playing a saxophone. And it gets stranger from there.

Ape City – published from August to November 1990 – was Adventure's first foray away from the main narrative of its monthly *Planet of the Apes* title, and, as such, was afforded quite a bit of creative freedom. Forget the misleading title; this has nothing to do with the locale of the same name that will one day house Cornelius, Doctor Zaius, and pals. Instead, think of this as *Planet of the Apes' European Vacation*.

Written by Charles Marshall (the writer for the monthly series) with art by M.C. Wyman, *Ape City* explores what happened after *Conquest of the Planet of the Apes*. Viewers are already all too familiar with how North America went down, but what about the rest of the world? *Ape City* answers that question, at least in part, by looking at Paris and its surrounding environs.

After the fall of man and the rise of the apes, Western Europe has fared far better than the United States. Infrastructure is still intact, leaving the ape inheritors with electricity, running water, and even broadcast television.

In a June 1990 interview with *Comics Scene*,[2] writer Marshall offered this perspective:

> To me, it's the next logical step when apes take over. You have apes that are emulating humans. In their part of the world, *nothing* has been devastated. You still have the buildings, the clothing stores, and the restaurants. These apes who have been the servants to the humans, who have seen how they acted, are all suddenly in the same shoes. I can't imagine that they would just throw everything away.

In *Ape City*, they haven't.

In the first issue, "Monkey Business," readers are introduced to Mongo, a chimpanzee nightclub singer (performing, of course, a differently spelled version of the theme from *The Monkees*). Growing weary of the lounge act, he bids *adieu* to his friend – club owner Fats – and takes off in search of adventure. From there, the scene shifts to a landing spacecraft, and soon the Vindicators make their entrance. A gang of five mercenaries from the past (Scab, Devon, Moriah, MX, and π), the Vindicators have been sent to the future to try to eradicate the ape menace early enough that future Ape-o-nauts Cornelius and Zira will never make their way back to the past and begin to eradicate the future.[3]

Time travel is confusing.

While the Vindicators are busy slaughtering every ape they see, one chimp – Flannagan – makes his way onto the vessel and discovers the crystal that powers the ship. He takes it back to his friend and mentor Doctor Benday (named, presumably, as a nod to Ben-Day dots[4]), an orangutan scientist busily trying to find a new power source to replace the aging and failing human power plants. So, naturally, the aforementioned power crystal is tossed into a basket and summarily ignored for the rest of the first issue, because Flannagan has to go and feed Cong (who, or whatever, that is).

---

[2] Gross, Edward. "Welcome Back to the Planet of the Apes." *Comics Scene*, No. 13. June 1990.

[3] As seen in *Escape from the Planet of the Apes* (1971)

[4] Small, colored dots of equal shade, usually cyan, magenta, yellow, and black in color, which are part of the four-color printing process used in comic publishing for several decades in the 20th century, and named after illustrator and printer Benjamin Day.

Cut back to Mongo, walking the Earth like Caine and singing "I'm a Believer."[5] He is soon beset by a sai-wielding ninja baboon – a baboonja, natch – and a hundred or so of its compatriots, but is rescued by Rox, a female chimp with a katana blade and an attitude, who is on her way to an appointment. Mongo decides to join her on her way (to keep her safe, of course).

The final group to be introduced comes in the form of Big Mal and associates, who look like they took their cues from *Chicago Mobs of the Twenties*. Also susceptible to the looming power crisis, Mal learns that the foremost authority on electricity is the aforementioned Benday, so he sets out with his goons to pay the doctor a visit.

They're not the only ones. The baboonjas, in search of a power source, seek Benday as well. The Vindicators, meanwhile, discover that their crystal is missing and head out to hunt it down. And the appointment that Rox has to keep? Also with Benday; she's to be his bodyguard. As they're talking, Mal's gang bursts through the front door, the baboonjas crash through a window, and the Vindicators break through the wall.

...aaaand scene.

This is quite a bit to process in one issue, but it works well as the first act of a four-act story arc. It introduces the main players and sets up the problems: an energy crisis, mercenaries from the past, gangsters, and ninjas; essentially, just about every early-'90s movie trope in one convenient package. Not exactly what one would expect from a *Planet of the Apes* story, but Marshall knew that going in.

As he told *Comics Scene*:

> When they presented me with the opportunity to do a *second* series, one set in Europe, I didn't want to do more of the same. We had done our homage to the movies, so I couldn't get excited about that. But to give Adventure all the credit in the world, they gave me carte blanche on everything, and I told them, 'If I do another series, it's going to be *weird*,' and they had no problem with that whatsoever.

Weird or not, *Ape City* presents an entirely different view of simian society, one far more advanced than that which George Taylor will eventually encounter in 3978. The apes have inherited all of man's technology and are using it to live the life that their hominid forbears left behind. Aware of the possible resistance

---

[5] Presumably the original version by The Monkees, not the remake by Smash Mouth. I wish I could tell you this would be the last in-your-face gag like this.

by some of his readers, Marshall started the second issue with this contrite message:

> First off, let me apologize to any diehard *Planet of the Apes* fans who suffered from seizures upon viewing the first issue of *Ape City*. I'm quite certain you weren't expecting to see gangster chimps in pinstripe suits and a battalion of ninja baboons. [...]
>
> This is a different, more fun look at the *Planet of the Apes* concept (actually, it owes quite a bit to Pierre Boulle's novel that started it all – *Monkey Planet*). [...] this book centers around one primary idea: survival in a dangerous and uncertain world.[6]

That danger and uncertainty is at the heart of "See No Evil, Hear No Evil, Speak No Evil" in *Ape City* #2. Picking up right where the first issue left off (and named after the famous trial scene from the 1968 film), the issue finds Doctor Benday and company surrounded on all sides by attackers. One whistle-blow later, though, two things happen: Benday's crew is saved, and we finally find out who (or what) Cong is: a gargantuan gorilla[7] with the mind of a child, the result of Benday's experiments with genetics. While the rival assailants fight with one another and with Cong, Benday, Mongo, Rox, and Flannagan beat a hasty retreat. They make their way to the Vindicators' ship, and therein discover that a sixth member of that team had stayed behind: Jo Taylor, daughter of once-and-future astronaut George Taylor.

Jo recounts the story of her father to Benday, and recalls how it led her to also join the space program and eventually the Vindicators. Meanwhile, Mongo takes off to recover the crystal from Benday's place. As Rox and Flannagan leave to go after him, Benday stays behind to tell Jo what gave rise to the Planet of the Apes.

This issue gives readers both more exposition and more action than the previous chapter. The conflicts and scenery changes help move the story along, and make up for the length of Jo's narration in the middle. Not only do we learn about Taylor's heretofore unknown daughter,[8] but we also get a more in-depth look at each Vindicator.

---

[6] *Ape City* #2. Adventure Comics, September 1990.

[7] Not to be confused with another copyrighted giant gorilla with a differently spelled name, or a similarly giant pixelated gorilla of video game fame with a differently spelled name.

[8] A second one, Tammy, would eventually be revealed once Mr. Comics held the comics license in the mid-2000s, and both would be referenced in the 2011 novel *Conspiracy of the Planet of the Apes*.

Regarding the Vindicators, Marshall told *Comics Scene*:

> The humans in the past basically know their future, that apes are going to
> take over the planet. I can't imagine that they would have that information
> and not try doing something about it. [...] I think they would try to do
> something more drastic, and from that I came up with the idea of sending
> a suicide squad[9] into the future to change the human/ape balance.

Of course, humanity could also have simply *not* enslaved apes in the first
place, but then there wouldn't be much of a story here.

One thing that becomes increasingly distracting as *Ape City* progresses is
the stream of anachronistic references to 20th-century American pop culture,
which often come from Mongo. Besides the aforementioned Monkees songs
that he sings, he makes references to The Three Stooges, Wheaties cereal, and
Bewitched (by calling Benday "Doctor Bombay," a character from that TV show),
and carries an American Express card. In France. In the future. In a civilization
run by apes. It's possible that Marshall threw these references in to help
readers identify more with the material, but it's far more likely that they were
peppered throughout the story in a failed bid to be tongue-in-cheek clever.

Speaking of confusing references, *Ape City* #3's "Monkey Planet"[10] opens
with an ape analogue for another American institution: the motorcycle gang,
appearing here in the form of the Hell's Apes. They come upon Mongo, and it's
quickly revealed that he and the leader of the pack,[11] Dinga, are old pals. While
they catch up and get very, very drunk, the action cuts back to the Vindicators,
who are still embroiled in battle with both the baboonjas and Big Mal's gang.
Benday and Jo, meanwhile, are enjoying a nice cup of tea as the doctor
continues her ape history lesson.

From there, the action escalates quickly. Two of the Vindicators encounter
Cong again, while Mongo – having departed from the Hell's Apes – infiltrates
Mal's gang, though not quite as successfully as he had hoped. Flannagan and
Rox are attacked by baboonjas at what used to be Benday's house, which gives
other Vindicators enough time to find the crystal. One of Mal's boys takes it,
but then a baboonja steals it with some hoodoo incantation before it goes *back*

---

[9] A term closely identified with the DC Comics title of the same name, featuring a
group of criminals sent by a government agency on what are likely to be suicide
missions in order to work toward having their sentences commuted.

[10] So named after Pierre Boulle's original novel

[11] Incidentally, "Leader of the Pack," the 1964 song by the Shangri-Las, is another
tune with which Mongo is familiar, as he is singing it when he encounters the
motorcycle gang.

to Mal's boys, who lose it to Flannagan. Just when all looks well and good, more Vindicators show up – with Benday and Jo as hostages – demanding the crystal, but before Flannagan can give it to them, Mongo and Dinga ride by and grab it... right before riding off a cliff.

In Europe, ape civilization developed quite differently from its North American counterpart, as seen on the cover of *Ape City* #3 (Oct 1990).

This issue strikes an even better balance between action and exposition than the last. Benday's explanation about the demise of humanity gives the story some much-needed context, particularly regarding why European simian society so closely mirrors humanity's (though no explanation is given as to the

Americanization of it). This is accented well by quick scene changes, continued gunplay, and the game of hot potato that everyone plays with the crystal.

Marshall also throws in a nice jab at another common Hollywood trope: stealing clothing that is coincidentally the perfect size. Everyone, from Captain Kirk to Indiana Jones, always happens to knock out an enemy who wears the exact same-sized clothing as the intrepid hero. Pop-culture *aficionado* Mongo must have no doubt been aware of this, as he beats up one of Big Mal's boys and puts on his suit... only to find that it's too small. He tries again, but the next suit is too big. Finally, with the third kayoed gangster, Goldilocks (err... *Mongo*, rather) is able to find a suit that seems tailor-made.

The final issue of *Ape City*, "Monkey See, Monkey Do," doesn't immediately pick up where the third issue left off. Instead, it takes a few pages to give readers a look at simian television programming – including MTV (Monkey Television, of course), *The Mating Game*, and *Gorillado* (a riff on *Geraldo*, hosted by a gorilla sporting Geraldo Rivera's trademark 'stache) – and uses an *ABC* (Ape Broadcasting Corp.) *Special Report* to recap the events thus far. This actually works to far greater effect than the straight recaps in the previous two issues, which sometimes came dangerously close to breaking the fourth wall. Here, the device is utilized well and is reminiscent of Frank Miller's usage of a similar narrative technique in *The Dark Knight Returns*.

From there, the story jumps right back to Mongo and Dinga seemingly plummeting to their doom, until Dinga jams the power crystal in the motorcycle's gas tank and – to the amazement of onlookers (and, presumably, readers) – the bike starts to fly. While E.T. and Elliott cruise the Parisian skies, zooming past the Eiffel Tower and the Arc de Triomphe,[12] the rest of the Hell's Apes make quick work of Big Mal's gang and the baboonjas. Before the Vindicators can step in, Jo takes control of the situation and threatens to blow them all up if they don't stand down, which they do. She promises to disable the Vindicator ship, but needs the crystal to do so. Benday hands it over and she flies off, but her plan hits a snag when Flannagan appears and takes the crystal out of its power housing. The ship starts to crash, but Cong appears out of nowhere to stop it, rescues Flannagan, flicks Jo into a lake, and throws the ship in the drink for good measure. At story's end, the Vindicators forgive Jo her

---

[12] To the strains of Dionne Warwick's "Up, Up and Away," with Mongo changing the lyrics to fit the situation

trespasses, the crystal is safely around Cong's neck, and the rest of the apes drink at Fats' Palace while Mongo sings "Born to Be Wild."

Yes, the result is as ridiculous as it sounds. It's understandable that Marshall wanted to end the story where he began it – with Mongo on stage – to bring it full circle, and that he wanted to have Benday and pals in attendance, to show that they had all become a family and that Mongo was no longer a loner. Unfortunately, the actual result is far too '90s-tastic, and would fit better in an episode of *Beverly Hills 90210* or *Saved by the Bell* than in a *Planet of the Apes* story – even one as bizarre as this.

The disappointing *dénouement* notwithstanding, *Ape City* #4 does a decent job of bringing the storyline to a close. It leaves enough open-ended questions to allow Marshall to revisit the story if he wanted to – What happened to the baboonjas? What will the Vindicators do now that they're stranded? How does the crystal help extend the European ape way of life? – but doesn't make those questions feel like hanging plot threads. In addition, with the conclusion of *Ape City* came the promise of a return to normality on the Planet of the Apes.

Urchak's Folly

Charles Marshall wasn't the only writer at Adventure with an *Apes* story to tell. Gary Chaloner – who provided cover art for *Ape City* #3 – threw his hat into the ring and created *Planet of the Apes: Urchak's Folly*, a four-part mini-series that premiered in January 1991. It takes place at roughly the same time as Adventure's monthly title, sometime during the time of Caesar's grandson, Alexander, roughly in the year 2140.[13] And it is apparent, at the outset, that this story is going to be wildly different, at least tonally, than *Ape City*.

Urchak's Folly #1, "The Valley," introduces us to the narrator, a human in a strange land – whose name is presented in promotional materials as Sebastian Thorne – with no idea who he is or how he got there. An ambush by a tribe of aboriginal troglodytes that Thorne possesses at least some fighting skills, but he is still overpowered by their sheer numbers. His world becomes immediately more complicated when he is rescued by a regal woman clad only in a V-string[14] and a headband (one *must* retain *some* modicum of modesty, after all).

---

[13] Handley, Rich. *Timeline of the Planet of the Apes: The Definitive Chronology*. New York: Hasslein Books, 2010.

[14] A variation on the G-string, first introduced by Victoria's Secret, in which the string that goes between the buttocks connects directly with the waistband to form a V shape.

Shortly after the rescue, while Thorne is admiring the reverence with which the troglodytes regard the woman, a group of horseback-riding gorillas attack, intent on killing all but the woman. Thorne barely has time to process the reality of what he sees before he becomes embroiled in life-or-death hand-to-hand (hand-to-paw?) battle with one particular gorilla, Renko. The human emerges the victor, but has no time for revelry or reflection, for he and the woman are taken into custody by a gorilla identifying himself as Sergeant Caspian. When they arrive at the apes' encampment, Thorne tries to fight his way out, but is quickly subdued and is ordered to be crucified by an ape he describes as "an ancient silverback gorilla draped in a cloak of vermillion": Colonel Urchak.[15]

The first aspect that immediately sets this series apart from *Ape City* is evident on page one: Chaloner's artwork. His stark lines and intense shadows – reminiscent of the early work of Kelley Jones – provide atmospheric foreboding even before the first troglodyte attacks. His mystery woman is sexy but not overly sexualized (even while wearing erotic underwear), a study more in strength than in sensuality. As well, the level of technology presented here is far more in keeping with that shown in *Battle for the Planet of the Apes* (and which, but for the invention of flash photography, doesn't seem to progress that much for the next 2000 years).

Throwing a human into that society certainly isn't new, but throwing an amnesiac into the mix gives *Urchak's Folly* a Barsoom feel, with Thorne cast in the John Carter role. (Now *there* would have been an interesting crossover!) There's even a bit of Jason Bourne in Thorne's character, who possesses martial skills but doesn't know where they came from. (Considering that Robert Ludlum's novel *The Bourne Identity* was first published in 1980, it's entirely possible the character was a source of inspiration.) Regardless of Thorne's origins – be they narrative or literary – one thing is certain: having a man with no memory serve as narrator allows readers to better connect with the material, learning about the environs at the same time and in the same way as the intrepid hero.

One caveat about the narrator, though – the narration is told in the past tense. Traditionally, when that tense is used, it indicates that the narrator is

---

[15] A character named in homage to Edgar Rice Burroughs' Tarzan novels, in which the titular Lord of Greystoke was raised by a tyrannical, human-hating ape warrior named Kerchak.

reflecting from a point in the future about events in the past. In other words, we know from the first caption box that Thorne's probably going to survive whatever ordeals come his way.

And those ordeals are legion, as *Urchak's Folly* #2's "The Bridge" shows, when Thorne wakes up on an examination table, staring at two rather astonished chimpanzees. When one, Doctor Titus, recognizes his intelligence and deems him non-threatening, he loosens the straps binding Thorne to the table, which is met with consternation from the just-arrived Caspian and Sergeant Chenko. After a brief kerfuffle between Chenko and the human, Caspian intercedes, and it is here that readers first learn of a growing enmity between the two gorillas.

The arrival of the camp administrator, Maximus, stirs something in Thorne's memory, and he gets glimpses of Victorian-era men (based on one fellow's A La Souvarov[16] and his use of the vernacular "Guv") discussing a lab experiment in what was presumably a prison. When Thorne snaps out of his sudden recall, he is in a cell once more, but he is not alone; he has a cellmate, William – a mutant from the Forbidden Zone, like those first seen in *Beneath the Planet of the Apes*. He relates his history and that of Urchak, a colonel in the army of General Ollo who was cast out of Ape City by Alexander.[17] William also talks about the savages and their priestess, who await the coming of a savior – George Taylor. Urchak plans to finish a bridge that will allow him access to their tribe so that he might destroy them, but William is under orders from Titus to blow it up before that happens.

Which he does.

But for the occasional fight, there isn't much action to be had in this issue. There's quite a bit of exposition and backstory, though, which help to provide a better understanding of both Thorne and Urchak. More importantly, though, William's story provides an interesting development in the *Apes* mythos – that of Taylor as savior, which is a theme that will be revisited several times during Adventure's run. How or why the human savages know of Taylor's eventual coming remains to be seen, though.

Those answers come in the third issue, "The Savages," which begins with Urchak blaming Caspian for the bridge's explosion. It is here that his mental

---

[16] The combination of mustache and sideburns with the lower half of the face left clean-shaven.

[17] *Planet of the Apes* monthly, issue #4 (August 1990).

instability truly begins to manifest, as he violates the apes' most sacred law and stabs Caspian to death. Elsewhere, Thorne awakens after the bridge explosion in the presence of William, Titus, and Morris (Titus's lab assistant). They soon come upon Argo DiVincenzo,[18] protector of the Taylorites – the followers of Taylor – who have decided to rescue their priestess, Miranda.

An unwary Administrator Maximus comes upon Urchak, deep in the midst of a psychotic break and terrorizing Miranda and Sebastian Thorne in *Urchak's Folly* #3 (Mar 1991).

Thorne convinces Argo to let him try to rescue her, instead of the entire tribe risking what would likely be certain death. But during his attempt, he is discovered by Urchak, who proceeds to beat him to a pulp. This throttling does

---

[18] A mandrill, the first and one of the only of its kind seen throughout the *Apes* franchise (the only other instances being Adventure's *Planet of the Apes Annual* and Ubisoft's 2001 *POTA* video game)

serve a positive purpose, though, as much of Thorne's memory begins to return, but that doesn't matter to Urchak. When Maximus tries to calm the gorilla's nerves, Urchak strangles him. He then has Miranda and Thorne locked up, where they proceed to get to know one another better.

It's evident at the beginning of the issue, but quite clear by the end, that Urchak is in the midst of a psychotic break. He personally murdered Caspian, yet has no memory of it and even calls Chenko "Caspian." His rationale for strangling Titus is that the chimp was actually a little demon that vexed him. And he shows no remorse for either act.

This issue also provides the origins of the Taylorites. Their holy book is actually the journal of Doctor Lewis Dixon, one of the humans who aided Cornelius and Zira in their escape in the third film. In it, Dixon discusses the two chimps and their revelations about how Taylor's arrival signaled the beginning of the end of their world. More of the journal is shown in the final issue of the series, detailing the couple's baby – Milo, who would later become Caesar – and how Dixon was instrumental in hiding the baby with Armando.

Urchak's Folly #4, "The War," starts smack in the middle of the troglodyte invasion, and Thorne and Miranda soon find themselves rescued. A brief skirmish ends with Chenko getting shot and the human couple fleeing for their lives. As they run, Thorne's memories come flooding back to him, revealing that he is actually from the far past – an unwilling participant in a Victorian time-travelling experiment. He and Miranda somehow make it to the very laboratory from which he came – miraculously intact, almost 300 years later – and it is there that Urchak finds them. Mad, crazy Urchak, still calling for Caspian. He attacks Thorne with a feral ferocity befitting his species and almost bests the human, but is tricked at the last second into leaping headfirst into the time machine. Thorne activates it, sending the gorilla into the distant past, and is next seen as a stuffed exhibit in the laboratory, apparently having been there the entire time. When the humans return to the ape encampment, they find it in flames. In his last act, the mortally wounded Chenko finds Titus holding Dixon's journal and murders him before being killed himself by Argo. They all part ways, and Thorne and Miranda set off together for parts east.

Introducing the time-travel element in this issue works well enough, but it seems like a bit of an easy crutch to fall back upon. Making him a stranger from the past puts him in the same league as Taylor, Brent (from *Beneath the Planet of the Apes*), Virdon and Burke (from the *Apes* TV series), and even Hudson, Allen, and Franklin (from *Return to the Planet of the Apes*). Granted, making him a Victorian traveller does set him apart somewhat – and suggests that the experiment that sent him there may in some way be related to H.G. Wells's *The Time Machine*, in which the Time Traveller is simply referred to as such and not given a name. It's a clever touch, for sure, as is naming the machine's inventor after Léon Foucault, the French physicist who took some of the earliest measurements of the speed of light. But in a franchise replete with time travel, it seems a bit of a cop-out.

Despite that, *Urchak's Folly*, as a whole, works quite well. Chaloner crafts a compelling tale full of love, betrayal, hope, mystery, and (mostly) believable fight sequences. He leaves no loose threads at the tale's end, either, though one does wonder what ever became of Thorne and Miranda. Unfortunately, they exist only within the confines of this mini-series, and are never utilized elsewhere during Adventure's *Apes* run (the Taylorites, on the other hand...).

Ape Nation

The next *Apes* mini-series that Adventure Comics put out premiered in February 1991. Despite the misleading title, it was not, in point of fact, a bigger, bolder sequel to *Ape City*. Besides *Planet of the Apes*, Malibu was home to a number of licensed properties, *Terminator*, *Tarzan*, *Star Blazers*, and *Star Trek: Deep Space Nine* among them. In July 1990, they published the first issue of a mini-series for their most recently acquired property, *Alien Nation*, based on the 1988 film starring James Caan and Mandy Patinkin, as well as the 1989 television series starring Gary Graham and Eric Pierpoint.

Perhaps you can see where this is going.

According to Malibu co-founder and creative director Tom Mason, the idea originally started as a lark.

> Malibu's head bean-counter Scott Rosenberg [...] was comparing the heights and weights of various Malibu beans and noticed that both *Alien Nation* and *Planet of the Apes* were 20th Century Fox properties.
>
> "Wouldn't it be neat if we could team-up the two titles," he blurted out from his inlaid oak cubicle one lazy California afternoon. [...]
>
> "Ha! Ha! Ha!" we all laughed.[19]

Enter Charles Marshall, Malibu's *Apes* scribe extraordinaire who, according to Mason, approached the company a scant two weeks later with the very same idea. Mason told him:

---

[19] Mason, Tom. "Apes, Aliens and Humans: A Lesson in Ape Management." *Ape Nation* #1 (February, 1991)

You have to figure out a way to bring them together. [...] Make it sane and believable. Don't bring them together through some goofy science experiment gone horribly wrong or for something like the Interplanetary Boxing Title. If you can do that and sustain it for four issues, we've got a series.[20]

Marshall, no stranger to writing unconventional *Apes* tales, did exactly that, and *Ape Nation* is the result. Taking place during the time of Adventure's monthly title (and, by extension, *Urchak's Folly*), *Ape Nation* shows what happens when a Tenctonese slave ship crashes onto simian-controlled Earth.

It also has the singular distinction of being the first comic book that Adventure – and Malibu as a whole – put out in color.

The first issue, "Plans," was released in two editions: the standard 28-page newsstand/direct market version and a 40-page "Limited Collector's Edition" put out by Diamond Comics Distributors. The latter featured a painted cover by Peter Hsu, character sketches and designs by artist M.C. Wyman, an *Ape Nation* "Who's Who," and an additional six-page prequel story, titled "Twice Upon a Time." The story itself is a nice addition but isn't much to speak of – it uses the same text, floating down the center of each page, to detail an ape fight with a bear and a perilous Tenctonese spaceflight. It does, at least, perform the task of showing the similarities between the two species, but it ultimately does nothing to add to the narrative to come.[21]

At the heart of the story is Heston,[22] a minor character from the monthly title, who warns Alexander's council of the crashed space vessel. He is given authority to assemble a team to go investigate and takes Packer (an aptly named packrat primate), Winnipeg (one of the Lightfeet[23]), Roto (a convict who claims to be the strongest ape of all), and Bartholomew (a precocious youth) with him.

Elsewhere, General Ollo – the Aldonite[24] gorilla banished by Alexander – meets with Simon, a talking human known as a slaughterer of apes. A third party soon joins the meeting: Danada the Destroyer, a Tenctonese villain. Ere

---

[20] Ibid.

[21] Though that perilous spaceflight *may* be revisited later on...

[22] Named, obviously, after Charlton Heston

[23] An ape tribe who lived like Native American humans, sought enlightenment, and were known as skilled trackers, the Lightfeet were first introduced in Adventure's monthly *Apes* title.

[24] A follower of General Aldo, Caesar's rival from *Battle for the Planet of the Apes*

long, they team up with plans for – what else? – nothing less than world domination.

As with the first issue of *Ape City*, Marshall shows with "Plans" that he is quite adept at setting up a four-act story from the very beginning. This issue immediately introduces all of the important players and lays out the main conflicts. In addition, he doesn't take the same tone of absurdity with *Ape Nation* that he did with his previous mini-series, nor does he take the material too seriously. He knows that, at its heart, this is a comic book about talking apes meeting aliens, and treats it with the appropriate balance of seriousness and humor.

He also succeeds in making the Tenctonese arrival on the Planet of the Apes a believable one. As Danada describes to Ollo and a disbelieving Simon, their ship – under the capable command of their captain, Caan[25] – flew too close to a black hole. By passing through it, they also moved through an area in which space and time became intertwined, so that by flying through one, they were also flying through another. This is, of course, a common sci-fi trope, reminiscent of any number of other instances, not the least of which is the very same principle employed in 2009's *Star Trek* reboot, and may be tied tangentially to the *Apes* franchise's own Hasslein Curve which transported Brent's vessel to the 40th century.

"Pasts," *Ape Nation*'s second issue, opens with an invading horde of gorillas, Tenctonese, and humans ravaging the ape countryside. Simon, Ollo, and Danada are embroiled in plans to conquer Ape City, but the scene suggests that Simon isn't as enamored with the plan as he was in the previous issue. From there, the scene shifts to Heston, who – along with his merry band – has been captured by the aforementioned horde and is chained next to Caan, who relays how he came to be there... and that he is Danada's brother. A rescue attempt by Caan's sister, Elysa, goes awry when she is felled by Simon, but that prompts both Caan and Heston into action, as they break free of their chains and go on the offensive.

On the road, the two unlikely partners come to a farmhouse, where the Tenctonese finds a pail of sour goat's milk (which has the same effect on his species as alcohol does on mammals) and proceeds to get blotto. He soon runs

---

[25] So named after James Caan, who portrayed cop Matthew Sykes in the *Alien Nation* film. Marshall was nothing if not consistent in his less-than-imaginative-but-seems-to-be-clever naming of characters.

afoul of an escaped Roto, who doesn't know Caan and only sees him as yet another of his captors. They begin to scuffle, with Roto plainly the stronger, and only stop when Simon, of all people, intercedes.

The tale that Caan tells to Heston makes for a nice call-back to the six-page prequel in the Limited Collector's Edition, and the reveal of the kinship between him and Danada adds an interesting dynamic to the story. As well, the first signs of Simon's dissent with his would-be conqueror allies make themselves evident in the early pages of this chapter, leading readers to wonder what his motivations are when he appears at the end of the issue.

The artwork, however, begins to get a bit distracting by this point in the story. The depictions of the Tenctonese, in particular, don't seem authentic to their portrayal on both the large and small screens. In those versions, the sides of their head are almost flush with their jawline, giving their skull a fairly human shape to them and only jutting out slightly. Wyman's aliens, however, have a head that bulges considerably above the ears, making their skull far more bulbous than those of their on-screen counterparts. It *is* possible that the movie's Tenctonese ship that landed on Earth in 1988 contains a different race than those in *this* ship,[26] but that doesn't seem very likely.

Whatever the case, things certainly start to heat up for the Tenctonese, particularly Caan, in "Pawns," *Ape Nation*'s third issue. After Simon "rescues" them from Roto, the three find themselves staring at the business end of a Tenctonese battleaxe. A group of the aliens has come to take them all back into custody, but this band of three quickly overcomes them. It is here that Simon learns of Ollo's treachery – the gorilla had ordered this hit squad to take out the human in the previous issue – and switches allegiances to his new cohorts.

Meanwhile, aboard the alien vessel, tensions are mounting between Ollo, who disapproves of the non-Aldonite ways of his ally, and Danada, who – after the gorilla's departure – orders him killed. At the same time, Heston makes his way onto the ship in search of Caan, but finds a surprisingly alive Elysa. They go off to stop Danada and to search for her other brother,[27] who is preparing, along with Simon and Roto, to take on the invading horde.

---

[26] Not unlike the Klingons on *Star Trek*; some have forehead ridges and some don't, owing to a genetic condition stemming from an artificially created virus.

[27] The two share some quiet scenes together in an *Ape Nation* tie-in tale in monthly issue #13, titled "Drunken Interlude," as discussed in the previous essay.

There isn't much purpose for this issue, really, except to set the stage for the fourth and final act. Much of it is also a bit hard to swallow. Caan watched Simon stab his sister in the previous issue and fully believes her dead, yet teams up with Elysa's murderer with virtually no hesitation. And speaking of Elysa, she tried to help Caan escape, and yet when Heston finds her, she's sleeping comfortably in what appear to be her regular quarters. If Danada was so easily willing to overthrow and imprison his own brother in a mad power grab, wouldn't he then want to lock up the sister who tried to let that brother go? At the very least, shouldn't she be in the ship's brig, or chained to a bed in its medical bay or something?

In the fourth and final issue, "Pains," Heston and Elysa find Danada, who tells them that there's no way to stop the advancing alien, ape, and human army. He tries to lay all of the blame on Ollo, but the gorilla overhears everything and kills the Tenctonese usurper. The alien woman and her chimp ally begin to sow discontent outside of the vessel; Elysa tells those of her kind that Ollo killed their leader, and Heston informs the surrounding apes that it was, in fact, Danada who killed Ollo (who is not actually dead). Their plan has the desired effect, and the two species begin to fight one another.

Apes, humans, and Tenctonese... oh my! Artist M.C. Wyman really shines in this two-page spread from *Ape Nation* #4 (Jun 1991).

On the battlefield, things do not appear to be going well for Roto, Simon, and Caan, but the cavalry soon arrives in the form of ten Lightfeet and the tide quickly turns. The fighting ends, and the compatriots make their way back to the alien ship to free those inside. Caan and his sister are reunited, Simon disappears into the wilderness, and everyone eventually parts ways, with the Tenctonese preparing for a long space journey.

This issue provides a satisfactory-enough conclusion to the mini-series. True, the ending seems a bit too easy – the approaching army is tired and possibly drugged, and the arrival of the Lightfeet at the last moment is awfully convenient. Still, there are some nice moments, including a subtle wink and a nod to *Star Wars*: Heston and Elysa escape from their pursuers by jumping down the ship's trash chute.

Wyman also shows here that he really knows how to draw engaging battle sequences. For much of *Ape Nation*, the army is shown as a dust cloud with faint hints of arms and legs, with the occasional panel-sized close-up. Once the Lightfeet get in on the action, though, Wyman really amps up the energy, particularly with the two-page spread on pages 16-17.

In his final editorial for the series, "Alien See, Ape Do," Mason mentioned that there were talks of a sequel for *Ape Nation*. Marhsall, he wrote, had everything already plotted, and everyone at Adventure was on board and ready to go. All they needed was the promise of sales. Unfortunately (or fortunately, depending on your opinion of the series), there must not have been enough sales promised, as that sequel never saw the light of day.

Blood of the Apes

The next mini-series to come from Adventure Comics was a four-issue reprint of Marvel's 1970s "Terror on the Planet of the Apes" storyline, written by Doug Moench and Gerry Conway, with art by Mike Ploog and Frank Chiaramonte. Sadly, only the first four chapters of that storyline were reprinted, despite Malibu's plans to repackage the entire saga. Instead, Adventure resumed its focus on telling new stories, the next of which represented a significant departure from the standard *Planet of the Apes* lore.

Caesar, son of Ape-o-nauts Cornelius and Zira, first decreed the Ultimate Law in *Battle for the Planet of the Apes*: "Ape shall not kill ape." This doctrine drove simian society for the next two thousand years, and was revered above all other laws. If indeed it was broken (as Aldo himself did in *Battle*), the act was met with absolute horror and revulsion.

So, naturally, Adventure decided to focus on a character who regularly violates that very rule. The result is *Planet of the Apes: Blood of the Apes*, written by Roland Mann and illustrated by Darren Goodhart.

At the very beginning of the first issue, we are introduced to the central character, Tonus the Butcher, who is pursuing a chimpanzee with a weapon and a book – a volume of the *Encyclopedia Britannica* – that he obtained from humans. When the chimp tries to escape, Tonus shoots him dead, then returns to the city of Phis, where he must explain his actions to ape Colonel Noorev. Across the Mizziphee River from Phis[28] is a human colony, home to a society of Taylorites who are considerably more advanced than those who were featured in *Urchak's Folly*.

Tonus, meanwhile, begins to wax elegiac in a bar about his lot in life and about his lost love, Deetra. As he stumbles out, he comes across Valia, an animal rights (read: human rights) activist whom he first mistakes for Deetra. When she verbally attacks him for his methods, he begins to bristle, but before their argument can escalate, an alarm sounds. There is an intruder in the armory: a human. A *talking* human.

The first, immediately noticeable difference in *Blood of the Apes* is the artwork. By now, readers were used to the fact that Adventure wasn't going to adhere to the ape look developed by John Chambers, but *Blood* represents an even further departure than that. His apes – especially Tonus – bear a striking resemblance to Kalibak, the DC Comics character designed by Jack Kirby. Some of their facial masks are recognizable as quasi-ape-like, but their overall Kirby-ness makes them a bit difficult to get used to. The rest of Goodhart's artwork is solid, though.

Incidentally, the artwork is not the only Kirby connection to appear in *Blood of the Apes*. In his opening editorial, Mason wrote: "Roland provided Darren with a loose plot. Darren breaks it down into pencil form. From there, Roland writes the final dialogue. This gives the artist more say in the actual story*telling* and gives Roland an additional challenge of writing dialogue in conjunction with something that's already drawn." This is a description of plot-first scripting, also known as the Marvel Method. It was devised by Stan Lee in the early 1960s and became his preferred method of collaborating with Jack Kirby and others.[29]

---

[28] Presumably the Mississippi River and the city of Memphis, Tennessee
[29] O'Neil, Dennis. *The DC Comics Guide to Writing Comics*. New York: Watson-Guphill, 2001.

In issue two, both camps – ape and human – are in a tizzy over the captured human, the apes because he can speak and the humans because, well, he was captured. One of the Taylorite leaders, Myndith, is particularly furious, as she doesn't even understand what the human, Marcus, was doing in Phis in the first place. They mount a rescue mission and bring him home, riling up the apes further in the process, with Tonus deciding to address the human problem on his own. While on his way, he once again happens upon Valia, who he believes is in league with the humans.

By now, it starts to become apparent that there will be several major personality changes by the end of the mini-series. Tonus absolutely hates humans, but his lost love was a supporter of them and so is the mysterious Valia. It isn't too much of a stretch to imagine that Tonus's views about humanity may start to change.

It's a bit difficult to believe that the Taylorites in this series can in any way be related to those in *Urchak's Folly*, however. There, they were little more than savages, clad in loincloths and V-strings. Here, they wear actual clothing – one even wears a *Flash* T-shirt – and they bear closer resemblance to the humans in Caesar's camp from *Battle*. In *Folly*, their hair was wild, even mangy. Here, they rock afros and mullets.

One thing that Mann does well, the wildly different Taylorites notwithstanding, is tie this series in to the rest of Adventure's *Apes* continuity. Tonus mentions getting his charter from General Ollo, seen both in the monthly title and in *Ape Nation*, and referenced in *Urchak's Folly*. As well, this issue in particular heralds the return of Argo DiVincenzo, the mandrill last seen in the final issue of *Folly*, who is far too cool a character to limit to a single appearance.

Predictably, *Blood of the Apes* #3 begins with a conversation between Tonus and Valia, who is trying to change the Butcher's mind about the worthiness of humanity. In Phis, Noorev receives a battalion from Ape City who have come to help take care of their human problem. The humans in question, meanwhile, encounter and quickly overcome Tonus, and set about trying to have a conversation with him regarding possible harmonious human-ape relations to no avail, so they knock him out.

Valia, it seems, is well known to the humans; they've been looking for her. At her insistence, they leave him alive and alone, so that he can see the mercy that they would like apes to bestow onto them. When he comes to, he starts to seriously consider her position, all the while climbing a tree to recover a cache of weapons. While in that tree, he notices the interaction between a human mother and child, who has learned in school of man's past mistreatment of apes and the need for a reconciliation between the species. As this occurs, unrest continues in the Taylorite camp, and Myndith decides on an unorthodox course of action: a peace march into the heart of Phis.

Planet of the Apes has long been successful not just because it's a planet full of talking apes, but also because of the social commentary that has been weaved throughout the franchise. *Blood* is no different, especially starting with this issue. At the heart of the problem is the fear of the other, spurred on by wounds of the past. The apes fear and hate mankind for what they've done. The humans fear the apes as well, but want to make amends and live in harmony. Each camp has its detractors – the apes have their animal-rights activists, while the humans have people like Richard, who feels that the answer to their problems is superior firepower.

These themes are universal throughout history; take any two warring nations, states, factions, or families and you'll find similar individuals in each and every one. For every warmonger there is a peacemaker, each trying to convert or obliterate the other, and *Blood* shows that the Planet of the Apes is no exception.

The final issue shows the continuation of Tonus's conversion from one to the other. The human child has spotted him in the tree, and gleefully waves and calls to him. Tonus, thinking of Deetra and Valia, lets him go, and soon comes upon the latter. She informs him of the upcoming peace march – how does *she* know? – and before he can talk her out of it, they encounter the army from Ape City. Tonus tries to stop them, arguing that the humans are unarmed and come in friendship, but he is brushed aside so, once again, he decides to take matters into his own paws.

The former Butcher goes to warn the approaching humans, but is too late. The ape army is right behind him, and thus begins the slaughter of the unarmed humans. All too quickly, the humans are fleeing, dying, or dead, and both Tonus and Valia are mortally wounded. As they lay dying together, Valia reveals her secret: she is no ape. She is Myndith, in disguise the entire time. In their last moments, she professes her love for Tonus, who has – against all odds – fallen in love with a human.

The ending of *Blood of the Apes* is a tad heavy-handed and more than a little predictable (not to mention somewhat far-fetched, for surely the apes would recognize a human wearing a mask), but it certainly drives home its point. Goodhart draws particularly grisly battle sequences, not so much for carnage but for their ability to instill disgust in the reader; one such panel focuses on a human toddler, surrounded by violent chaos, crying over the body of his slain mother.

A forbidden love ends tragically for Tonus the Butcher in *Blood of the Apes* #4 (Feb 1992).

The only complaint? In the midst of what was to be the final battle of his life, Tonus goes toe-to-toe with a gorilla assailant and, in a moment of fury, screams, "Kiss my butt!"

Really? Is that the best that Tonus the Butcher can do?

Surely he could have come up with something better. There's no logical reason why he couldn't have used the far-better-fitting "kiss my ass" instead. Remember, "damn" and "hell" were frequently employed throughout the *Apes* franchise in general (most famously in the '68 film, which was rated G) and also in these comics. Additionally, human nudity has abounded in several *Apes* titles; recall that Miranda only wore a headband and V-string, and nothing else, in *Folly*. Furthermore, Adventure's sister imprint, Aircel, was famous for putting out such erotic titles as *Flesh Gordon* and *Debbie Does Dallas*. Is it really possible that *showing* them was fine, but actually *saying* "ass" is where the creators drew the line?

A Day on the Planet of the Apes

In September 1991, Adventure released its first (and only) *Apes* annual, *A Day on the Planet of the Apes*. Written by Marshall, with art by James Tucker and clocking in at 54 pages, this issue offers up six stories. As Marshall told *Comics Source*, "This title was inspired by the photography book they did recently where they sent photographers all over the world to take pictures on the same day, so you got a feeling for what was going on everywhere. I wanted to tell stories that took place in one day all over the planet of the apes, so you got a feeling for what kind of place this was and how different it was."

The first story, "Morning Glory," features an unnamed ape returning from a long journey and trying to make his way back to his wife and child. It is told entirely through caption boxes, giving readers a peak into his mind. Marshall really shines here, having written the character in such a way that his thoughts of love could conceivably come from any one of us.

"High Noon" follows, and it is exactly what one would expect: apes in the Old West – or, at least, the *Planet of the Apes* version, which is actually mid-22nd century. It details an adventure involving the Ape Riders, a quartet consisting of Shiloh, one of the Lightfeet; Mojo, a travelling showman who banded the Riders together; Deadeye, a former bandit and a quickdraw; and The Monk, the group's doctor (and one of the best gamblers in the West). This is precisely the sort of tale that falls squarely in Marshall's wheelhouse: it's ridiculous, and it's as far afield from standard *Apes* mythology as you can get, but it's also fun.

And the story must have proved relatively popular with readers (or at least with Adventure's editors), as the team makes a return in the monthly series, with issue #20, "Cowboys and Simians," which focuses on the Riders. (Though they do meet their makers not long after, so maybe they weren't all *that* popular...)

Up next is "Afternoon Delight," starring everybody's favorite (or most reviled) guards, JoJo and Frito, the bumbling, comic-relief pair who made their debut in the monthly series' sixth issue and were the spotlight of one of three stories in issue #13. There, they came upon a cache of Hostess fruit pies (yes, really) and gorged themselves. In this story, they find a bomb shelter filled with beer and proceed to get hammered, all the while having an argument about whether the beer tastes great or is less filling (yes, really). They also come upon a generator and a boombox and jam out to Bob Seger's "Old Time Rock and Roll" (yes, really).

Marshall certainly liked his comic relief; however, even though Mason claims that they received no complaints about JoJo and Frito at all from readers,[30] it seems rather difficult to believe that these two characters were warmly received. It's also hard to accept that a gasoline generator or any magnetic storage devices – namely, cassette tapes – would function after two hundred years. However, according to a government report,[31] beer can, in fact, survive a nuclear blast and be perfectly drinkable (yes, really), so at least Marshall got the science right there.

Marshall continues the silliness with "Eternal Dusk." Here, a couple of kooky ape teenagers, Bobo and Jina, do their best impersonation of Michael Jackson's "Thriller" video and sneak into a haunted house, where they are attacked by a vampire mandrill, but the whole thing ends up being a campfire story told by the "real" Bobo. The end.

Moving on, the penultimate story is "A Night at Fats' Palace," a return to Marshall's *Ape City* stomping grounds. Big Mal and his crew crash the party, and Mal sets his eyes on that evening's entertainment: Monique, performing a heartfelt rendition of "I Wanna Be Like You."[32] When Fats protests, Mal's men strongarm him, but then Dinga and the Hell's Apes swing in to save the day – and wreck the joint in the process.

"Midnight Tales," the last entry in *A Day on the Planet of the Apes*, actually concludes the first tale. The intrepid traveler from "Morning Glory" finds his way home to his wife, who has been lighting a different candle for each night that he had been away. It's quite a touching sight, and – when combined with its bookend counterpart – is about as tonally different from the rest of the issue as a story can get.

It's a shame that the annual didn't feature more stories like its first and last one. If Marshall truly wanted to look at various aspects of the planet on the same day, it would have been much better served if less of the issue were full of slapstick and one-liners. "High Noon" and "Eternal Dusk" could have been taken completely out of here, perhaps to be replaced with another look at *Folly's* Thorne and Miranda, or maybe another aspect of the monthly series.

---

[30] See previous essay

[31] United States of America. Department of Health, Education, and Welfare. U.S. Food and Drug Administration. *The Effect of Nuclear Explosions on Commercially Packaged Beverages*. By E. Rolland McConnell, George O. Sampson, and John M. Sharf. Washington, D.C.: March 1956. Project 32.2a.

[32] The song sung by King Louie the orangutan in Walt Disney's *The Jungle Book*

Anything but cowboys and vampires.

The Sins of the Father

Adventure's next one-shot was published in March 1992. Written by Mike Valerio, with art by Mitch Byrd, *Planet of the Apes: The Sins of the Father* takes place thirty years before the 1968 film.

A murder has been committed in Ape City, and the victim is Camille, the young daughter of police prefect General Ignatius. The Minister of Science, Augustus, along with his son Zaius – yes, *that* Zaius – investigate. The prefect insists that the killer must have been his human slave, but Augustus, despite the Ultimate Law, insists that the murderer was an ape. A further examination of the body reveals that it *was* a human, but Augustus still insists publicly that an ape is to blame, in an effort to postpone the man's execution. That night, Augustus and Zaius witness the brutality with which Ignatius beats the man, and how the man finally lashes back at the gorilla. The prefect pushes the slave to admit that he killed Camille and, to everyone's astonishment, the human slowly verbalizes, "Y-y-yesss..."

Augustus threatens to kill Ignatius if he harms the human further, but the gorilla doesn't listen and is put down by the Minister of Science. Augustus then tells the incoming authorities that Ignatius killed his own daughter and the human witnessed it; terrified that the human would out him as the murderer – blasphemy, surely, because man can't speak, after all – he attacked his slave, and they killed each other in the process.

Zaius confirms the story, unsure why his father's mouth produced such lies. Augustus soon makes that clear, though, as they ride through the desert and arrive at the iconic, decrepit Statue of Liberty. It is here that Zaius learns of man's former dominion over the planet, and the threat that talking humans represent to simian society. He vows to follow his father's example and quash any instances of such human anomalies in the future.

The Sins of the Father is a welcome departure from much of the rest of Adventure's *Apes* offering because it ties directly into the original film. Valerio's portrayal of Zaius as a wide-eyed, almost idealistic young orangutan serves as a sharp contrast to the crusty old cynic of the first two movies. This story gives that character far greater depth, and provides a great deal of understanding into his fear and hatred for Taylor.

It is a bit surprising, however, to see the Minister of Science play so fast and loose with the Ultimate Law. He has no problems jumping to the conclusion that an ape was Camille's killer, and shows absolutely no remorse for taking Ignatius's life. Perhaps, though, the revulsion that this surely spawns in his son later contributes to Zaius's fanatical adherence to the Sacred Scrolls. And in keeping with the comic's title, the sins of the father (Augustus) are nearly repeated by the son (Zaius), who proclaims a death sentence on Zira and Cornelius in *Planet* (even if *Beneath* shows that he never actually followed through with it). Apparently, the Ultimate Law has its exceptions.

The Forbidden Zone

In December 1992, Adventure Comics began its final foray on the Planet of the Apes. Its monthly series had its last issue in June of that year, and, after a six-month break, *Planet of the Apes: The Forbidden Zone* was released. Written by Lowell Cunningham with art by Leonard Kirk, *The Forbidden Zone* takes place several centuries after the events of the monthly series. It completely eschews the silliness that had pervaded the majority of Marshall's work with the company, focusing instead on the more serious themes of human-ape relations presented in *Urchak's Folly* and *Blood of the Apes*. And, given the title, it's a foregone conclusion that the denizens of the Forbidden Zone – the mutants, from *Beneath* and *Battle* – play a major role as well.

Indeed, the first issue, "Forbidden Knowledge," starts off in the titular wasteland, where one of the mutants – Mendez 10^{33} – is being persecuted for blasphemy, insisting that the Alpha-Omega Bomb that his people worship as a god is, in fact, a weapon that is killing them all. He is sentenced to death but escapes into the desert, where he wanders until the point of collapse. A scout takes him back to the community of Primacy, where apes and talking humans have lived together in harmony for three hundred years. The arrival of Mendez 10 can threaten all of that, however, since the mutants intend to find him and kill him and everything else in Primacy.

One of Adventure's strong suits, while holding the *Apes* license, was to show different ape communities in different parts of the world during different periods in history. The introduction of Primacy is in perfect keeping with that goal. The idea that a city still exists that practices the ideals which Caesar set forth is a refreshing one, to be sure. In addition, there is a scene in this issue in

---

[33] A bust of Mendez X – presumably the same individual – can be spied in one of the corridors of the Forbidden City in *Beneath*. Despite his blasphemy and betrayal in this story, his people apparently still honored him alongside the twenty-four other past Mendezes.

which an expedition from Ape City in search of viable farmland discovers the ruins of a gas-station convenience store that has three restrooms: men, women, and apes. Such a discovery could surely challenge Ape City's accepted view of history about human-ape relations. With "Forbidden Knowledge," then, there is the potential to set much of the Planet of the Apes on its philosophical ear.

"Danger Zone" is the title for issue #2, and its contents certainly live up to its foreboding name. Mendez 10 comes to in a room full of apes and freaks out (using the fiery mind illusion exhibited by the mutants in *Beneath*) but is ultimately calmed by Primacy's human security chief, Pell Shea. (The fact that Primacy's Lawgiver, Dogen, put a human in such a high position of authority naturally drives some of the gorillas ape.) He warns of the coming of the mutant army and is met with initial distrust, but Dogen and Shea take a chance on him and invite the mutant to become a citizen of Primacy.

In Ape City, meanwhile, the expedition team's report of their findings is destroyed as heretical, and apes are dispatched to quiet them. At the expedition site, the two leaders – Martin and Julius – discover a map of the United States. Julius sets out in search of some of the other cities on the map and eventually comes upon Primacy, but is not met with open arms.

The interplay between Martin and Julius is one of the more compelling that Adventure presents. Here, Julius – a gorilla – is an archaeologist at heart, eager to learn about history before the rise of the apes. On top of that, he is both erudite and remarkably polite, qualities not often associated with gorillas but usually attributed to chimpanzees. Martin, a chimp, on the other hand, has seemingly little interest in the sciences – particularly archaeology – and wants to get as far away from the ruins as possible. This character reversal was a brilliant turn on Cunningham's part. All too often, the three most common ape types – chimp, gorilla, and orangutan – stay within their social stations and almost never exhibit anything but their castes' stereotypical attributes. Here, Cunningham forces readers to acknowledge those stereotypes, and to try to move past any preconceived notions based merely on species.

War is looming at the start of the third issue, "Battle Zone," as the mutants continue to advance on Primacy. Inside the community, Shea, in the midst of battle preparations with Mendez 10, comes face to face with Julius, and both are shocked. Shea – and all of Primacy – had been cut off from Ape City for centuries by a wide zone of radiation, and had no idea that life still existed there. At the same time, Julius is utterly floored by talking, intelligent humans.

As they speak, the apes dispatched to quiet the expedition – having murdered everyone there, Martin included – begin to descend on Primacy. The mutants arrive at the same time, putting the once-peaceful city of ape-human harmony in the middle of a two-front war.

Kirk's artwork is particularly strong in this issue. As with almost every other Adventure *Apes* comic, the apes bear little to no resemblance to their cinematic counterparts, but Kirk is so good at what he does that it's easy to gloss right over that. The apes presented herein look like their real-life counterparts; the gorillas actually look like gorillas, the chimps like chimps, and so forth. Additionally, Kirk finds ways to add different physical characteristics to each of them, making them as differentially identifiable as humans. He does the same thing with the mutants, which at first may not sound like much of an accomplishment since they're humans; however, these mutants aren't wearing their facemasks, so their actual visages are scarred, slagging, and replete with irradiated rot.

Things come to a head in "War Zone," the final issue of *The Forbidden Zone* (and of Adventure's *Apes* run in general). Primacy's troops are forced to retreat in order to regroup as both the mutants and the apes continue to advance. Shea convinces Mendez 10 to use the fiery mind illusion once more, this time on the ape front lines. This chases the gorilla army right to the mutants, and the two of them engage in mortal combat. The apes emerge victorious but the cost in life is high, and their commander, General Brak, yields his forces to Primacy.

At the tale's end, Mendez 10 and Julius become citizens of Primacy. Brak takes his forces back to Ape City where he is heralded a hero, while the true account of the battle is suppressed. The mutant leader, meanwhile, is pleased with the outcome of the war, as all of the soldiers he sent were, as he put it, "those whose minds were stunted" and whose defective genes were now gone from their gene pool. Glory be to the Bomb.

There are quite a few heady concepts in *The Forbidden Zone*. Besides the aforementioned prejudicial stereotyping, Cunningham also touches upon parents and the children who do not live up to their expectations: Julius, a scientist, is the son of Colonel Arvo, the gorilla who leads the ape army before Brak's arrival. It is Arvo's intention to attack Primacy at any cost, including the life of his disappointment of a son. Arvo is so morally bankrupt that he regularly eschews the Ultimate Law, as evidenced when he wipes out the entire expedition at the convenience store, as well as when he tries to murder his superior officer.

And Brak? Brak is military, through and through, but he doesn't have the lust for battle as do his fellow gorillas. He does his bit for king and country because he is a good soldier, and good soldiers follow orders, but the suppression of the truth and the outright fabrication leave a sour taste in his mouth, leading him to make the one conclusion that truly epitomizes the Planet of the Apes: "Truth is the ultimate Forbidden Zone."

Adventure's End

With the end of *The Forbidden Zone* in March 1993, Adventure Comics published no further *Planet of the Apes* material. Their contract with 20th Century Fox expired and Malibu chose not to renew. There would be no more *Apes* comic books, in fact, until Dark Horse Comics adapted Tim Burton's re-imagining of the franchise in July 2001.

What Adventure left behind, though, is an indelible mark on the franchise. The company kept the flame going in the long, lonely period between Marvel and Dark Horse, and their contributions, though varied, are notable. For every "High Noon," there is an *Urchak's Folly*. For every "Afternoon Delight," there is a *Blood of the Apes*. For every "Eternal Dusk" there is a *Forbidden Zone*. And for every JoJo and Frito, there is a Julius or a Tonus.

Thank the Lawgiver for *that*.

Dark Horse Goes Ape: Is There a Soul in There?

by Lou Tambone

The 1990s were not a very fruitful time for primate publications of the comic book kind. Adventure Comics, a division of Malibu Publishing, held the *Planet of the Apes* license from 1990 until 1993, and the company published a wealth of original content during those three years. After 1993, however, the well had run dry.

The development of a new *Planet of the Apes* film stirred the comic pot, but the planned film lingered in development hell for a number of years. When the new movie became a reality, Fox started up its merchandising machine and one of its first acts was to award the publishing license to Dark Horse Comics.

Dark Horse had proven itself a worthy comic book publisher after enjoying great success with franchise favorites like *Star Wars*, *Aliens*, and *Buffy the Vampire Slayer*. With the promise of a great film and the comics in good hands, the stage was set for a *Planet of the Apes* revival of epic proportions. What we got instead, however, was a *Planet of the Apes* re-imagining of underwhelming disproportion.

Then again, all science fiction is subjective, right?

When you're a child, the deeper meanings and themes embedded so cleverly in science fiction stories are apt to fly over your head like a simian swinging from branch to branch in the trees above. The rediscovery of great stories is one of my favorite pleasures, and that applies to other media as well, like music. Being a musician and a creator of music, I always enjoy going back and rediscovering a great album or band. It's no different when it comes to literature.

Delving back into *Planet of the Apes* after all these years has been a fantastic trip. It has given me a new appreciation for this very original concept that has since branched out into many directions. The series was so influential that, to this day, the name Cornelius immediately conjures up an image of Roddy McDowall in an ape costume. For as long as I live, whenever I hear that name, I'll see a chimpanzee in my head.

Thematically, the *Apes* mythos covers a lot of ground, but I think what really attracts me now is the topsy-turvy nature of its core premise. For a long time, humans have enjoyed supremacy on Earth, establishing ourselves as the dominant species. We've gotten used to this. Yet the device that forms the foundation of the *Apes* universe is the idea that humans might not be able to maintain that control – that we could lose our position of dominance. This sort of role reversal is very appealing to me. Everything is just so backwards.

We can relate to apes in a primitive way. The physical resemblance between mankind and our simian cousins is a bit uncanny, which makes it all the more easy to imagine a *real* world in which apes could become civilized and human-like, and perhaps even take over the planet, much like the robots in the *Terminator* films.

These apes are powerful, primordial, intelligent, and of course dominant. They are, however, just like humans. For all their talk of superiority, they have all the same strengths and weaknesses that we have. They don't all get along. Some are more liberal than others, while others are quite conservative. Debates and fights within ape society are common. And humans are the *real* animals.

What a concept.

One thing all the films did well, which carried over into the comics, was to reflect events happening in the human world of today. The 1970s were a time of upheaval – civil rights activism, anti-war protests, government corruption, and much more. The films picked up on a lot of this and were able to present alternate, almost mirror images of the goings-on in the real world.

Dark Horse Comics' *Planet of the Apes* series revisits this concept, starting with *The Human War* miniseries and continuing to the end of the monthly series that follows. The main story is set against the backdrop of an ape civil war on the planet Ashlar,[1] mirroring events in the history of not only the United States, but plenty of other nations as well, making the appeal a global one.

Put this together with an engaging story, and I'm all in. This is exactly what Dark Horse did with its *Planet of the Apes* comics.

It's easy to overlook Dark Horse's contribution to *Planet of the Apes*, as it comprised only a small group of comics published following the release of Tim Burton's 2001 cinematic re-imagining starring Mark Wahlberg.

I'll wait for you to stop groaning before I continue...

Say what you will about the Burton film, but examined in the context of that movie, these comics are fun, engrossing stories on their own, developed in a sandbox-within-a-sandbox: the so-called "Burtonverse" within the larger *Apes* cosmos. Put them up against other series, and the cracks begin to show.

Media tie-ins are always a risky venture. It takes a lot of tricky timing and finger-crossing to get everything released at the right time. If you want a comic, game or book to come out alongside a film, you need to have that piece of media in the works well before the movie is completed. This can be thorny, because those rascally directors and producers like to make changes to films up until the proverbial eleventh hour, which can render source material for the tie-in incorrect or completely irrelevant. On top of all that, the tie-in's success and continued publication (typically measured in sales) hinge on whether or not the public embraces the film.

The Dark Horse folks were smart enough to stay away from the movie's central plot with their releases, instead focusing (mostly) on events occurring decades later. They were given a great deal of freedom to play in Tim Burton's re-imagined *Apes* universe, and it showed. Judging by how poorly moviegoers received the film (particularly its ambiguous ending), this could be one of the main reasons this comic series sold any copies at all.

Since there are not many issues or one-offs to discuss, I'll examine each series one at a time. Let's see what happens, shall we?

Dark Horse Extra

Dark Horse Comics published a fifty-issue, newspaper-sized series from 1998 to 2002 titled *Dark Horse Extra*, containing serialized tales from most of its comics roster. A three-part *Planet of the Apes* strip was featured in three

---

[1] William Broyles' initial outline for the film provided the name Aschlar, which later became Ashlar in the script, though that designation was not spoken onscreen.

successive issues (36-38) that ran from April to June 2001, written by Scott Allie and illustrated by Eric Powell and Dan Jackson. Attar, from the Burton film, stars with his brother, Tolan, along with some damn, dirty humans in this telling of a hostage standoff between ape soldiers and human savages.

This strip introduces the theme of sibling rivalry into the expanded stories, while offering a little foreshadowing of Attar's conflicted mindset in the film and his subsequent role as an exiled general in the monthly comic.

Young Attar, before his tenure as general, with his brother Tolan (*Dark Horse Extra* #36, Jun 2001)

The relationship between Attar and Tolan is somewhat representative of one of the central themes of the saga itself: that of human-ape harmony. Apes are fiercely loyal beings, and revealing signs of doubt about that loyalty can be perceived as weak or empathetic to the human struggle.

Tolan believes in unwavering dominance and likes it that way. Capturing, demeaning, and even killing a human is just a way of life. You kill a human and other humans will fear you. You cannot crack or break down, or else you run the risk of losing your dominance. Attar is a bit more accepting of humans, while still remaining carefully dedicated to the ape cause. To openly come out in support of humans could result in death or (as seen in *The Human War*) exile.

> *"Sometimes a cage is just a cage."*
> – Attar, *Dark Horse Extra* #36 (April 2001)

Though this story takes place before the events of the film, the Attar from the comic seems quite different from the hardened warrior introduced on-screen. When we first see him in the movie, the gorilla is openly hunting humans, as his job (and the script) demands. No signs of doubt about what the apes are doing are evident until the end of the film, when Pericles arrives in his little white pod.

In the comic, we're shown right away where his conflicting ideas about humans and ape supremacy lie. I get the impression he doesn't disagree with who the dominant species should be, but more with how order should be maintained. Attar believes in setting good examples and showing mankind that the apes are better via their actions. Tolan, on the other hand, couldn't care less about such things, as illustrated in the strip's final chapter.

As the two brothers sit around discussing the finer points of ape domination, some humans attack their camp and a standoff ensues. One human holds Tolan at knifepoint, while Attar restrains the man's child in response. Attar agrees to let the youth go free in order to save his brother, but more importantly (and perhaps subconsciously) to show these humans that apekind not only *is* dominant, but *deserves* to be. As expected, Tolan ruins this by killing the fleeing human. Attar is very angry, causing Tolan to question his real motives in letting the humans go.

"Would you go into enemy ground to save my life, brother?" Attar wonders, seemingly praising the human's bravery – a distinct departure from his onscreen dismissiveness toward humanity. It could be that this incident makes Attar think a little differently about what he says, and to whom. I like to assume that he kept his future grumblings to himself.

Perhaps this strip was intended to provide some foreshadowing of Attar's change of heart later in the film, but having read the comic *after* watching the movie, I found it a little forced. In the context of this little newspaper-like strip, however, it works quite well: direct and to the point.[2]

General Thade attempts to avoid his downfall prophesied by the blind chimp Oracle in the *Toys"R"Us Collector's Comic* (Jul 2001).

Toys "R" Us Collector's Comic

Retailer Toys "R" Us distributed a mini-comic prior to the Burton film's release. Like the *Dark Horse Extra* strip, this so-called "Collector's Comic," written by Phil Amara and illustrated by Pop Mhan, is tightly focused and deals predominantly with two characters.

The mini-comic's story takes place prior to the film's events. This comic's main purpose is to introduce the world to the Burton movie's primary antagonist, General Thade, along with another character exclusive to Dark Horse continuity, known simply as Oracle. The chimpanzee is a blind "seer" and Thade's prisoner. The narrative use of a prophetic oracle is not on original idea by any stretch of the imagination, but it gives this little one-off comic a well-deserved feeling of intensity.

This comic works extremely well as a set-up for the film. When you're remaking or rebooting a popular series, it's smart to introduce certain new

[2] Incidentally, the existence of Tolan (and the mention of their father) contradicts the novel *Planet of the Apes: Force*, by John Whitman, in which Attar is said to be an orphan without any family.

characters beforehand so the audience is familiar with them when the movie is released. Viewers will relate to them a little better and perhaps enjoy the film more. Thade, however, is such an enjoyable villain that it wouldn't have mattered either way. (I exited the theater in 2001 declaring Thade my favorite character, with Attar coming in second.)

What's more, this comic feels like a deleted scene from the film. By that, I mean that it fits naturally within the movie's context and could have been dropped into the first hour without interrupting its flow. The *Dark Horse Extra* strip, on the other paw, seems to beat readers over the head with ape dogma. This comic is a little more sinister and accomplishes a bit more, as far as helping to establish the re-imagined *Planet of the Apes* universe.

> *"The fates are mounted against you."*
> – Oracle, *Toys "R" Us Collector's Comic* (July 2001)

I've often heard the phrase "deliciously evil" tossed around in reference to villains whom we love to hate. For me, Thade falls squarely into this category, especially considering the details revealed in this particular comic. Who else but a deliciously evil villain would not only imprison a gifted oracle in a dungeon, shackles and all, but also take her son from her and have him raised as an orphan – just to prevent the kid from growing up to seek vengeance on him?

On the surface, Thade seems very sure of himself. But as with most over-confident beings, underneath the hood he is not so secure and requires constant reassurance. Perhaps this is the reason he keeps Oracle around, although this visit seems to backfire on him. According to the dialogue, it appears as if he has visited her before and has asked about her visions. Presumably, these previous visits must have gone somewhat better, or else Thade would have simply had her disposed of. After all, why keep visiting this blind ape, just to get repeatedly kicked in the ego?

I believe this visit was the important one – the one in which she has reached her limit and would rather die than be Thade's seeing servant any longer. Oracle doesn't seem to give a damn about what happens to her after learning of her son's fate. She tells Thade that he's doomed and, in the process, vaguely gives away a big moment in the film, when Pericles lands near the end. She also mentions Attar and how he has been duped into believing a different view of ape history. When Thade asks about Ari, Oracle even tells him flat-out that she has "moved on" and is all about ape-human harmony. Oh, but she doesn't stop there. The writers also seize the opportunity to tease the upcoming comic series featuring Esau (a human) and Seneca (an ape).

Of course, Thade is not thrilled to hear any of this, reacting violently and leaving her in her cell. As he departs, he convinces himself that she's mistaken... but you can't help but get the feeling that, in the back of his mind, some doubt remains. He's still confident about his future, but...

The Human War

Set several decades after the events of Burton's remake, this three-issue miniseries[3] – written by Ian Edginton, with art by Paco Medina, Juan Vlasco, Adrian Sibar, Christopher Ivy, and Norman Lee – is where Dark Horse's main storyline begins. Instead of living on the film's fringes, this series brings us into the future, where the simian world is being ravaged by a civil war between those apes (and humans) fighting for integration, and those who believe apes should remain the powerful, dominant species. The new main characters of Esau and Seneca are introduced alongside a new enemy, Minister Shiva. This short three-parter leads nicely into the larger series that follows.

Esau (left) and Seneca, an unlikely pair of friends on the planet Ashlar in *The Human War* #1 (Jun 2001).

An ever-present concept in *Planet of the Apes* lore is the notion that "ape shall not kill ape" (the notable exception being the TV series, in which that rule seems to be nonexistent). In this series, it's right up front in a small textual introduction, offset by the image of a bloody ape sword.[4] We're told that a civil

---

[3] *The Human War*, along with Dark Horse's film adaptation, also ran in Titan Books' five-issue *Planet of the Apes: The Official Movie Adaptation* magazine.

[4] Which is, admittedly, not entirely consistent with the Burton film itself, in which Attar kills Krull, Thade kills two gorillas, the ape military opens fire on Limbo, Thade

war is happening before we even get into the main storyline. This works well as an intro, as it drops us right into the fray.

One strength of this Dark Horse series is that it is not bogged down with a thousand different characters (on the rebel side, at least). For the most part, all of humanity ends up being represented by Esau, the human freedom-fighter, while the ape rebels are represented by Seneca. This, I feel, helps to keep everything in focus.

Esau is the quintessential Willis-Schwarzenegger-Stallone wisecracking, pun-slinging, shoot-'em-up-and-ask-questions-later tough-guy rebel in tattered clothing. This underscores the "humans are savages" motif, since the well-dressed Seneca is more mild-mannered, and perhaps more civilized, by comparison. Once an ape senator, Seneca became a somewhat reluctant rebel, believing war to be the only way to save both humans and apes from wiping each other out completely.

> *"It's not enough that I succeed... but that everyone else must fail."*
> – Shiva, *The Human War* #3 (August 2001)

As villains go, it's difficult not to enjoy Minister Shiva as a simian baddie. She's very Thade-like – which isn't much of a stretch, since we later learn that Thade was, in fact, her grandfather. She's mouthy, ruthless, rebellious, demanding, and dressed like Ming the Merciless of *Flash Gordon* fame. What's not to love? Well, there is the fact that she's into genocide... but let's overlook that for now, shall we?

Not only is Shiva Thade's granddaughter, but there's a little more to the story that makes for an exciting twist. While talking to her assistant, Fyn (Seneca's brother and a spy for the rebelling forces), she discloses a few other facts. Thade wasn't about to wait for Ari to come around to his way of thinking, so he took up with a courtesan ape who was Shiva's grandmother – and a half-chimp, half-gorilla crossbreed. More importantly, though, the minister tells Fyn there is something out in the Forbidden Zone that could end the war in the apes' favor. If you've seen the film, you know what that is: nuclear power.

The motif of nuclear destruction, of course, carries over from other *Planet of the Apes* media. When the classic films were made, nuclear protests and anti-war demonstrations were commonplace, and so these issues made their way

---

tries to kill Pericles, and Ari's life is threatened several times, without anyone once commenting about apes killing other apes... but I digress.

into the screenplays. Portions of both *Beneath the Planet of the Apes* and the extended version of *Battle for the Planet of the Apes* involved a large nuclear missile, the Alpha-Omega Bomb, being worshipped by zealous mutant humans living beneath the planet's surface.

The "Holy Fallout" (from a nuclear war waged millennia prior) created the mutants, and the Bomb would ultimately (at *Beneath*'s conclusion) bring about the planet's destruction. It thus makes perfect sense to incorporate nuclear power into *The Human War*'s storyline, as Burton did in his film.[5]

> *"Glory be to the Bomb, and to the Holy Fallout. As it was in the beginning, is now, and ever shall be. World without end. Amen."*
> – Mendez XXVI (Paul Richards), *Beneath the Planet of the Apes* (1970)

The third act of this comic ends up being a race to the finish line between Shiva's forces and the so-called Insurrectionists, who find out (via Fyn and the exiled General Attar) what the sinister minister is actually up to. The writers use vague comic book terms like "destiny" and "the truth" to represent what Shiva is searching for, or what they'll find out in the Forbidden Zone.[6]

Some enjoyable connections to the 2001 film are naturally employed as we make our way through the three issues. For instance, Attar makes a cameo appearance, perhaps foreshadowing his larger role in the following series. He's used wisely here, as a link between the past and present. Fortunately, this cameo doesn't feel obligatory, but instead well-thought-out and necessary.

Attar's grandson, Commander Kharim, represents another parallel to the film. Perhaps it's something in their bloodline, but Kharim basically performs the same role as Attar does onscreen: namely, he's the hardened brute who experiences an epiphany at an important moment in the plot and flip-flops his position. The fact that Shiva is an ape-racist (an apist?) and a half-breed – a taboo, at least in the comics[7] – affects Kharim's loyalty. When he discerns that she is fundamentally reckless and insane, he takes matters into his own paws.

---

[5] The most recent films have opted for a virus, as opposed to nuclear power, as the instrument of man's downfall. Perhaps this is a reflection of the changing times, but you can still spy the old biohazard symbols in the background.

[6] Those who have suffered through the film know what it is they'll find: Calima (a bastardization of a "Caution: Live Animals" sign aboard the space station *Oberon*).

[7] Senator Nado (an orangutan) and Nova (a chimp) openly enjoy an interspecies romance onscreen, so the taboo notion seems questionable in the film's context.

She's turning on a nuclear device without even knowing what it might do! If we follow the logic of *Beneath the Planet of the Apes*, the whole planet could be destroyed. No worries, though. Some fancy button-mashing saves the day, and the good guys manage to shut the whole thing down.

Let's talk about tension for a moment. This miniseries is loaded with it. You'd think Esau and Seneca, being on the same side, would be best buddies, right? It seems that their alliance is a fragile one, however, and that makes things more interesting. They frequently question each other's motives and loyalties. Esau thinks Seneca has some kind of authority complex ("You keep on giving the orders, monkey boy") while Seneca subconsciously views Esau as a savage, which manifests itself in his speech at times ("...so vile and brutish...").

I like to think that Seneca's tension is caused by risk. He once held a high position in the Senate, but gave it up for the greater good in order to fight for something he considered greater than himself. Being out there, aligned with rebel humans and their followers, puts him in constant danger. He also knows that his brother is even more at risk, acting as a double-agent. Seneca has no time for Esau's bravado and "kill-'em-all" attitude. He wants things over with as quickly as possible. It's not all wine and roses in Derkein (the Burtonverse's analog to Ape City) either, it seems. It's mostly political, but the tension is pretty thick – and everywhere you turn. Just about every character has some beef with someone else. Minister Rodi and the ape chairman go at it, for instance, while Shiva fights with just about everyone.

Examined through a critical eye, the series is fulfilling but a bit formulaic toward the end. I enjoyed the little twists and turns it takes, and particularly the inclusion of Attar, but I wasn't thrilled with the notion that Shiva would blindly hunt down this nuclear device and turn it on without having a single clue what it might do once activated. For someone so sharp and calculating, she comes off as uncharacteristically reckless and chancy.

The positives outnumber the negatives, though. The bottom line is that it's a good, engaging *Apes* story. And, really, that's about all you can hope for in a spinoff comic.

Planet of the Apes Monthly Series (*Old Gods* and *Blood Lines*)

This is it, folks: the "Big Kahuna" of Dark Horse's *Planet of the Apes* run. Or, rather, it would have been, for what was intended as an ongoing title ultimately lasted a mere six issues. So I guess it's more of a "Little Kahuna."

The short-lived monthly series, simply titled *Planet of the Apes*, was released as six standalone issues that were later grouped into two graphic novels collecting three issues apiece, titled *Old Gods* (#1-3, written by Edginton and drawn by Medina, Vlasco, Sibar, and Lee) and *Blood Lines* (#4-6, written by Dan Abnett, with art from Mhan, Lee, Sibar, Medina, Vlasco, and Sanford Greene). In addition, the first three chapters were packaged under an alternate title, *Planet of the Apes: The Ongoing Saga*.

Both *Old Gods* and *Blood Lines* are loaded with action, adventure, mystery, and a cast of new characters, as our heroes (Esau and Seneca) continue their struggle to somehow create harmony between man and ape, mostly by fighting a lot and making snarky wisecracks.

Did I hype it up enough? Good. Now I'm going to pull the rug out from under you. This series ends abruptly at what feels like the halfway point. You might say that it's "gone in six monthly issues." Feel cheated? I did.

As wacky as the Burton film was, when introduced to a compelling offshoot in another medium, I was head-first in the pool. I hadn't read these when they were originally released, and can only imagine how disappointed I would have been to have enjoyed these six issues, only to then have the story end without any notice or resolution. I would have been highly annoyed, after having waited a month between new issues, but I think that's just my completest nature at fault. It's a character flaw. I'm working on it.

As for the story, everything revolves around the omnipresent theme of the pursuit of peace, harmony, co-existence, and all that happy stuff. During this search, our band of integrated heroes follows the exiled Attar (quite blindly, I might add) on a quest to find someone none of them know, but who we readers do: Ari. Yes, the Ari from the film, played by Helena "I'm-in-Every-Tim-Burton-Film-Ever-Made-for-Obvious-Reasons" Bonham-Carter. Somehow, an older and wiser Ari holds the key to all of this. She's been on the run for the past two decades, searching for... well, something. We're not sure what, as the series ends before telling us, but we are led to believe it's the *Planet of the Apes* equivalent to the old philosophical question of "the chicken or the egg." In this case, you might call it "the human or the ape."

While the road to Ari is paved with good intentions, hope is lost before it can be restored at the onset of the first issue. Esau and Seneca, having been captured by Kharim, are about to be hanged for their crimes. Luckily, they are saved at the last minute by none other than Attar himself, disguised as their executioner. One exciting escape later, and they're back on the road, where Attar explains, albeit vaguely, their next moves.

In the course of their travels, they come across an outpost inhabited by apes with human servants. This area is routinely assailed by a group of brutish apes whom Attar identifies as the Chimerae, an ancient sub-race of orangutans and gorillas who have inbred themselves into deformity and madness.

After helping to rebuff a Chimerae attack on the outpost with the help of a female human slave named Crow and some homemade grenades, the trio set out to follow the retreating mix-breeds to their camp among the remains of a mythological place known simply as the the First City. A fight ensues in the ruins and, with more help from Crow, we find the travelers back on the path to Ari, this time with Crow in tow.

Now pursued by Lord Scarak and his group of Ultimar soldiers, our group is brought to their knees in a snowy wood until an enigmatic figure, fully armored from head to toe, saves them from the ape army. This same figure leads Attar, Crow, and Seneca to a human settlement while the injured Esau follows in secret. The camp is hostile toward apes, binding Attar and Seneca while trying to decide their fate. Soon enough, Esau shows up to save his friends. While debating everything, the Ultimar return and attack the camp. The ghostly, fully armored figure (a gorilla named Keyser, whom the humans call "the Ghost in the Trees") gives his life defending the human camp, revealing that he was cast out of simian society long ago simply due to his belief in ape-human harmony. From there, it's back on the road to finding Ari.

The most disappointing part of it all is that after the grand quest for peace and harmony takes many twists and turns, after discoveries are made, and after new characters and facts come into (and out of) the picture – whammo! Series canceled. Poor Ari is still out there somewhere, waiting to be found, and for all the build-up, she never actually makes an appearance in the comic.

"Living to fight another day's the best kind of revenge."
– Esau, *Planet of the Apes* #1 (September 2001)

The Dark Arts

Artwork in comics can be a mixed bag when it comes to style. Depending on the circumstances, a rough, unfinished look can sometimes win out over more detailed artwork. The *Planet of the Apes* comic books from Dark Horse are certainly not sketch-like; they're just detailed enough not to appear overdone.

It's important to me that artistic style not detract from storytelling. I have a bit of a love-hate relationship with comics like Frank Miller's *The Dark Knight Returns*, because the art looks very amateurish and there is text all over the place, making it difficult to establish reading order. Dark Horse's *Apes* artwork is not like that. It's very straightforward, consistent, and easy to follow. In fact, I was surprised to find out that more than ten different artists shaped the entire body of work.

In 2001, Dark Horse felt the need to release a so-called "interactive" online sketchbook with pieces by Paco Medina, J. Scott Campbell, and Davide Fabbri. I suppose you'd have to climb into your DeLorean and go back in time to figure out *why* they did this, as it wasn't really necessary. Remember, the Internet was still growing back then. Many people didn't yet have home computers or broadband connections. Perhaps it was viewed as hip or trendy to put something on the Internet as an exclusive of sorts.

Whatever the reason, this online sketchbook seems like something shoe-horned into the marketing campaign to help promote the film. All of the sketches appear to be precursors to panels or covers from the comic, and all are framed with text from a "record keeper" named Secturus. In the text, Secturus seems to be in a state of denial that these sketches could ever be produced by a human... and there's the gag, folks. At best, it's a nice peek behind the scenes, but not much else.

Flogging a Dark Horse

My frustration with the series' cancellation is a bit displaced, I'll admit. It's not fair to blame Dark Horse or the creative team for the series' cancellation when it was the film's supposedly "poor" performance that caused the plug to be pulled. I personally don't believe it was the movie's monetary performance that killed everything ape back in 2001, though. After all, the reboot's budget was around $100 million and it made about $180 million (U.S. domestic), so it *was* profitable from a certain point of view.

Rather, I think it was the public's reception that sank the film. It fizzled out very quickly, and viewers soon realized that no sequel would be forthcoming. With that realization came the abrupt halting of not only Dark Horse's storyline, but Harper Entertainment's excellent spinoff novels. Since then, Twentieth Century Fox has entirely distanced itself from the film, other than a Blu-ray re-release. (Can you blame them?)

So we got what we got as far as the comic goes. Some folks might say, "Half a story is better than no story at all." Others might ask, "What good is half a story?" Both assertions have some merit, though I tend to agree with the latter. That being said, the monthly series started off ridiculously fun and entertaining, and never really swayed from that vibe. The story was becoming increasingly interesting as it built up, before disappearing mid-stride.

You have to hand it to Dark Horse's writing team, though. It's difficult to avoid becoming wrapped up in the stories they created in this run. They took what Burton started and put some real thought into expanding that universe in a smooth way – minus the movie's substantial acting, writing, and directing deficiencies – while keeping the overall *Planet of the Apes* mythos intact. That's quite an accomplishment, which makes the cancellation that much more depressing. Imagine where it could have all gone?

Thankfully, we don't have to imagine too hard, because in issue 15 of *Simian Scrolls: The UK Apezine*, writer Rich Handley, in a piece titled "Time-Lost Tales from the Planet of the Apes," interviewed Abnett and Edginton and asked them how the series was supposed to end if all had gone to plan.

In their joint answer, the authors revealed that Ari would eventually have been found living among the descendants of the *Oberon*'s human crew, along with other human-friendly apes. These humans had not been wiped out, but had moved around, raising the *Oberon*'s remaining apes as equals and not as slaves or pets.[8]

Eventually, according to the two scribes, evolution took hold and the apes became dominant. Those original humans' progeny had survived throughout the years, and Ari had found them and all of their secrets of the past, which is why she had sent for Attar in the first place. Edginton and Abnett had also considered bringing back film characters Daena and Limbo, as well as exploring the nature of the infamous "Ape Lincoln" Thade memorial featured in the film's controversial and confusing conclusion.

In addition, the writers mentioned a possible twist by which some of the main characters would have taken off in pods and time-traveled to another world technologically similar to the planet Soror, from Pierre Boulle's original

---

[8] The novels *The Fall* and *Colony*, by William T. Quick, detailed a different fate for the *Oberon* crew. But, then, fans of other franchises, *Star Trek* and *Star Wars* chief among them, are no strangers to contradictions between various media, particularly comic books and novels, so why should *POTA* be any different?

source novel, *La Planète des Singes* (*Monkey Planet*). This would have led to infinite possibilities and tie-ins to other films. Imagine Seneca, Esau, and Attar meeting up with Taylor in the Dark Horse universe?

All of that sounds like a lot of fun to me. Of course, things usually change from concept to page. Some of these ideas, or even none at all, might have ended up in the finished product.

I find myself a bit conflicted while trying to decide if I enjoyed the monthly series as much as I did *The Human War*. I've read them both a number of times, and while I liked each one, I think *The Human War* was great up until the end. The monthly series showed a lot of promise, but we were cut off midway. It's difficult to overcome the disappointment of not knowing what happens in the end. A story without an ending is just an excerpt, after all.

Wrapping It Up

Comic book universes tend to be enormous. (You would need an advanced degree to figure out all the ins and outs of the Marvel Universe alone.) Then just when you think you have it down, they reboot everything and start over.

I have not read any other *Planet of the Apes* comics besides the Dark Horse titles. Perhaps I will, after all is said and done, but I couldn't possibly begin to take these comics out of the Burton universe, put them side by side with other series, and come up with an in-depth analysis. These comics belong on a rogue branch jutting off some kind of *Apes* space-time continuum diagram, if they're even connected at all.

Completists and die-hard fans may want them, mostly to fill a gap in their collections or to say they've read them. In the grand scheme of things, though, they're just not that important, mostly because they weren't allowed to reach their full potential (at least, the monthly series wasn't). They also become a lot less interesting when you compare the characters to those we all know and love from the classic films.

Therein lies the conundrum: They're worth reading if you can get your stinkin' paws on them, but although they are undeniably entertaining, there is nothing truly spectacular about them. It's maddening trying to make sense of it all, really. (Don't bother.) The extent to which you might enjoy them depends on your personal point of view and the context into which you place them. Should you include them as part of the global *POTA* mythos, you might be disappointed (not to mention confused).

However, if you think of them as standalone tales with a beginning and an (abrupt) ending, you might like them a good deal more. After all, it's not every day that you come across spinoff material that is inarguably superior to the original media from which it spawned. I tried to forget they were from the *Apes* universe (and from the Burtonverse, specifically), and that seemed to make them more fun. Besides, these comics were *meant* to be a standalone series, and I firmly believe they should remain that way, tucked away in their very own little pocket universe. Perhaps it's best, in the end, to think of them as forgotten byproducts of a film that never should have been made in the first place. Trying to fit them into the greater *Apes* saga is just asking for a gorilla of a headache.

In a wonderful example of simian kismet, *Dawn of the Planet of the Apes* was released while I was writing this piece. I went to see the film on opening night and was blown away. I doubt many people would hesitate to label it one of the best films – if not *the* best – in the entire series, second only perhaps to the original 1968 movie (even if only out of loyalty). You rarely see filmmaking of this high caliber anymore, and it's prevalent in every aspect of the film, from the writing, acting, and effects to the editing, directing, and so forth.

If only the same could be said of Burton's efforts.

Assessing the Revolution: Mr. Comics Flies the Flag

by Edward Gross

Red flags.

Even before the meaning of that phrase was clear to me, my twelve-year-old self felt their rising presence back in 1972, as I sat in the Kings Plaza Theatre in Brooklyn, New York, watching *Conquest of the Planet of the Apes*. Marketing-wise, 20th Century Fox had certainly done its job. It began with one-sheet posters announcing the forthcoming film, followed by the theatrical trailer and, of course, television commercials, all heralding "the revolt of the apes."

It wasn't all that necessary to prime the *Apes* pump for me, as I'd become enamored with the film series right from the release of the original *Planet of the Apes* in 1968 (even at age eight, there was no question in my mind that something special was there), and its first two sequels, 1970's *Beneath the Planet of the Apes* and 1971's *Escape from the Planet of the Apes*. By the time of *Conquest*'s release, Cornelius, Zira, and all the rest had become part of my pop-culture obsessions, joining the ranks of James Bond, Superman, the Universal Monsters, and Barnabas Collins. Caesar, in inspiring a revolution on the planet of the apes, was invited to the gang.

Conquest genuinely impacted on me, particularly in Roddy McDowall's portrayal of Caesar, a character entirely different than the actor's Cornelius had been in previous films. Even back then, I recognized him as someone who was in a state of innocence at the outset, but who evolved over the course of the movie into a savior to his "people," whom he set free during the so-called "Night of the Fires." I was blown away by Caesar's speech during the closing moments, which was unbelievably powerful as he laid down, point by point, his goals for the soon-to-be-free fellow simians. If you haven't seen it recently, go back to watch McDowall's performance – it's *electric*, despite the fact that he has to convey it all through makeup.

Yet as great as that sequence is, it also marks the rising of the aforementioned red flags. It begins when a female chimpanzee named Lisa looks at Caesar and somehow utters the word "No," which, in turn, seems to trigger a complete change of heart in Caesar. The fury is gone from his voice, the fire from his words. The city burns, with human bodies lying everywhere, and Governor Breck sprawled before him, death seemingly imminent at the butt-end of gorilla-held rifles. Yet at that moment, at the very height of the revolt, Caesar apparently decides to go Gandhi on humanity,[1] proclaiming that if man is to be dominated, then it should be with compassion and understanding.

This would have been the perfect moment for Gary Coleman to pop up and ask, "What'chu talkin' 'bout, Caesar?"

Of course, at the time, I had no idea that test audiences were turned off by the movie's original cut, nor that series producer Arthur P. Jacobs – who worried that the filmmakers were on the verge of losing the much-coveted family audience who had flocked to see the previous films – working in conjunction with 20th Century Fox, had decided to tone down the violence. This resulted in Caesar's change of heart *and* the desperate editing done to hide the fact that McDowall's voice had been badly dubbed over some previously shot footage.

This reversal didn't matter much at the time, because it was all wrapped it up with Caesar's statement, "Tonight, we have seen the birth of the planet of the apes." And that was more than enough to send a chill up the spines of *Apes* fans everywhere.

---

[1] At least until the Blu-ray version of the movie restored the original ending, replacing Caesar's sudden change of heart with a much more violent, bloody revolt and closing speech befitting the rest of the film's grim tone

In a sense, it felt like the *Apes* saga had come full-circle – that *Conquest* could have faded out with Caesar standing there while human civilization burned, and then faded up with Charlton Heston's arrival on a planet of apes some two thousand years in the future, as seen in the 1968 original. *That* would have been perfect, but instead, a year later, we were given the fifth and final installment in the series, *Battle for the Planet of the Apes*. *Battle* ultimately raised more questions than it answered and, as far as I was concerned, should have been called *Red Flags on the Planet of the Apes*.

Set several years after *Conquest, Battle* picks up after a nuclear war has decimated much of the population, and the first generation of *Beneath*'s mutants are residing underground with the Alpha-Omega Bomb in what would seem to be Los Angeles (and *not* New York, as they would be in the second film). Simultaneously, the apes have moved into the forest, built a city in the trees, and inexplicably acquired the power of speech only one generation following Caesar's uprising. Some, like Virgil, have proved as eloquent as Caesar, while others, such as the gorilla Aldo, tend to grunt their words. Governor Breck and his aide, MacDonald, are dead, and the latter's brother is now Caesar's most trusted confidant. In essence, *a lot* has happened in those years between films, and viewers are left with the distinct feeling that an entry in the series has gone missing. It's a fun film, sure, but it raises a lot of red flags.

This is where *Revolution on the Planet of the Apes* comes in, bridging the gap between the films and filling in some of the holes for viewers. Suddenly, after all these years, those red flags are finally lowered.

Issue One

Published by Metallic Rose Comics (Mr. Comics) between 2005 and 2006, the six-chapter story for *Revolution* was written by Ty Templeton and Joe O'Brien. The miniseries commences with "The End of the World," illustrated by Salgood Sam, which opens with a text prologue encapsulation of the twenty-two years prior,[2] beginning with the disappearance of George Taylor's spacecraft, the *Icarus*, and its return two years later with Doctors Cornelius, Zira, and Milo onboard.

We learn that the virus that killed all dogs and cats (as discussed by Cornelius in *Escape*) has come to pass, as has the notion of apes becoming the

---

[2] It should be noted that the span of time between Taylor's 1972 launch and *Conquest of the Planet of the Apes* (set in 1991) is only nineteen years.

new pets and eventual slaves to humanity, with simians out-numbering humans three to one. (This, of course, recalls a red flag going all the way back to *Escape*, though – given that Cornelius had laid out all of this so distinctly while being interrogated, why on Earth would *anyone* proceed to replace cats and dogs with apes?)

The *Planet of the Apes* films are strong on social commentary, and *Revoluton* continues this trend. Arthur Trundy is elected President of the United States, running on the platform of "Manifest Human Superiority," which culminates in the U.S. Constitution being amended to drive home the point that the human species is superior to all other creatures on Earth. As Trundy rises in power, the country moves with him toward dictatorship, with the Pentagon taking control of the media and all private broadcasts being deemed illegal. Thus is born the American News Network (ANN), a government-run cable channel modeled after Fox News and other biased TV networks.

It is into *this* environment – with slave apes making up the work force – that Caesar and Armando enter at the outset of *Conquest*, and in which the events of that film play out. The story cuts to the bedroom of pirate video blogger Chris Leung, who watches an unauthorized broadcast of Caesar's speech on the Internet (interestingly, both the Internet and blogging seem to have developed decades earlier under the fascist regime than they have in the real world). His father refutes everything being shown, refusing to believe that an ape can talk – mirroring the apes' reaction to Taylor's speaking ability in the original film – but is proven wrong when a gorilla bursts in through the living room window, killing the man and his wife.

Caesar, meanwhile, awakens in what seems to be a hotel room, with Lisa sleeping by his side, after experiencing his father's memories of Earth being destroyed. This establishes a major aspect of this storyline: because Caesar was conceived prior to Earth's destruction but was in the womb during the journey backwards in time, his brain was somehow affected so that he has memories of both the past and the future. In essence, Caesar exhibits mental abilities beyond those of normal apes or men. In this way, the writers begin to lower one of the biggest red flags raised by *Conquest*: namely, Caesar's inexplicable ability to inspire rebellious attitudes among other apes, seemingly by his mere presence. More on that later.

The comic establishes that Breck is still alive, and is being held as a prisoner. MacDonald, the one human whom Caesar continues to respect, frequently appears by his side in New Ape City (the former San Diego). For his part,

MacDonald still attempts to reason with Caesar, as though he has any chance of talking down this revolution (which, of course, he doesn't).

At the White House, President Trundy receives a visit from a discredited, wheelchair-bound scientist, Doctor Karl Reich. The scientist offers a disturbing theory that Caesar views the world non-linearly, always knowing his own destiny, which shakes Trundy's confidence. "Past, future, action, reaction," Reich explains. "The mechanism of casualty may mean nothing to such a mind. He may approach every choice as merely a path to a predetermined outcome." He also has a monkey crawling around his shoulders at all times – Reich literally has the proverbial monkey on his back, representing the burden of knowledge that is his alone.

Reich's words are juxtaposed with powerful images showing Caesar demanding order and law by *any* means necessary. But as he's about to crack open the skull of a belligerent gorilla with a slab of concrete that he quickly drops, Caesar proclaims the first law: "Ape shall not kill ape." This is an important moment, as it shows that Caesar is already attempting to change the future, and to take a more peaceful approach in the hope of altering Earth's seemingly inevitable destruction. Caesar's final speech during *Conquest*'s theatrical ending seems less jarring as a result, as the comic melds Caesar's violent nature with his peaceful intent. Another red flag lowered.

Part one ends with a shift to Hasslein Air Force Base and the lab of one Doctor Constantine. Aldo, a gorilla servant from the base's cleaning staff (and later the fifth film's brutish antagonist), is led into a chamber, where he is to be strapped to a chair with electrodes attached to his brain, like other gorillas already present. But to the shock of his human handlers, he utters the word spoken to him time without number: "No!" The ape repeatedly grunts the word while brutally beating to death his handlers and, presumably, Constantine. It's a pivotal moment, smoothing out a continuity error between the third and fourth movies. In *Escape*, Cornelius claims that Aldo is revered as the first ape to say "no," and yet both Caesar and Lisa precede him in *Conquest*. *Revolution* shows Cornelius's account to be mostly accurate (aside from the utterance occurring hundreds of years sooner than stated). Another red flag eliminated.

Following the main story is the first entry in "Caesar's Journal," a series of backup features offering the chimp's longhand observations, written in the hope of preserving the early days of the world's new history. This first entry is dated three days following the Night of the Fires, firmly establishing the comic's setting. The journals provide insightful glimpses into Caesar's inner thoughts, showing us his hopes, concerns, and insecurities. We learn that he fears mankind's reprisals, but has taken human hostages as a precaution, providing a plausible reason why the U.S. government didn't re-take the city following *Conquest*'s revolt (red flag down). Each issue's journal is spotlighted by illustrations from Bernie Mireault, which intriguingly show Caesar's sketched portraits of apes drawn in various styles reminiscent not only of John Chambers' award-winning on-screen makeup, but also artwork from Mr. Comics' predecessors, Marvel and Malibu Comics. Could Caesar, in dreaming the future, have foreseen the events of those stories as well?

Finally, the issue wraps up with a short Ty Templeton tale illustrated by Attila Adorjany. Titled "For Human Rights," it takes place three years prior, at a presidential rally for a campaigning Trundy, who conveys to a crowd his desire to ensure that simians remain subservient to humans:

> Out in San Francisco, they're teaching gorillas to talk with "sign language." They say these apes can ask for things. Give me a banana. I want a shot of rum. Next thing they ask for is a book to read. Once they ask for things, they're going to ask for the vote. It happened before with women. And Blacks. And the Chinese. And those were positive steps for human rights, but we have to stop the liberals before they give our country away to the animals.

The thinly veiled racism (not to mention misogyny) of Trundy's speech fits well with *Conquest*'s Civil Rights Movement parallels, creating a dystopian vision of the United States that (aside from ape servants) is not that dissimilar to where some might say the nation is currently headed. It's easy to believe that in such a political climate, someone like Breck, with his fascist policies and his unconstitutional title of "His Excellency," could rise to the rank of governor.

As the rally gets underway, an angry Chris Leung attempts to assassinate Trundy. However, a nearby gorilla senses his actions and attacks, saving Trundy's life but ultimately being shot dead by the Secret Service. Trundy refuses to recognize that the ape was protecting him, or that a fellow human was the would-be killer. The revelation that Leung, a protagonist in the miniseries, had once tried to assassinate a presidential-hopeful is surprising and effective.

That being said, although Trundy's blindness to reality is intriguing, this aspect of the scenario being laid out – that Trundy ran on an anti-simian agenda – falls a little flat. While it's true that the *Apes* films, particularly *Conquest*, were seen by many as an allegory for black and white relations of that time period, this notion that humans would need to guard themselves against apes by drawing comparisons between them and women, blacks, and Chinese is a bit dopey, unless the collective IQ of Americans has dropped dramatically by the time of this story's setting.

Issue Two

"Lines of Communication," once again featuring art by Salgood Sam, picks up where the first issue left off: at Hasslein Air Force Base, with an armed Aldo approaching a squad of jet fighters, surrounded by similarly armed gorillas. On a nearby TV, the voice of Nora Rhodes, the Pentagon's secretary of media (a strong condemnation of the trend toward a government-controlled press), assures viewers that "everything is under control," and her spin-doctoring has an ironic effect on the gorillas, who utter guttural chants of "control" while commandeering the aircraft.

We learn that Doctor Bryce Evans (Rhodes' ex-fiancé) is capturing chimps for an experiment that will allow him to save the world from the apes, and that organized ape revolts are occurring across the country. Somehow, "word" of Caesar's revolution is spreading among the world's simian population – just as Caesar had predicted in *Conquest* – and while Trundy's advisors recommend that a military strike be directed toward Caesar and San Diego, the president first wants to ensure that something called "Churchdoor" is secured.

An aide informs the president that a print publication called *People News Monthly* features the first interview with Caesar, but Rhodes dismisses the threat, saying, "Nobody pays attention to print media." It's an interesting statement, as the miniseries takes place in 1991, several years before electronic publishing would overtake print journalism in the real world, but it makes sense given the earlier rise of the Internet in this timeline.

In Los Angeles, as military forces contain a violent ape uprising, one soldier snaps, firing on an unarmed crowd of humans. "Wooley's gone ape!" another solder yells, echoing an iconic line from the 1978 film *Dawn of the Dead*. The parallel is a strong one. For fans of George Romero's classic zombie trilogy, in which the living are just as much a threat to survival as the undead, it's a moment laden with a great deal of subtext. Swap out "living" for "humans" and "undead" for "apes," and the message is clear.

Meanwhile, Caesar straps Breck to the same electric table on which the former governor had him tortured during *Conquest*, and says he dreamed the end of the world his entire life, with apes and humans at each other's throats. "I always wondered how hate could consume someone so totally," he states.

"And then I met you." Caesar then shocks his adversary, demanding to know more about the mysterious Churchdoor. At this point, the reader has not been told what that project entails, though there is foreshadowing in images of Taylor's death at Saint Patrick's Cathedral in *Beneath*, as well as in Caesar's description of his dream of a "great golden sword" poised to destroy everyone.

The second chapter ends explosively, with jet planes, piloted by Aldo's gorillas, shooting down an airplane in which Rhodes and Cully Sparks, Trundy's secretary of defense, are traveling. Sparks plummets to his death as the aircraft is ripped apart, but not before warning Rhodes that with Churchdoor, Caesar could destroy them all.

The true strength of "Lines of Communication" comes from the brief but powerful moment between Caesar and Breck. Even facing electrocution, the former governor remains defiant, telling Caesar that his mother butchered humans (as seen in the original film), while his father beat an unarmed orderly to death (in *Escape*). Refusing to believe such things, Caesar grows furious almost to the point of savagery, and throws the switch. In the aftermath of *Conquest*, this is the type of sequence that audiences were hoping to see in *Battle,* but which never happened since actor Don Murray elected not to reprise the role of Breck.

Dramatically, the animosity between them is tangible and similar to that which existed between Zaius and Taylor. Each is representative of his entire species, and each is driven by fear and a deeply felt hatred that figuratively keeps them both locked on a seemingly inevitable path toward total destruction.

And yet... in the pages of this issue's "Caesar's Journal," Caesar offers up a determination to change that course, to alter the future he – and we – have seen. He writes:

> Tomorrow I will go see Breck. Mr. MacDonald tells me he remains defiant. I must do everything in my power to remain calm when I see him. But even writing his name fills me with anger I can barely contain. The things he has done, the things he planned to do. If my revolution is to be more than a bloody uprising, I must first show this man – this human who once called himself my master – the true meaning of civilization.

Just as Breck previously fixated on breaking Caesar on screen, the reverse scenario plays out in the comic, echoing Breck's damning film dialog: "When we hate you, we're hating the dark side of ourselves." It's a haunting series of panels, carrying the uncomfortable realization that Caesar and Breck are more similar than either would admit.

Caesar teaches Breck a shocking truth about revenge and karma in *Revolution on the Planet of the Apes* #2 (Jan 2006).

The back-up story, "People News,"[3] written by Templeton with artwork by Gabriel Morrissette and Bernie Mireault, deals with the *People News Monthly* magazine issue mentioned in the main story. The Pentagon Bureau of Information forces the issue's entire print run to be pulped, with claims that the Caesar story is a hoax. The writer of the piece, though, hides a copy of the issue in a titanium steel wall safe.

Brilliantly, the story jumps ahead two thousand years to an excavation site, where Cornelius and Zira retrieve the now ancient magazine from the safe (for some reason, Zira is a member of her husband's archeological team, despite her being a neurosurgeon). But just as Zira comments that the chimpanzee on the

---

[3] Originally released as a free online preview with the longer title "People in the News."

cover looks like Cornelius, Zaius rips it from her hands, dismisses anything it has to say, threatens Cornelius's career if he pursues the matter, and tears it to shreds when he reads a cover blurb that asks, "Can he be the fabled 'lost child' of Cornelius and Zira?" Two ends of the time stream are joined by those in power purposefully turning a blind eye toward the truth, and dooming their respective societies in the process.

Issue Three

The third issue kicks off with another installment of "Caesar's Journal," much of which is focused on the chimp leader's dreams of the past and future, though one section teases what's to come: "I remembered a word – spoken by Governor Breck and others in front of me when they did not know I could understand them. It was a secret word. A word they always whispered, even in front of me. That's why I remember it. 'Churchdoor.'" By this point, it's probably safe to assume that most readers had figured out what Breck's secret project involved, especially given the signifigance of a particular church to the second film's reveal.

The main story, "Intelligent Design," illustrated by Tom Fowler, opens with Breck and Caesar. The former governor, held by gorillas, sneers that those "damn dirty apes" should get their stinking paws off of him (it seems that *everyone* enjoys using a variation of that one). Caesar demands to know the location of the security bunker containing Churchdoor. Breck breaks free and leaps toward his nemesis, but the chimp slams him down to the ground and savagely beats him, much to the frustration of MacDonald, who (perhaps a bit naïvely) urges Caesar not to lower himself to seeking vengeance. Caesar then orders him prepared for trial, setting the stage for the issue's events.

Observing from outside, Kolp (Breck's security chief in *Conquest* and the main antagonist of *Battle*), along with fellow future mutants Mendez and Alma (also from *Battle*) plan to attack and kill Caesar, with Kolp noting that Breck is merely a "target of opportunity." Although Alma and Mendez have only small roles in *Revolution*, their presence helps to bridge the gap between films, by showing that they had worked for Kolp for years before *Battle*, making their decision not to carry out his final order (to detonate the bomb) in that film's extended edition that much more powerful.

Bryce Evans continues his experiments and seemingly creates a virus capable of killing all non-human primates. Rhodes, meanwhile, parachutes into New Ape City and runs up against Leung, who, in the aftermath of his parents' death, has a burning need to spread the truth about what is happening in San Diego via a series of "vidblogs" that are frequently disrupted by the government in accordance with the American Truth Act. The two verbally spar over the government's suppression of the truth (an argument we've heard several times in the *Apes* franchise, with Rhodes cast in the mold of Zaius and Hasslein), until Caesar interrupts, noting that truth is manipulative, and that the world needs to see *facts*, not truth, so that they can make up their own minds.

We learn of the growing ape assault on humans around the country. The situation is growing increasingly dire, and Reich suggests that if Caesar has Churchdoor, Trundy should initiate something called "the Inferno Protocol." Given the ominous name, anyone with knowledge of the first two films should be able to figure out what *that* involves: a nuclear strike.

Gorillas lead Breck, accompanied by MacDonald, to Ape Management's Ape Pit for his trial. En route, the two men have an interesting exchange:

> BRECK: You're a bleeding-heart traitor.
>
> MacDONALD: Is it treason to act humanely?
>
> BRECK: "Humane?" You've lost the right to use that word.
>
> MacDONALD: I did what I thought was best.
>
> BRECK: You've sold out your species to a pack of animals.
>
> MacDONALD: They're not animals, Mr. Governor... they're *us*.

With this exchange, Templeton and O'Brien capture well the flavor of Paul Dehn's dialogue, and both MacDonald and Breck ring true to their on-screen portrayals. One red flag raised by *Battle* was the absence of actors Hari Rhodes and Don Murray, with a new MacDonald brother and a promoted, irradiated Kolp taking their places. Scenes like this one illustrate how unfortunate it was to lose both Rhodes and Murray from the fifth film (with no disrespect intended to Severn Darden and Austin Stoker, of course, who both turn in enjoyable performances in their own rights). But at the same time, *Revolution* helps to lower that flag, by revealing *why* they were absent.

The trial begins, and Leung illegally broadcasts the proceedings on the Web. When Caesar accuses Breck of being involved in a conspiracy to destroy the world via Churchdoor, the president, watching the vidblog, orders it shut down immediately. At that moment, the area is rocked by an explosion as Kolp and his people break in. Kolp shoots Caesar and stands above him, gun in hand, proclaiming the revolution at an end (and thankfully not calling Caesar a "clever ape," which would have taken the *Battle* parallel too far).

The next feature in the issue is "Hasslein's Notes," by Joe O'Brien, a written memorandum to the President of the United States from Otto Hasslein, expressing his belief that he must personally rectify the situation pertaining to Cornelius and Zira. Since he is the one searching for a means of traveling to the future, the troubled scientist reasons, everything that has happened is his fault. Hasslein writes:

> It has become clear to me now that mankind's greatest threat may not be these two apes and their child at all. If we are ultimately to prevail, we must conquer our own ignorance. Perhaps, one day, we will. But for us to ever have such an opportunity, it seems I must take present matters into my own hands. It is only fitting. As I said, Mr. President, it is I who am responsible. It is therefore I, and I alone, who set things right.

It's an intriguing letter that goes far toward humanizing Hasslein even more than actor Eric Braden did in those moments during *Escape* when, while talking to the president, the scientist expressed his feelings regarding the simian threat. Hasslein is no mustache-twirling villain (his Marvel and Power Records portrayals notwithstanding), hurting others in the pursuit of personal gain; he is, to some degree, a man with noble motives, despite his willingness to murder innocents to carry them out, and we see here that he feels genuine regret for what he knows must be done. He takes no pleasure in it. His stance in this letter is a logical leap for the character to make – that the fate of humanity and the planet itself has been altered by his creation of the space drive that propelled the *Icarus* into the future and back again. It is, thus, his burden to carry.

The issue's final feature – "Little Caesar," by Templeton and Sam,[4] is a six-page tale that takes place during Caesar's days as a performer in Armando's circus. When SPCA member Paula Dean threatens to launch an investigation into how the animals are trained to do such amazing things at his circus, Armando realizes it's time to pull up stakes before the truth about his chimp foster-son is discovered. The nature of that truth is not so much the acrobatics that Caesar and his fellow chimps can perform, but rather the influence he seems to exert on others.

As Caesar explains to Armando (apparently for the umpteenth time, given the circus owner's reaction), whenever he dreams of the animals doing tricks and routines, they are somehow able to do so a few days later. "Am I seeing the future?" he wonders. "Am I dreaming things into reality?" He has foreseen

---

[4] Previewed in issue #1 of Mr. Comics' other simian-themed comic book, *Big Max*, under the title "Armando's Marvelous Menagerie Circus"

"explosions, bombs, wars, men with scars who wear masks, gorillas on horses hunting people," and so forth, all of which viewers know will happen in the classic film sequels. The implication: Caesar made it all possible with his dreams.

The idea, while seemingly far-fetched, actually has its roots in *Conquest*, which shows apes mesmerized by Caesar's mere presence, and then suddenly committing acts of rebellion, as though compelled by Caesar's own disgust at viewing simian servitude. It also harkens back to the film's closing moments, when Caesar proclaims to MacDonald that an emperor moth can communicate with another over a distance of eighty miles, and that an emperor ape might do better. This helps to explain how the rebellion could possibly spread around the world, and how it could be organized elsewhere while Caesar is in California. Telepathy is not only a viable explanation for what happens on screen, but an eminently logical one.

Caesar contemplates that the circus's deaf and dumb strong-man, Pierre the Mute Mountain, might one day regain the power of speech – and that very thing happens a few panels later. This raises the most intriguing possibility of all, while simultaneously lowering several red flags: Could Caesar have willed the apes into gaining speech and intelligence... and could he also have taken those capabilities away from mankind?

Issue Four

In "Truth and Consequences," by Templeton, O'Brien, and Sam, Kolp's attempt to assassinate Caesar is interrupted when an armed gorilla shoots the commando, giving Caesar the upper hand. Recognizing Kolp as the man who murdered Armando, the chimp nearly kills him to avenge his human foster-father's death, but MacDonald reminds him that such behavior would be exactly the opposite of what the circus owner would have wanted. Roddy McDowall's voice and manner resonate in the scene, as Caesar alternates between calmly pensive (as in *Conquest*'s theatrical ending) and brutally angry (as in the film's uncut ending). It's something the writers consistently do well throughout the miniseries.

When Kolp's team takes off with Breck in hand, both Leung and Rhodes – despite representing diametrically opposed views of journalism – elect to stay behind to witness the facts about Caesar for themselves. In this moment, Rhodes seems capable of redemption, as though awakening to the truth about the fascist administration for which she has worked. She and Leung watch first-hand as Caesar waffles between peaceful opposition and animalistic violence.

Sadly, no introspection on either human's part is provided in the face of Caesar's inner turmoil, as it would have helped to flesh out each character.

At the Pentagon, the powers that be view the nuclear destruction of an unnamed country that has dropped a bomb on its own people from an orbital platform in order to take out apes rising within that nation. President Trundy and Doctor Reich discuss other options, including a military program to train gorillas as combat soldiers – thus explaining the ease with which Aldo's team, in the previous issue, had been able to pilot fighter jets. They do so again in this chapter, targeting San Diego.

Caesar pursues Breck and the others to a security bunker, but *just* misses stopping them before they seal themselves in and proceed to Churchdoor. MacDonald leads Rhodes and Leung toward the bunker, but Evans, armed with a machine gun, knocks Caesar's advisor unconscious. The reunion between Rhodes and her fiancé quickly turns from joyful to angry when he boasts of having saved her "sweet ass" – and it's the one truly false moment in the issue, as this otherwise strong woman runs away from him in tears. With everything else going on, *that's* what puts her over the edge?

At the White House, the gorillas launch an attack. As this is happening, Reich ponders whether Caesar merely dreamed about mankind's dystopic future or actually willed it into being. "The circle has no beginning and no end," he decides. "You create the future and the future creates you. You have conquered causality, and in doing so become its prisoner. But how can you choose when the outcome is already known?" Reich then puts a bullet in his own brain, uttering "Heil Caesar."

It's clearly intended to be a shocking moment, but it's not meaningful enough. The truth is that Reich is underdeveloped as a character. He serves merely as exposition, an attempt to explain Caesar's ability to see the future (in essence, he's a much less effective version of Hasslein and Virgil, who exhibit developed personalities outside of their expository duties), but beyond that, his primary functions appear to be to state the obvious to Trundy, and to be the voice of pessimism. Moreover, his final words offer a rather unclear message. The comparison to Julius Caesar makes sense, given the chimp's chosen name and the fact that his influence is fast spreading worldwide... but how is Caesar in any way (as "heil" would denote) like Adolf Hitler? (Of course, the fact that the man's name is Reich could imply that the scientist himself has Nazi sympathies... either way, the message here is a bit unclear.)

In *Revolution* #4 (May 2006), Aldo assumes the Oval Office.

The chapter concludes with Aldo sitting behind the desk of the Oval Office, lighting up a cigar, the bodies of dead Secret Service agents strewn across the floor. It's a comical and effective image, nicely setting up the gorilla general's lust for power that would be his eventual undoing in *Battle for the Planet of the Apes*.

This issue's "Caesar's Journal" reflects on the revolutionary's dreams of the future, including visions he has had of his sons and daughters yet to be born — particularly one son (presumably *Battle*'s Cornelius) dying violently. In that regard, the authors remain true to Malibu Graphics' monthly *Apes* title, which, in introducing Caesar's grandson Alexander, had already implied that Caesar and Lisa produced at least one more child.

The chimp describes dreams of his grandchildren fighting in a global war with humans, culminating in the Moon being destroyed in "an orgy of violence and madness." The cryptic statement, in the original film, that Earth no longer has a lunar satellite is almost a passing thought, never spoken of again. It's jarring, and leads to one of the movies' biggest mysteries (alongside "Why didn't Taylor know he was on Earth if the apes spoke English and had horses?" and "Why would unthinking animals wear loincloths?"). This journal entry sets the stage for a planned sequel to *Revolution*, titled *Empire on the Planet of the Apes*, which apparently would have lowered that particular red flag but was unfortunately never published.[5]

"Paternal Instinct," a backup feature written and illustrated by Sam Agro,[6] focuses on Tammy Taylor, a police officer who happens to be the daughter of Colonel George Taylor. The cop, whose thought balloons betray the massive daddy/abandonment issues with which she is dealing, must stop a group of human thugs from murdering a chimpanzee baby, but one of those punks takes her by surprise and knocks her unconscious. When she awakens, she discovers the infant chimp dead and the humans slain by a pack of gorillas. Things get worse when the chimp mother takes a human baby to replace hers, and Taylor must talk her into handing the child over. Though successful, she shoots the chimp dead after rescuing the infant, realizing this makes her a "magnificent bastard" like the father she barely knew.

It's a strong vignette, made more so by the similarities between father and daughter. That being said, the revelation that George Taylor, in signing up for a one-way space mission, left behind a wife[7] and daughter is *huge*. Taylor's a deadbeat dad! In the 1968 film, Taylor makes it clear that he has no regrets about leaving the 20th century, and he tells Nova that he experienced "lots of love-making, but no love." It's certainly possible that his marriage was a loveless one, but the idea that he would willingly abandon a four-year-old daughter – and then indicate he has no regrets about it – is pretty horrible, and perhaps inconsistent with his on-screen portrayal. Heston's Taylor was cynical, rough, and easily angered, and "magnificent bastard" would certainly fit with how he

---

[5] BOOM! Studios recently addressed the Moon's destruction in *Planet of the Apes: Cataclysm*. See the essays by Joseph Dilworth Jr. and Dafna Pleban, elsewhere in this volume, for more information.

[6] "Paternal Instinct" was written to replace another tale by Agro, "The Believer," which was pulled due to concerns about religious overtones. That story was later printed in *Simian Scrolls* issue #16, with Agro's permission, and is further discussed later in this anthology.

[7] Named Gillian Taylor in the novel *Conspiracy of the Planet of the Apes*... no relation to the same-named marine biologist from *Star Trek IV: The Voyage Home*

goaded Landon, but he in no way came across as villainous. Amazingly, Malibu Graphics' *Ape City* miniseries previously revealed *another* abandoned daughter, Jo Taylor, though neither story references the other offspring.

Issue Five

The reveal of Churchdoor's nature happens quickly in "Weapon of Choice," another tale featuring art by Salgood Sam, though given all the foreshadowing, it likely comes as a surprise to very few readers. It's an Alpha-Omega Bomb, similar to one that would be the instrument of Earth's destruction some two thousand years in the future, and Kolp safely whisks Breck away to the weapon's bunker so the president can order a full ground assault.

In San Diego, gorillas apprehend Evans (who comes off as pretty powerless compared to his introductory scenes as mankind's potential savior), Rhodes (who has apparently stopped crying between panels), and Leung (who has strangely become a background character during *Revolution*'s second half). Evans accuses MacDonald of helping Caesar to destroy the world, but MacDonald insists that the ape is actually attempting to *save* it. Meanwhile, as nuclear strikes escalate around the world, a helicopter carries President Trundy and General Norman Akins to Fort Liberty, in New York. The president's team sees things in flames and the Statue of Liberty destroyed, setting the stage for Taylor's discovery two millennia in the future.

As the ape revolution spreads, a news broadcast is taken over by an orangutan, who (apparently mimicking Rhodes' repeated messages, and speech-empowered by Caesar) tells TV audiences that "everything is under control," a claim the network itself makes moments later after cutting the feed. Shortly thereafter, with Leung's help, Rhodes sends a broadcast to the president to let him know just how out of control the situation really is. Breck plans to detonate a doomsday bomb, she says, recommending that San Diego be targeted for a thermonuclear strike to prevent the world's destruction.

While all this is going on, Doctor Evans says he needs time to create a new batch of his anti-apes virus. But his relevance to the story seems a bit superfluous at this point.

Breck tells Caesar that he himself conceived and commissioned the Alpha-Omega Bomb, overseeing the "black budget" that funded it. While it's certainly in keeping with his character to be involved in such a project, the timeline might not bear out his claim. The bomb's conception must have occurred before Taylor left Earth in 1972, since he tells Brent about it in *Beneath*. *Conquest*, however, is set in 1991, 19 years after Taylor's departure. When *Conquest* was filmed, actor Don Murray was 42 years old. If we assume Breck's age to be the same as Murray's, then that would mean Breck was only 23 years old when Taylor left. As such, his being in a position of such great power seems doubtful... though not impossible. If Breck is *older* than his actor counterpart, however (quite possible, considering that 42 is often considered young for a governor), then the timeline works much better.

For trivia buffs, issue five contains three cool connections to previous *Apes* titles from other publishers. The inclusion of Fort Liberty pays homage to Ubisoft's *POTA* video game, in which the Statue of Liberty is shown to contain a secret bunker. Trundy also mentions a secure bunker at Mount Rushmore, which Marvel Comics had established in its "Terror on the Planet of the Apes" storyline (it's up Abraham Lincoln's nose). The third connection involves Templeton's backup story, "Ape Shall Not Kill Ape," illustrated by Kent Burles and Bernie Mireault, a tale set in a classroom of humans and apes during an unspecified future period beyond Caesar's lifetime. Burles had previously drawn the first eleven issues of Malibu's *Apes* comic, using an identical art style.

Greybeard, a local Lawgiver, preaches the lessons of cohabitation that audiences witnessed at the conclusion of *Battle*. But Augustus, a Lawgiver from a different village, arrives, bringing not only armed gorillas and chimps, but savage humans, whom he lets loose on his more peaceful counterpart. With Augustus assuming control, the humans of that village are stripped and cast into a river, and the new Lawgiver proclaims apes cohabiting with "animals" a thing of the past. Although the law that "Ape shall not kill ape" remains important, he says, the new truth is for apes to "Beware the beast man..."

Though only six pages in length, this story captures the inherent pessimism of the *Planet of the Apes* films, reinforcing the idea that no matter what a character's intentions or actions may be, things will always move inextricably toward the future that Taylor finds, in which apes rule supreme, humans are nothing more than mute savages, and the world will end in destruction. It also serves to lower a particularly large red flag in the films: the discrepancy between the Lawgiver's hateful condemnation of mankind as recited in *Planet* and *Beneath*, and his optimistic outlook toward peaceful co-existence as seen in *Battle*. The establishment of multiple Lawgivers throughout history provides a simple, elegant solution to the inconsistency.

The final installment of "Caesar's Journal" removes a red flag raised in earlier issues of *Revolution* itself: namely, if Caesar can foresee the future, why does he not know about his parents in *Battle*, or about the mutants' impending attack? We learn that Caesar no longer recalls any of the dreams he chronicled in prior entries, nor even writing about them. The chimp's precognition has apparently faded away, taking with it his knowledge of future events. This harkens back to issue four's journal, in which he pondered, "What if I have been dreaming the world into being... what happens if I stop dreaming? Does that stop the sky from catching fire?" It's an intriguing question and, in keeping with the films' ambiguity about whether the timeline is changing or circular, we never discover the answer. But it certainly gives us a lot to think about.

Issue Six

The final installment of *Revolution on the Planet of the Apes'* main story, "Survival of the Fittest" (once again featuring art by Salgood Sam), begins with a fleet of fighter jets piloted by gorillas arriving to serve as Caesar's reinforcements. They are led by Aldo, who has apparently evolved far more quickly than other apes, as he salutes Caesar upon arrival, noting, "General Aldo reporting for duty!" This might make sense given his enhancements at Area 51, but it flies in the face of Aldo's on-screen depiction in *Battle* as a dimwitted, monosyllabic brute incapable of advanced reasoning.

Elsewhere, the soap-operatic debate between Rhodes and Evans continues (he's still just talking about his virus instead of doing something more productive, like actually working on it). Leung, meanwhile, announces that his broadcast is done since his camera is out of juice.

In preparation for the final battle, Caesar has Lisa and many others, humans and apes alike, seek safety in the mountains. MacDonald insists on joining Caesar, explaining, "If man's destiny turns on today's actions, then men must take responsibility for those actions. Whatever that destiny may be." Those who have watched *Battle*, in which his brother replaces him as Caesar's advisor (and it's hard to imagine that anyone reading this anthology has *not* watched *Battle*), can see where this is going.

Trundy learns that the Russians and Chinese have launched nuclear strikes against all major European targets. At that moment, Breck chimes in, reporting that everything is under control (which is no more true in this instance than the several other times throughout the miniseries that characters make such a claim), but Aldo's gorilla pilots launch an explosive assault and penetrate the bunker. With no choice left, Trundy orders the activation of the Inferno

Protocol, which will launch nuclear strikes at every major U.S. city, in the hope of wiping out the apes – despite the human casualties that will ensue.

A dreaming Doctor Zaius kills Milo to alter history, in *Revolution on the Planet of the Apes* #6 (Aug 2006).

The apes quickly overwhelm the security bunker. Caesar and Breck engage in a pitched battle that echoes the final moments between Taylor and Zaius in *Beneath*, with the impression that the Alpha-Omega Bomb will detonate. MacDonald prevents that outcome, but is fatally shot in the process and, in one of the miniseries' sadder (though not unexpected) moments, dies in the grieving chimp's arms.

Outside the relative safety of the bunker, bombs begin to drop. Rhodes and Evans die holding hands after admitting they still love each other, while an unnamed observer (Leung, most likely) muses, "One day, someone will ask, 'How did this happen? How could we, with all our technology and civilization, be defeated by simple apes?' The answer is, we weren't. We did it to ourselves. Apes didn't *conquer* the planet. They *inherited* it."

The story concludes with a dialog-free montage foreshadowing the status quo of *Battle for the Planet of the Apes*. Caesar leads San Diego's surviving apes and humans into the wilderness, away from the exploding city, and a man who just might be the second MacDonald brother has an unspeaking cameo among the refugees. Aldo's forces trade in their jet planes for wild horses, and Kolp's commandoes seek shelter in the bunker's lower levels, where Alma reports an increase in radiation, setting the stage for the rise of the underground mutant civilization.

In the final panels, Lisa musters the ability to speak a full sentence, reassuring Caesar that everything will be all right, and providing a nice counter-balance to everyone else's claims of things being under control. Nearby, survivor Chris Leung chronicles this next chapter in human-ape relations, only this time with pencil and paper. It's a fitting conclusion to a satisfying story arc that leaves the reader wanting more. If only Mr. Comics had followed through with its plans to give readers what they wanted.

"Catch a Falling Star," penned by Templeton and drawn by Steve Molnar, is the final backup tale, and perhaps the best one, with a twist ending worthy of Rod Serling's *The Twilight Zone*. Set in what seems to be a modern-day metropolis, this surreal story opens on a robed orangutan rushing past a building ablaze with fire, which armed apes force human slaves to battle using a contemporary firetruck hose. The orangutan turns out to be Doctor Zaius, who visits a beer-chugging Doctor Milo in an urban apartment complete with modern appliances and furniture. As if that were not bizarre enough, Zaius shares with his young friend The Divinity of Taylor and Caesar – which turns out to be Caesar's journals as presented throughout *Revolution on the Planet of the Apes*, and which he has kept hidden from the masses.

The documents foretell the arrival of Taylor's crashing spacecraft, Milo's temporal journey with Zira and Cornelius, and the resultant birth of Caesar, which Zaius believes was never meant to happen since the Sacred Scrolls state that God's chosen savior was a talking gorilla named Aldo (yes, that is indeed another of the films' red flags). To that end, he murders Milo to prevent Caesar's birth, only to discover that Milo's name throughout the documents has now been replaced with his own, indicating that time has been altered so that the elder orangutan will bring the chimp couple back in time instead of Milo. The reader's brain explodes at the insanity of the situation, and...

Zaius suddenly awakens on a lounge chair in the desert, where Cornelius is conducting an archeological expedition. Zaius, it seems, has merely been dreaming... or has he, like Caesar, been foreseeing the future? Moments later, Cornelius introduces the latest member of their team, and it's Milo. Zaius no longer recalls his eerily prophetic dream or Milo's involvement in it, nor does he recognize the significance of a falling star that passes overhead. But readers do; it is, of course, the arrival of Taylor's crashing spacecraft.

Final Thoughts

While imperfect, *Revolution on the Planet of the Apes* is nonetheless among the most significant and well-told comics to be set in the *Apes* universe. This is notably due to its attempts to fill in canon (such as providing first names for Breck, Kolp, and MacDonald[8]), bridge the gap between *Conquest* and *Battle*, answer many questions asked since *Battle*'s 1973 release, and thereby remove a number of those pesky red flags.

It's fun to spot homages in the naming of characters. Nora Rhodes, for instance, is named after actor Hari Rhodes, *Conquest*'s MacDonald. Arthur Trundy is named for producer Arthur P. Jacobs and his wife, Natalie Trundy, who played *Beneath*'s Albina, *Escape*'s Stephanie Branton, and Lisa in *Conquest* and *Battle*. Norman Akins is named after Claude Akins, the actor beneath Aldo's makeup in *Battle*, and Norman Burton, the first film's Hunt Leader and Galen's father Yalu on the *Apes* TV series. Bryce Evans is the namesake of Maurice "Zaius" Evans, while Paula Dean borrows her name from *Apes* screenwriter Paul Dehn. It can be slightly distracting at times (much like the many such in-jokes in *Rise of the Planet of the Apes*), but some of the homages are actually quite subtle, and thus easy to overlook until the second or third readings.

Where *Revolution* falters, frankly, is in its handling of the supporting cast. Although Leung's parents were killed by gorillas, we don't get a sense of what is driving his determination to see Caesar in action and broadcast that to the world, or why he went so far as to try to murder a man running for president. This is especially frustrating when you consider that the blogger, despite being a would-be assassin, is one of the story's protagonists, not a villain. Rhodes, meanwhile, is a government stooge, but isn't fleshed out as a human being. Her relationship with Evans (who spends a lot of time talking about his virus, but doing nothing about perfecting it) isn't given any depth at all. They're engaged, yet seem to have a love-hate relationship without any basis provided for those feelings. Their reunion thus has no impact on the story or on readers.

---

[8] Arnold, Vernon, and Malcolm, respectively. Breck, amusingly, is named after Arnold Schwarzenegger, who was California's governor at the time of *Revolution*'s release. It's interesting to note that Jason Clarke's character in *Dawn of the Planet of the Apes*, who serves a similar role to MacDonald's brother in *Battle*, is named Malcolm.

Reich, despite his revelations about Caesar, serves little purpose and gradually becomes little more than the curmudgeonly uncle you're obligated to invite to family gatherings, even though you'd prefer not to. President Trundy hates apes and wants to preserve human superiority, but where are those feelings coming from? What is driving him? In *Conquest*, Breck at least had the opportunity to address this question when confronted by Caesar. Added to this, most of the sequences involving the president and his cabinet are repetitive, with the same points being made over and over again, issue after issue.

But there are a number of highly significant elements of *Revolution on the Planet of the Apes*.[9] As noted, the most brilliant concept is the notion of Caesar, due to the nature of his gestation period during Zira's trip through the time barrier, being endowed with the ability to dream visions of the future while actually influencing the real world around him. This further develops the character, explaining why Caesar needs, in *Conquest*, to actually see apes as slaves in the big city, and why, after the Night of the Fires, he is so determined to change things – to alter the course of history so that somehow, in the end, apes and humans can live in some sense of harmony, and thereby prevent Earth's destined destruction. (Never mind the *massive* time paradox that would result – if the timeline is altered, Zira and Cornelius won't travel back in time, and Caesar will never be born in our present, and thus won't be able to lead the ape revolution in the first place.)

There is true power in the moments between Caesar and Breck, the emphasis on the hatred each has for the other, and Caesar's recognition that he must put aside that hate if there is *any* hope for the future. Above all else, it is *those* scenes that make one regret the fact that we never got to see McDowall and Murray act against each other again on film. They serve as a revelation in how their dynamic mirrors the adversity between Taylor and Zaius in the first two films. Indeed, there are certain inversions in the *Apes* saga – Caesar/Breck to Taylor/Zaius and *Escape* to *Planet* – that not only serve up powerful variations, but prove how hopelessly the events of this saga are locked into place, despite the intentions of anyone involved.

Writers Ty Templeton and Joe O'Brien should be credited for what they achieved in this scenario. The beautifully illustrated *Revolution on the Planet of the Apes* – in essence, the fourth-and-a-half film – lowers several red flags

---

[9] Not the least of which are fan letters written by four of this anthology's contributors: John Roche, Dayton Ward, co-editor Rich Handley, and yours truly

raised by the classic movies, making the mythos as a whole (and the fifth movie, in particular) that much stronger.

Thanks to *Revolution*'s intricately plotted scripts, much of what once made little sense is now under control, and it is regrettable that we never got the chance to see what the authors had planned for future story arcs. As revolutions go, this one represents a successful campaign.

A Tale of Two Cities: Sibling Rivalry on BOOM!'s Planet of the Apes

by Joseph Dilworth Jr.

By the time that BOOM! Studios officially announced that it had picked up the *Planet of the Apes* license and would be publishing a new comic book series, it had been roughly six years since an *Apes* comic had hit stands. As this was during the lead-up to a new movie (a reboot of the film franchise), it was a surprise that BOOM! would be placing this new series within the original continuity. Issue one would begin 1,300 years[1] prior to the 1968 *Planet of the Apes* and ten years after the framing sequence of the original series' final entry, *Battle for the Planet of the Apes*.

By 2011, BOOM! had already established itself as a solid comic book publisher with an exciting stable of original titles, most notably *Zombie Tales* and Mark Waid's *Irredeemable*. It also had been successful with many licensed properties, such as *Farscape*, *Eureka*, Clive Barker's *Hellraiser*, and an

---

[1] Early issues and press materials initially placed the series 1,200 years before the first film. However, this was in error, as the comic was set in 2680, while the movie took place in 3978. The span was thus corrected, in later issues and in trade-paperback collections, to 1,300 years.

adaptation of Philip K. Dick's novel *Do Androids Dream of Electric Sheep?*, which had served as the basis for the acclaimed film *Blade Runner*.

Among the licenses that BOOM! had acquired were a couple from 20th Century Fox. *28 Days Later* and *Die Hard: Year One* had done well for the publisher, so when it came time for a return of Fox's *Planet of the Apes* franchise to comics, it would appear the choice was clear. BOOM! made the popular decision to start out with a continuing monthly title, with an idea to build upon that with additional miniseries. However, an idea can only go so far on its own, and in any media, it is only as good as the creative team chosen to nurture it. On top of that, in order to be successful, the new *Planet of the Apes* comic would have to satisfy stalwart *Apes* fans, as well as draw in the mildly curious or those completely unfamiliar with the concept.

Daryl Gregory was already an acclaimed and award-winning writer prior to entering the world of comic books. His first novel, *Pandemonium*, won the Crawford Award for best first fantasy novel and was nominated for three other awards as well, including the World Fantasy Award. *The Devil's Alphabet*, his second novel, was named one of the best books of the year by Publishers Weekly and was nominated for a Philip K. Dick Award. His collection of short fiction, *Unpossible and Other Stories*, was similarly acclaimed by Publishers Weekly.

It might seem odd that a novelist from outside the industry would be chosen for such a plum assignment, however acclaimed he might be, but Gregory had an ace up his sleeve. In 2010, BOOM! had hired him to co-write the series *Dracula: The Company of Monsters* with Mark Waid. This series received modest acclaim and quite the fan following. Waid was then BOOM!'s chief creative officer and appeared to enjoy his collaboration with Gregory, and there is little doubt that this played a part in the author being at the top of the list to helm the new license.

Gregory brought two key strengths to this comic: an ability to write clearly defined and distinctive characters, and to construct an entertaining story with a well-thought-out narrative. The writer knows, from the start, how the actions on page one will inform the last page of the final issue. There is an old adage that tells us the journey is more important than the destination, but Daryl Gregory spoils us by writing an epic journey that brings the reader to an equally epic and intriguing finale. The characters involved in this rich tale are three-dimensional and dynamic. Each personality enhances the story, and is difficult to let go of when that character exits the stage.

An assassin murders the Lawgiver, setting human and ape society on a dark path in *Planet of the Apes* #1 (Apr 2011).

In the visual medium of comic books, a well-written story only gets the book so far. The artwork gets the comic the rest of the way over the finish line, and is equally as important as the words in terms of storytelling – perhaps more so. Great art can elevate a poorly written story and enhance a terrific one. Bad art, on the other hand, can destroy a comic, no matter how beautifully constructed the prose may be. There is no exact science to putting together the perfect writer-artist team. Most pairings work serviceably well on any given title, but nowadays, it is rare to strike creative gold the likes of, say, Stan Lee working with Jack Kirby, or Chris Claremont and John Byrne, or even Marv Wolfman and George Pérez. In the case of *Planet of the Apes*, BOOM! managed to catch lightning in a bottle with the team of writer Daryl Gregory and artist Carlos Magno.

Magno had previously been honing his penciling skills at DC Comics, most notably on the final four issues of the *Tangent: Superman's Reign* limited series and several issues of *Countdown to Final Crisis*, as well as some issues of *The Phantom* for Moonstone and various comics for Marvel. He was a relative newcomer to BOOM!, having only previously done some penciling for *Zombie Tales*. Clearly, editor Ian Brill saw something in the burgeoning artist to not only pair him with Gregory, but give him full artistic control by letting him ink his own pencils.

On *Planet of the Apes*, Magno exhibits clean, concise, and detailed artwork that is in the same style as Pérez and Phil Jimenez. It should be stressed that he does not imitate those two artists, but rather has line-work and character detail that put him in the same caliber. Magno excels at giving all characters their own individual body language and face, without repeating himself. No character would be mistaken for another, which is especially welcome when it comes to the apes. Just as Gregory writes everyone in their own unique personality, so, too, does Magno draw them. Consistency is also on display with the characters' own physical continuity.

One of the more unique stylistic choices is in the appearance of the ape characters. The biggest challenge lies in keeping an appearance similar to how the apes are represented in the films, while at the same time updating them to fit a comic book look and allowing the artist to put his own stamp on the design. Magno succeeds and exceeds in all aspects. His characters are beautifully rendered over richly detailed backgrounds, and he brings to life the story in new and unexpected ways. This contribution to the ongoing storyline is very apparent when, in the final three special issues concluding the story, the artwork is handed off to someone else.

The main monthly series was abruptly cancelled at issue sixteen, leaving the story unfinished. Fortunately, BOOM! published three additional, oversized one-shots (*Planet of the Apes Special*, *Planet of the Apes Spectacular*, and *Planet of the Apes Giant*) to finish what Gregory had begun. For whatever reason, Magno did not go along for the ride, so art duties fell to Diego Barreto. Barreto's artwork is more in the vein of Tom Grummett and Keith Giffen and, while still adequate in the storytelling department, lacks some of the clean line-art that Magnos exhibited. It takes a few pages to make the adjustment, but the epic story is such that the transition is easily made. It is unfortunate that Magnos could not have finished what he started, but that is certainly not Barreto's fault. While his artwork may shift the tone darker visually, he still holds true to the story.

The tale itself is broken up into five story arcs[2] across nineteen full issues, as well as a short story presented as part of a 20th issue, the *Planet of the Apes Annual* one-shot. Within those five arcs, Gregory delivers a superlative tale that accomplishes something rather difficult. This is a story that anyone can read and enjoy, especially those completely unfamiliar with the *Apes* franchise. Yet for those of us intimately familiar with the complicated continuity of the five classic films, there are hidden treasures to unearth. Gregory tells a wholly original story, while also helping to close the loop largely unexplored between the end of the final film and the beginning of the first.

The catalyst for the entire epic tale hangs on one of the most incongruous and near-mythical characters of the entire franchise: the Lawgiver. This is the ape whose Sacred Scrolls set down the laws of simian society. His anti-human teachings were spoken of often, yet his words to a group of ape and human children during his only brief appearance (in *Battle*) seemed to espouse coexistence and peace. That incongruity starts to take shape here, as very soon after the start of the story, the Lawgiver's words are re-written and embellished to serve a darker purpose.

Like any great work of drama, this *Planet of the Apes* series starts small and builds. The Lawgiver is assassinated by a masked human, an event that informs

---

[2] The first four arcs, published in the monthly comic, were titled "The Long War," "The Devil's Pawn," "Children of Fire," and "The Half Man." The fifth arc, from the one-shots, was collected as a trade paperback under the title "The Utopians."

everything to come. The already tenuous relationship between apes and humankind deteriorates further, spiraling into all-out conflict. Eventually, the very pillar of simian society is attacked and a newborn child is stolen from his mother. Some try to stave the escalating violence, while others fuel the fires. Just as all seems lost for humanity, Daryl Gregory hits us with a narrative conceit that sets up the long game: a time jump, ten years into the future.

Occurring at the end of issue twelve, this is clearly meant to mark the halfway point in the saga. The original plan was likely to tell the second portion over the course of another twelve issues. However, with the series cancelled at issue sixteen, the story was left incomplete. The three extra-sized issues at least provided closure, but I can't help but wonder how much richer the narrative would have been had it played out as intended. The size of the audience always dictates the continued publication of a comic book series. One can only speculate as to whether or not there was even more story to tell and, had the readership been there, how much more we could have seen of Gregory's saga.

The new primary setting for the comic is the City State of Mak, named after the two MacDonald brothers who served as human advisors and friends to Caesar, the liberator of the apes, in the films. The Lawgiver is the leader of Mak, and has worked hard to make it an integrated society of both mankind and apes. Despite his efforts, the humans have been primarily relegated to a section of the city called Southtown, nicknamed "Skintown" by the apes. Southtown is essentially a slum area, while the apes inhabit the more affluent areas of Mak. It is here that the Lawgiver has raised the story's two main characters: his adopted daughters, Sullivan (a human) and Alaya (a chimp).

While the Lawgiver is initially relegated to little more than a glorified cameo here, we do eventually gain further insight into the character via flashbacks woven into the narrative. In the short story from the annual, for example ("First and Last Days"), we see that, in continuing his agenda of co-existence, the Lawgiver has enrolled Sullivan in a simian school. On her first day, she is assaulted by a human male, who is chased down and killed by the albino ape General Nix. As the Lawgiver has extended the meaning of Caesar's first law that "ape shall not kill ape" to also include humans, he orders the fierce but honorable general arrested and sent to jail.

This short story adds much weight to the motivations of Sullivan, Alaya, and Nix, as well as how all three react to the Lawgiver's death, and in the way they treat each other. The two women think of the elderly orangutan as their "grandfather," even though neither shares a bloodline with him, nor are they even of the same species. They are both devastated by his loss, yet have different reactions. Though they want the assassin brought to justice, their methods and mindset are worlds apart. It is fascinating to see each woman's way of dealing with such devastating personal loss, with each reaction setting the stage for the destinies of their respective species.

Alaya, for her part, becomes vindictive and swears vengeance, determined to capture and kill the human murderer. This is where old prejudices rear their ugly heads, as anti-human apes rally to the side of their new leader, and Alaya's thirst for retribution is only slightly tempered by Sullivan asking for time to find the killer herself. Alaya allows for only a fraction of the time requested, but clearly doesn't intend to live up to her word, as she immediately starts marshalling her forces and working to ferret out the killer.

Alaya's grief paves the way for racism and hate to overcome any sense of rationality, and she uses a key moment to rally the troops, as it were, and to resolve a long-debated topic amongst *Planet of the Apes* fans. She essentially assumes the role of de facto Lawgiver and, as such, is expected to speak at her predecessor's funeral. Sully hopes that her sister will use the opportunity to quell the rising tensions on both sides and unify the citizens of Mak peacefully. However, Alaya does the opposite. Defying tradition and sacred ape laws, she writes her own scroll and presents it as the Lawgiver's words, driving a permanent wedge between apekind and humanity.

The final classic *Apes* film, 1973's *Battle for the Planet of the Apes*, ended with the Lawgiver's words, "...as I look at apes and humans living in friendship, in harmony and at peace, now some 600 years after Caesar's death, at least we wait with hope for the future." However, the first movie had Cornelius read from the Sacred Scrolls, "**Beware the beast Man, for he is the Devil's pawn. Alone among God's primates, he kills for sport or lust or greed. Yea, he will murder his brother to possess his brother's land. Let him not breed in great numbers, for he will make a desert of his home and yours. Shun him; drive him back into his jungle lair, for he is the harbinger of death.**"

Gregory, at last, reconciles these two worldviews. The Lawgiver lived by the former quote and worked his entire life toward that end. Alaya herself amended the Sacred Scrolls with the latter quote and presented those words as though from the Lawgiver himself, and as proof of his changed view of humanity. This shows that while the trip back in time by Cornelius, Zira, and Milo in *Escape from the Planet of the Apes* may have, indeed, resulted in a kinder, gentler Lawgiver than in the original timeline, his harsh and decisive words would still manifest themselves and form the basis of relegating mankind to little more than cattle in the apes' eyes.

Of course, the tragic events that unfold in the comic book aren't entirely the apes' fault. Sullivan, the unofficial mayor of Skintown, does her best to temper the rising emotions within the human population. She, too, wants the killer of her adoptive grandfather brought to justice, but finds it difficult to believe that it could be anyone in her community. As the ape presence and sanctions increase in Southtown, the other humans grow more hostile and rebellious. Sully isn't against defending her people, but goes to great lengths to avoid violent conflict. And there is an added factor for Sullivan to work hard to keep the peace and push for a better future: she is pregnant.

While the Lawgiver's death informs the first twelve issues of the series and all the events therein, the birth of Sully's baby and what happens to him thereafter are the catalyst for what occurs following the ten-year jump. Parents mark many milestones in a child's life, but none is as inherently powerful and important as his or her birth. In the world in which this story takes place, more and more human children are being born mute, though there is no discernable reason for this. As fate would have it, Sullivan's son is born alive and healthy, but does not cry or make any sound. While shocking, this revelation pales in comparison to the circumstances of his birth.

Skintown is eventually cleared of its occupants, with the humans either being rounded up into captivity or fleeing into the mountains to fight another day. Sully is among those unable to escape capture. She is brought before Alaya, who demands that her baby be removed. Once Sully's son is brought into the world, Alaya claims the infant for her own and leaves. The loss of a child may be the most traumatic event a person can endure. Having that child stolen and never seeing or knowing him thereafter must be unimaginably painful. This is the breaking point for Sullivan, and, as we see ten years later, she has abandoned any sort of peaceful solution and has gone to war against her sister.

Then there is Nix, the other primary character in this tragedy and probably my favorite character of this series. Perhaps even the most interesting ape in the entire franchise, Nix rose through the ranks of the simian army, despite facing prejudice for being an albino. Nix has his own moral code of fair, yet swift, justice. He doesn't seem to harbor any particular hatred towards humans, but metes out harsh justice to ape and human alike, as evidenced by his protection of the young Sullivan. The fact that Alaya releases him from prison to lead her army against mankind, rather than selecting a decidedly anti-human general, suggests that she might hold out some hope of eventual peace between the species.

Ayala seeks help from an imprisoned General Nix in this panel from *Planet of the Apes* # 11 (Feb 2012).

While Nix obviously holds affection for Sullivan and regards humans as more than just animals, he still becomes Alaya's right-hand ape and stays by her side through the decade of war with humanity. Even when she is later deposed, he still visits her in prison and keeps her informed of everything that transpires. He ultimately stands beside both Sullivan and Alaya, nobly helping to resolve the story.

The early revelation of the Lawgiver's assassin does nothing to prevent all-out war from breaking out. At that point, both sides are resolutely determined to march along their respective paths, and no amount of common sense or reason can dissuade them. The primary suspect is Bako, Sullivan's most trusted friend and confidant. Years prior, Bako had been part of the army that brutally razed the Red Creek settlement (the event that orphaned both Sully and Alaya). Shortly thereafter, his wife and son were killed in the responding attack that left him and his mute daughter, Chaika, alive but devastated. Surprisingly, it is Chaika and not Bako who turns out to be the assassin, and after she is slain, Bako intensifies his fight against the apes. His last act is to try to retrieve Sullivan's infant son, but he loses his prize – and his life – at the hands of Alaya.

One of the few characters to switch allegiances during the story is Hulss. Loyal to the Lawgiver, the ape gradually becomes disillusioned with Alaya's methods. He secretly starts aiding Sullivan and the humans, but eventually makes a stand and fully defects to Sully's side. During the time jump, he is able to acquire weapons for his new friends from the Great Khan, an East Asian ape who rules his domain. After negotiating an alliance between Khan and Sully, Hulss discovers that the former plans to conquer all he surveys and thus add to his empire, betraying his new allies. Hulss is tasked with keeping Sully's son, Julian, safe when the final battle begins.

The Great Khan himself is a striking and decadent figure, having chosen to shave his body and act like a human, even going so far as to take a human wife. He seems to have adopted many Asian customs and traditions, and is definitely more human than ape in his actions and attitudes, especially in his empire building. Having played the long game of slowly building trust with his would-be allies, he uses cunning and deceit to bring himself within striking distance of his goal. It is perhaps his lack of understanding of his duality and the nature of each that leads to his undoing. However, as with any conqueror, it is his inability to conceive of having flaws, as well as his over-confidence in his own power, that ultimately results in his defeat.

The final story arc, as relayed in the last three one-shots, is told by Julian many years after the events occur. Julian is the son of two "sisters:" the human Sullivan, his biological mother, and the ape Alaya, the chimp foster-mother who raised him for the first ten years of his life. The later event has the curious effect of bringing Alaya back around to the idea of apes and mankind coexisting. There is no doubt that Alaya loves her human nephew as though he were her own. As Alaya says, "Hate what humans do, but do not hate humans."

Julian seems to have been raised with this sentiment. He is later kidnapped by humans and returned to his biological mother, whom he has grown to resent because of her militant ways. Interestingly, after ten years of conflict, Alaya and Sullivan seem to have reversed their stances, with the latter embracing violence and war, while the former is content and at peace. Both women having lived through and understanding both sides probably contributes to their eventual reconciliation and decision to work together. One can only speculate that Julian lives his life having been influenced by the positive aspects of both apekind and humanity. It would appear so, as we see him, at the very end, living in a household comprising both sides.

Of course, with any story of this magnitude and this many layers, there is always a "man behind the curtain" who is ultimately responsible for much of what transpires. In this case, that would be Brother Kale, the leader of a cult that broke off from a larger human sect. He is the primary source of arms and armaments for Sully's people, and has provided Chaika with the means to kill the Lawgiver. Gifted with the ability to mentally manipulate people, Kale occasionally speaks of an "ultimate weapon," later revealed to be a small nuclear device. Fans of the films will quickly recognize Kale's cult and the sect they broke away from as being precursors to the bomb-worshipping mutants seen in the second film, *Beneath the Planet of the Apes*.

It's difficult to know just how much of what transpires is a direct result of Kale's influence, either indirectly or by overt mental control. Certainly, he provides the means for the Lawgiver to be assassinated, but did he also further compel Chaika to do the deed, or did he merely let that play out as it did? We see moments in which he overtly directs someone using his mind, such as exerting control over an ape politician named Nerise when she deposes Alaya, but there might be many more instances that are more covert. He ultimately falls prey to his own hubris, as his plan to unleash his "god" becomes his undoing, and Sullivan leave him to the mercy, or lack thereof, of the apes.

Hint: It doesn't go so well for him.

Ayala and Sullivan travel to meet with the Golden Khan in *Planet of the Apes Giant* (Sep 2013).

The entire story comes back around full-circle as the sisters, once divided, reunite to stop Khan from conquering Mak. Alaya, Sullivan, and Nix, the fragmented trinity at the beginning of the saga, provide a distraction so that the remnants of Kale's cult can detonate their nuclear bomb and put an end to all the fighting, both internal and external. It is a grand conclusion that cements this as an epic and unforgettable tale. It began as a story destined for tragedy, and yet we are left with some hope for the future of the survivors. However, the impending arrival of a human astronaut named Taylor, his meeting with a mute savage named Nova, and their eventual, even more devastating fates temper that hope with imminent doom.

The original film franchise left thousands of years unseen as fertile ground to mine for stories within that continuity. Daryl Gregory's storyline fits wonderfully within established continuity, while also enhancing and adding to it. This story is feature film-worthy itself, as well as being the strongest *Planet of the Apes* comic book series in a long time, if not ever. It is unfortunate that it didn't quite unfold as planned, but at least we eventually got the complete tale. It leaves me wanting more, which is as it should be. While BOOM! has given us more stories within the original *Apes* continuity,[3] my fervent hope is that one day, Gregory will revisit the world he brought to life and show us what happens next.

---

[3] Discussed in the following essay.

Reopening the BOOM! Box: Prequels and Sequels on Parallel Planets

by Joseph Dilworth, Jr.

With the success of their first ongoing *Planet of the Apes* series, BOOM! Studios decided that the time was right for some more *Apes* comics. For this spinoff series, BOOM! chose an idea pitched by the husband-and-wife writing team of Corrina Bechko and Gabriel Hardman, which was strong enough for the publisher to upgrade from a one-shot to a full miniseries. On the success of that first four-issue series, *Betrayal of the Planet of the Apes*, the pair were allowed to continue their story in *Exile on the Planet of the Apes* for four additional issues, before expanding into a longer form with twelve issues of *Planet of the Apes: Cataclysm*. While separate stories in their own right, *Betrayal* and *Exile* also serve as terrific prologues to the epic that is *Cataclysm*.

Starting twenty years before astronauts Taylor, Landon, and Dodge crashed into ape society from the past, these issues bring things full-circle by concluding with the events that brought three apes back to the past during the destruction of Earth in *Escape from the Planet of the Apes*. These issues work well as direct prequels to the classic 1968 *Planet of the Apes* film. Depending on your frame of reference, they could also be considered sequels to the last two original *Apes* movies (which were themselves prequels) or just as a prequel to the third film.

It's all rather confusing and the subject of another essay for another time.

Corrina Bechko is possibly the most uniquely qualified writer ever to take on *Planet of the Apes*. She has a zoology degree and worked for many years as a researcher at the Los Angeles Zoo, specifically studying the behavior of chimpanzees and orangutans. Bechko has written comic books for Marvel Comics, DC Comics' Web imprint Zuda, and Image Comics. Subsequent to writing about apes, she and Hardman also penned eighteen issues of *Star Wars: Legacy* for Dark Horse Comics, as well as the creator-owned series *Invisible Republic*.

Gabriel Hardman, meanwhile, has worked for more than fifteen years as a storyboard artist for multiple films, starting with *Austin Powers: International Man of Mystery*. He also storyboarded *Superman Returns*, *Inception*, *The Dark Knight Rises* and, most recently, *Interstellar*. Hardman wrote a few books for Marvel and other publishers, and provided artwork for many more. He created the art for his past series with Bechko, *Heathentown*, as well as their most current collaboration, the aforementioned *Invisible Republic*. Hardman gets to flex his artistic muscles here by providing the artwork for *Betrayal of the Planet of the Apes*.

The writing duo craft an epic journey for several characters across twenty issues that is full of intrigue, conspiracy, betrayal, and character drama. From ape plotting against ape to the marginalizing of humans whose actions say what their muted voices are unable to, to the threat of all-out war that some are desperate to avoid while others are actively fomenting, it's all there. These are things that would be expected in any story set in the world of *Planet of the Apes*. However, Bechko and Hardman go a bit further.

The original film series was a product of its time, giving us allegories to such hot-button topics as the Civil Rights Movement, protests of U.S. involvement in the Vietnam War, and the fears raised by the Cold War between the United States and Russia. Some forty years later, those are once again major concerns, even if the players have changed. Whether intentional or not, all of these things are in the DNA of *Betrayal*, *Exile*, and *Cataclysm*. The end result is the flavor of a 1970s science fiction film in a modern comic. More directly, these comic book tales "feel" more like a *Planet of the Apes* movie than any that have been published before.

Each of the three series is drawn by a different artist, with Hardman handling *Betrayal*, Marc Laming illustrating *Exile*, and Damian Couceiro penciling *Cataclysm* (with Mariano Taibo inking the latter). The changing of artist from one series to the next works well as, rather than being a distraction, it feels more like a changing of directors from one film to another. Thankfully, each artist illustrates every issue of his respective story, so the tone remains constant. The costuming and architecture are consistent and recognizable throughout, further reinforcing the idea of these being separate movies in a series, as opposed to printed comics. In short, think of these comics as adaptations of movies that were never released, and you'll get the idea of how seamlessly it all fits into the continuity of the original films.

Betrayed and Exiled

Bechko and Hardman make the interesting choice of shining the spotlight on Doctor Zaius, the main antagonist of the first two feature films and one of the most layered characters of the whole franchise. As an orangutan, he presided over the council that arbitrated legal matters in ape society. He also harbored a secret, as he was possibly the only living ape who knew that man had once dominated the Earth and subjugated apes, instead of the widely held and reinforced belief that apes had always ruled the planet.[1] In the first four-issue miniseries, *Betrayal of the Planet of the Apes*, we get to see how Zaius acquired this knowledge and became the orangutan depicted on screen.

It is interesting to see a Zaius who is idealistic and happy. He is newly appointed to the ape High Council and, as *Betrayal* begins, he is presiding, along with Councilors Quintessa and Tenebris, over the trial of Doctor Cato, an elderly orangutan accused of heresy for having taught sign language to his pet human, Tern. Cato is being defended by the one-eyed Aleron, a well-respected gorilla war hero and elder statesman. Aleron is more progressive and passive than his peers and, like Cato, is one of the few apes to treat humans with dignity and respect. The verdict in the case is "not guilty," and it's difficult to discern if Zaius is happy about the verdict, or merely that the elder councilors allow him to read it. Either way, he doesn't yet have the disdain for humanity that he displays in the films, but it's only a matter of time – or, in this case, pages – before he will.

A couple of things are set in motion in the first issue that forever alter the destinies of both apes and humans. These plot points carry over not only into *Exile* and *Cataclysm*, but also into the films themselves. First, there is the

---

[1] Yet somehow, Cornelius indicated, in *Escape from the Planet of the Apes*, that *every* ape knew about it, and that simian society even had a holiday commemorating the great liberator Aldo. When it comes to reconciling the sequels' contradictions, this has always been the 800-pound gorilla in the room.

murder/staged suicide of Cato by Ursus and his gorillas. In the films, Ursus is Zaius's henchape, but here, twenty years prior, the gorilla has another master. Tern is an accidental eyewitness to the events, initially attempting to save his simian friend before winding up a fugitive from the assassins trying to cover their tracks. Tern becomes the fall guy, and it isn't long before Aleron becomes embroiled in the proceedings, but the military veteran has his own secret which leads him to think the human isn't a murderer.

General Aleron, soon to face a devastating betrayal in *Betrayal of the Planet of the Apes* #1 (Nov 2011).

Many years prior, Aleron was involved in a scuffle with another ape, Lieutenant Varus, because of the latter's mistreatment of a group of humans. This fight has remained a secret until present-day, when a group of archeologists have uncovered evidence that Varus was shot and killed. As man is thought to be incapable of wielding a gun, the logical conclusion is that Aleron must have broken the cardinal rule of ape society, namely that "ape shall not kill ape."

The fact that the investigation and assassination are orchestrated by the same individual, Tenebris, is not a coincidence. The councilor is trying to kill two birds with one stone, by stopping the advancement of humans with the death of Cato, while simultaneously discrediting the most vocal and popular human sympathizer, Aleron. Tenebris has a very specific, if not psychotically paranoid, reason for doing both of these things, as Zaius will soon discover.

Zaius conducts his own investigation into the history of humans, which leads to his being kidnapped by Ursus and secreted away to an undisclosed location. There, he learns a terrible truth, one so devastating that it would completely unravel simian society were it to become known to the general populace: Instead of being animals of the wild, humans had once ruled the Earth above primitive apes, but were brought low by their own war-like ways. Thus were formed the Forbidden Zones, where technology proving the former dominance of mankind could be kept safely away from apes.

The "suicide" of Cato, the trial and imprisonment of Aleron, and the murder of Quintessa are all intended to squelch any further enabling of man to become more than the mute animal he now is. Understanding the need for someone to carry on his crusade, Tenebris has indoctrinated Zaius into the fold. Of course, this all leads to further tragedy, for when Tenebris confronts Aleron upon the gorilla's escape from prison, Tern kills the orangutan. Zaius, acting on his newfound disgust for man, orders all humans driven out of the city and into the Forbidden Zone. It is also revealed that Varus was, in fact, not killed by fellow ape Aleron, but by a human.

It's interesting that *Betrayal of the Planet of the Apes* plays like the original film, but from the perspective of the apes instead of the humans. The elements are there: an orangutan who guards an Earth-shattering secret, an exceptional human who threatens preconceived notions regarding both simian and human pasts, and a plot to keep everything suppressed that goes not quite according to plan. Maybe it's a case of seeing something that isn't there, nor should it be inferred that there is any intentional copying of the original, but it all provides some nice symmetry with the classic *Planet of the Apes* film. And whereas the first sequel movie seemingly ends the forward momentum of the franchise (by blowing up the planet), the next story in this sequence leads us to an even grander realm.

Exile on the Planet of the Apes picks up two years after the tumultuous events of *Betrayal*. There is civil unrest within ape society as the humans, exiled out of Ape City, have formed a rebellion from within the Forbidden Zone and are savagely attacking simian towns. Doctor Zaius finds himself in the barely tenable position of trying to unite his fellow apes while also looking for a way to quash the human uprising. Even worse, it is becoming increasingly obvious to him that an ape must be aiding and abetting the humans, and the situation becomes even more explosive as he attempts to root out the betrayer while being hampered by the rest of the council.

Exile sets aside the political intrigue and conspiratorial maneuverings of *Betrayal* in favor of heightened action and increased tension. Zaius has been led to think that humans are only warmongering savages who do nothing but consume what they can and destroy what they cannot. The books that Tenebris exposed him to support this supposition, as do the attacks that the humans continue to perpetrate. Like many before him, though, Zaius chooses the iron fist and no compromise and, although both seem to allow him to vanquish those who oppose him by the end of the story, they further the separation of the chimpanzees from the others within society. By crushing one rebellion, Zaius only sparks the flames of another. In a way, it is somewhat ironic; if Zaius hadn't so zealously guarded the secrets of humanity's violent past and the apes' subservience to the "monstrous" man, he could have twisted the history into a tool to unite all of his people.

There are several suspects who could be helping the humans, chief among them Cato's former pupil, Prisca, and former scribe, ex-inmate Timon. As it turns out, the suspicions of both are correct, more or less. Prisca remains staunchly sympathetic toward humans, as was her mentor, and eventually leaves the city to join up with them. Timon, for his part, has been selling goods pillaged during the human raids and using the money to buy supplies for the rebellion. Unfortunately, Timon, in a possible attempt to hedge his bets and play both sides against each other, betrays the humans and leads Ursus and his gorillas through the narrow passage to the encampment in the Forbidden Zone. Prisca is aided in her defection by a familiar face from the film series, Doctor Milo, before discovering the true leaders of the human army: a human and an ape, both very familiar to her personally.

Aleron and Tern are the silent partners in the human rebellion. The human is the field leader, while the aged gorilla strategizes and plots from behind the scenes. It's worth noting that Tern has the support and backing of his people in the actions he takes, whereas Aleron further betrays his people and alienates himself from them with everything he does. It doesn't matter that his actions are noble and right; Aleron has forever branded himself an old ape with no country. He knows that he will only face prosecution and an ignominious death should he every return home. For his part, Tern can ever only really hope to be martyred for his cause, as there are far more (and better-armed) apes than there are humans.

Both escape their inevitable fates, Tern by sailing out to sea with the surviving humans and Aleron by giving up his life to seal off the passage to the Forbidden Zone. Tern's escape even invokes a provocative image from the end of *Planet of the Apes*, this time eliciting awe and wonder instead of crushing despair. The traitorous Timon becomes trapped in the Forbidden Zone, seemingly alone with his remorse at having betrayed Aleron. Eventually, he discovers a still-alive human child among the dead. These two will appear again, at a moment that is both the best and the worst.

General Aleron is no longer one to trust the word of an ape in *Exile on the Planet of the Apes* #3 (May 2012).

In the end, Zaius openly admits that his actions (leading the assault on the humans, resulting in many deaths on both sides) may not have been the best possible choice, but he fervently believes that it was the right one, according to the laws of the apes and the teachings of the Lawgiver. He isn't quite the religious zealot whom we meet in the first film, but he has taken another step along that path. Ruthlessness is now a part of his nature, and he only needs a few more nudges to reach the point of no return. Unfortunately, he is about to get a few shoves toward completing his journey as the story continues with a massive *Cataclysm*.

Surviving the Cataclysm

Anton Chekhov said, "If you say in the first chapter that there is a rifle hanging on the wall, in the second or third chapter it absolutely must go off. If it's not going to be fired, it shouldn't be hanging there." With that in mind, the fact that the opening flashback of *Planet of the Apes: Cataclysm* ends with an unfired Earthbound nuclear missile aimed at the Moon should give the reader an idea of how the writers intend to pay off the title. It is with no small amount of hyperbole that it can be said hellfire rains down upon the apes in general, and on Ape City in particular, following the Moon's destruction. The first four issues chronicle the resulting destruction that ensues.

In flashbacks, we see the last great human war, the conflict that most likely removed man from being the dominant species on the planet. One side controlled a base on the Moon, and before the other side could fire a nuclear missile at it, they were destroyed. Around two millennia later, and eight years before Taylor *et al.* arrived in their spaceship, a lone ape fires the missile and blows up the Moon. Chunks of the lunar satellite impact the Earth's surface, decimating Ape City and bringing chaos to the main characters.

Zaius tries desperately to save his people, most specifically his wife, Siena,[2] and pregnant daughter, Valentina. Unfortunately, Valentina goes into labor while the sky is falling and dies during childbirth. During all of this, there is a palpable sense of terror in all of the characters, and the full scale of destruction and devastation is portrayed very well. It's ironic that in just eight short years, George Taylor will destroy the entire planet. It makes the apes' will to survive, and the trials and tribulations that follow, all the more tragic.

Unbeknownst to anyone, there is another party at work, using the chaos and destruction to foment further discord among the apes. The mutant humans from *Beneath the Planet of the Apes* are using their mind-control powers in insidious ways. Zaius discovers the traitor responsible for all of it, and at the same time uncovers a dangerous secret. The mutant responsible has disguised himself as an ape, and he reveals that he is not the only wolf in ape's clothing. The fact that Zaius doesn't immediately become paranoid beyond all reason is a credit to his stoic nature.

In the wake of the destruction, Zaius takes charge to help rebuild the city and provide for his people. However, in so doing he ends up making two decisions that initially seem like great ideas, but nearly incite a full-scale civil

---

[2] The novel *Conspiracy of the Planet of the Apes* named his wife Ambrosine.

war. Interestingly, Zaius seems racked with indecision at times, mostly due to the scale of the destruction and the loss of his daughter, and it is Siena who urges him down the paths he takes going forward. Granted, she is an advisor to her husband, but she has more cause to fall apart than he does, since she was actually present when their daughter died. She has channeled that grief into aggressive action, though, and it is hard to tell whether Zaius acting on her advice is for the best or not.

The first best/worst decision that Zaius makes involves a way to provide food for his people. Nearby to Ape City is the Painted Valley, an agrarian community of chimpanzees. Zaius sends an expedition to barter for food, led by his son-in-law, Vitus, and the chimps Milo and Cornelius. While in the Valley, the group learns some terrible secrets that threaten further food supplies and the very foundations of ape society. Many years earlier, an earthquake had poisoned the community's water supply with radioactive water from the Forbidden Zone. The end result is that all of the children became telepathic mutants, just like the humans who worship the Alpha-Omega Bomb in *Beneath*.

Vitus, Milo, and Cornelius also discover why there are only chimpanzees in Painted Valley. Years before the water poisoning, the chimps rose up against the orangutans and gorillas who were oppressing them, and indirectly slaughtered them all. While they didn't technically violate the most sacred primate directive, they did act maliciously. Ultimately, everyone agrees that the Ape City group will return with a small amount of food and report that the debris from the Moon decimated the valley and killed its inhabitants. The mutant children, meanwhile, will use their powers to visually reinforce the illusion for any visitors who may possibly arrive, thereby ensuring that the secrets remain buried.

Would that it were that simple.

Zaius's second great decision gone bad involves a legitimate attempt to unite the already fractured castes within society. The chimp sector of the city was more or less completely decimated, instantly disenfranchising one-third of the population. Orangutans and gorillas have always been disrespectful to their more passive brethren, we learn, and rounding up the chimps into camps, however well-intentioned at the outset, has not gone well. Of course, Zaius erroneously interprets the unrest as folks needing something to do. He then presents to the chimps the idea that they will be the ones to rebuild their own city. The chain reaction to disaster continues, as this is perceived as forced labor, a notion reinforced in how the gorillas treat the chimps.

A group led by Prisca begins to meet in secret, in order to formulate a plan to gain equality. Zira joins this group and, when her special friend Cornelius returns from his expedition, he can't help but be swept up in the fervor. Innocently, he tells the group what he learned about the chimps in Painted Valley and how they rose up to liberate themselves. The group takes this as a call to arms and proof that only violence can grant them their freedom. And then Timon (remember him?) arrives from the Forbidden Zone with the human, Pin, whom he has been raising during his many years in exile. Turns out, Pin can talk, although this is eventually revealed to be a cleverly orchestrated ruse. Eventually, this all reaches a fever pitch and Zaius finally unleashes Ursus and his troops to end the growing insurrection by any means necessary.

Ursus means to use guns, but is stopped at the last, near-fatal moment by trusted ape soldier Marcus, who convinces the gorillas to stand down and, standing hand in hand with Cornelius and Timon, is able to avert a bloody civil war. In the chaos leading up to the stand-down, Siena is accidentally killed, all but guaranteeing that Zaius will take the final steps to become how we see him in the first film: uncompromising and unrelenting. That film also shows how this is but a temporary easing of tensions, for in just a few years' time, the chimps will once again be marginalized by the orangutans and gorillas.

The final issue of the series serves as a coda narrated by Milo, with a lot of information laid out in the epilogue. The key points are that Milo had discovered that the Earth was radically changing and slowly dying due to the loss of the Moon, but Zaius had refused to listen to the evidence and forbade Milo from discussing it with anyone else. So, the chimp doctor started making plans to escape. The arrival of Taylor's ship from the past was just what the doctor ordered, and scavenging that vessel, along with a second ship that crashed (Brent's from *Beneath*), made it so that he, Zira, and Cornelius were able to leave Earth shortly before its destruction via the detonation of the last remaining Alpha-Omega Bomb.

In all honesty, the final issue's coda feels rushed and rather contrived. It might have served the story better had it been left off, with the prior issue closing the epic. One wonders if Bechko and Hardman had more story to tell, but other factors led to their saga ending when it did. Certainly, the massive information dump of the final issue would have worked more effectively had it been allowed to play out over several more issues, and the final punctuation of ending at the beginning of *Escape from the Planet of the Apes* would have packed a lot more punch. Regardless, the writers were at least able to tie up their major plot points and bring the bulk of the story to a satisfying conclusion.

If there is one thing to learn from *Betrayal*, *Exile*, and *Cataclysm*, it's that the Earth is no better off being ruled by another species than by man. All of the tragedy that transpires is due to a secret being held by, or a series of very poor decision on the part of, the apes. In fact, it would seem that their entire history is marred by secret upon secret upon bad decision. Then again, every secret is harbored out of a desire to protect and serve ape society as a whole, as is every decision that is made. Perhaps if they had been more open and forthcoming about their own history, and the complete history of the planet, apes like Zaius could have avoided everything that went horrifically wrong. However, the final page reveals the ultimate tragedy of the *Apes* franchise – that (in Cylon fashion) this has all happened before and will happen again.

This brings us to the *Planet of the Apes Annual*. The first story in this extra-length issue was discussed in the previous essay, but there are three others that bear examining, including two by Bechko and Hardman that have a direct connection to the series just discussed.

"A Boy and His Human" is a humorous tale amidst a dark event. Written by Bechko and illustrated by John Lucas, this short story tells the tale of a boy chimp, Adrian, who befriends a human boy during the purges in *Betrayal*. "Befriends" may be too strong a word, as Adrian sees the wide-eyed mute human more as a pet and brings him home like a stray dog with the intention of convincing his mother to let him keep the human. After a chase by angry gorillas, Adrian decides to set free his would-be pet, only for the human to then be captured by the soldiers. A hopeful coda includes Adrian possibly heading off to the human pens with a friend who is learning about locks.

Hardman, meanwhile, writes and illustrates "The Scroll," which reveals a few key pieces of information about Aleron and Tenebris. The story relates an excursion by some gorilla soldiers, chief among them a young Lieutenant Aleron. The gorillas are trying to retrieve a text that may be from the time of the Lawgiver. Unfortunately, the temple on Mount Lam, where text is being translated, has been cut off by an earthquake. Aleron risks his life to reach the temple, only to discover that the surviving orangutan has been driven mad by the scroll – mad enough to take his own life via shotgun.

The firing of the weapon unleashes a landslide that traps Aleron, who is helpless in preventing a crow from plucking out his eye. Aleron is rescued and the scroll is returned to Tenebris, who burns it as a forgery. Revealed to the reader is part of the burning scroll text, "...ape and man should live together in friendship and share dominion over the world in peace..."

We learn how Aleron lost his eye, but also see that his strength and resolve for doing what is right was always there. He is horrified when the orangutan takes his own life, though he never learns the reason for the suicide. Tenebris is the sole caretaker of the true history of man and ape at this point in the timeline, and is terrified of any other ape learning the truth. So, of course, he must destroy the scroll and play it off as a forgery, even if he is destroying the actual words of the revered Lawgiver, as narrated in *Battle for the Planet of the Apes*. It seems, even centuries later, that the poignant message of co-existence between ape and man espoused by the Lawgiver is still being edited to propagate ape superiority over humans.

The final story in the annual, "Old World Order," is an oddity in that it doesn't fit in with the comic book continuity. Written by Jeff Parker and drawn by Benjamin Dewey, this chapter tells a kind of a horror story. A gorilla official and his armed escort from Ape City are visiting the backwater city of Port Simian. The official is determined to bend the port to fit in with civilized ape society and conform with all laws. In fact, Port Simian's citizens and its leader, the orangutan Trajan, lead a decadent life, eschewing most of the laws that other apes have always followed (a trait he shares with the Golden Khan, from Daryl Gregory's ongoing storyline). The gorillas soon learn that the most sacred law is ignored in a horrific fashion. Cargo from an unknown land is offloaded from a ship, containing feral razorback gorillas, something the official and his bodyguards find out in person – and fatally.

Dawn Rises on the Coming War

What worked so well for the original films' continuity seems to have been a good idea for the new movies as well, as BOOM! Studios also published a Web series that serves as a prequel to *Rise of the Planet of the Apes*, as well as a San Diego Comic-Con exclusive comic book, a second Web comic, and a six-issue published miniseries intended to bridge the gap between *Rise* and *Dawn of the Planet of the Apes*.

The *Rise of the Planet of the Apes* prequel spanned six online episodes, each consisting of five pages, and was published in weekly installments leading up to the film's theatrical release. Daryl Gregory, the writer of BOOM!'s main *Planet of the Apes* series, shifts his pen from the old film continuity to the new. Gregory shows a keen understanding of apes at any point in their evolution as he tells a tale of Caesar's parents (more specifically, his mother, Bright Eyes), and how she came to be at Gen-Sys Laboratories in the movie.

The artwork is provided by two veteran BOOM! Studios artists. Tony Parker, the illustrator for the company's *Do Androids Dream of Electric Sheep?* adaptation, handles the chores on episodes one through four and six, while *Nola and Hawks of Outremer* penciler Damian Couceiro takes care of episode five. Both do an excellent job considering how ape-heavy this series is. Presumably, any art school student can adequately draw chimpanzees, but it takes a skilled, accomplished artist to really bring them to life and give them realistic and nuanced expressions and body language. Parker and Couceiro do so in a captivating way (pardon the pun), to the extent that the human characters become all but forgotten in their brief appearances.

In the comic-book prequel to *Rise of the Planet of the Apes* (Jul/Aug 2011), Bright Eyes misses her home and her mate in the African jungle.

The story starts with a group of poachers attempting to round up a bunch of chimps in Africa. They manage to capture a blue-eyed female, whom they nickname Bright Eyes, and kill the rest, including Bright Eyes' mate, the group's alpha male. Bright Eyes is sold to Gen-Sys Labs, where she is included in the ALZ-112 testing group. While other test subjects are driven mad by the drug, Bright Eyes instead sees her mental capacity increased. Because of this, she becomes even more aware that her situation is dire and she needs to escape. She actually manages to sneak out one night, but quickly discovers that she is no safer in the outside world than she is in her cage, to which she morosely returns. The first few minutes of the film reveal Bright Eyes' tragic fate.

There are a couple of Easter eggs in this story for the eagle-eyed *Apes* fan. The poaching scene, shown briefly at the beginning of *Rise*, is significantly expanded upon in Gregory's version. The author most likely worked from what was originally scripted, since, in a foreword to the series, he notes that he was privy to a sneak-peek at the screenplay as research. In addition, three of the other test chimps are nicknamed Verdon, Burke, and Chambers, named after the two astronauts who journeyed to the ape-controlled future Earth in the *Planet of the Apes* TV series,[3] as well as *Apes* makeup guru John Chambers. Plus, one of the Gen-Sys scientists shares the same first name, Rita, as the deceased first wife of Malcolm, the main human protagonist in *Dawn of the Planet of the Apes*.

Before the Dawn is a very brief Web comic consisting of six pages of collage-style artwork that provide a quick summary of how humans were devastated by the simian flu and the challenges Caesar faces as he tries to build a home for his fellow apes. A printed copy of this promo comic was distributed at the 2013 San Diego Comic-Con. Curiously, there appears to be no information as to who wrote and/or illustrated it, nor is it available online anymore. The images and words are presented in a rather provocative way, and definitely set the tone for the then-upcoming film.

The following year, at the 2014 San Diego Comic-Con, BOOM! released a one-shot book only available at the show, titled *Dawn of the Planet of the Apes: Contagion*. This hard-to-find comic was written by *Steed and Mrs. Peel* writer Caleb Monroe and illustrated by long-time DC Comics artist Tom Derenick. The story details a few key moments in the life of Ellie, Malcolm's second wife and one of the key characters in *Dawn of the Planet of the Apes*.

The issue begins tragically, with the death of Ellie's daughter, Sarah, from the simian flu, an event that all but cripples the mother, but leads to a critical discovery. It turns out that Ellie is one of the very few humans – one out of every five hundred – who has a natural immunity to the plague. She keeps this knowledge secret as she eventually returns to work at a research facility attempting to develop a cure. They are, of course, using chimps for testing, but are humane and decent to the apes. One of them, Betty, has a particular fondness for Ellie and eventually helps her escape when the facility is overrun by murderous protestors. In the end, Ellie and Betty are the only two beings, human or chimp, who leave alive.

---

[3] Though on the TV show, the character's name is spelled "Virdon."

Contagion is a poignant tale that informs much of Ellie's characterization in the 2014 sequel film. We understand not only why she is particularly protective of Malcolm and her stepson, Alex, but also why she also has an affinity for the apes in Caesar's camp. She is one of the few humans who do not blame the apes for the plague that has mostly wiped out humanity, not just because she is a scientist who knows better, but because of, and perhaps despite, the death of her daughter and her work with chimps, which have made her kinder and more compassionate. The apocalypse has actually made her more caring, while it has hardened and instilled more hatred in most of the survivors.

The final sequel-prequel series takes place two years after *Rise* and about eight years before *Dawn*. While it occurs over a short span of time, the story provides some crucial pieces of character insight into three of *Dawn*'s major players. Caeser, Koba, and Malcolm are highlighted here, and we see part of what made them the characters as depicted in the 2014 film.

For this story, BOOM! chose Michael Moreci, the writer of the high-concept series *Roche Limit*, as the authorial voice. Moreci has no problem handling mind-boggling sci-fi concepts, but he is exceptionally good with characters and accentuating their distinctiveness. That serves this story very well, as it is essential that a small character piece be punctuated by some action. Moreci also manages to humanize the ape characters, as well as the humans themselves, who are facing no less than the extinction of their species. It may be lacking in science fiction foibles, but this story nonetheless gives us heady concepts with its emotional content, especially considering how it informs what we see on the screen.

British artist Dan McDaid provides the artwork for all six issues and does a wonderful job. He manages to capture the apes from the new films beautifully, and also renders the humans in a way that feels real. His art is very reminiscent of Peter Snejbjerg's, without being at all derivative. A humanizing tale requires a humanizing artist, and McDaid nails it in every panel.

As for the story itself, it is set up as a parallel between Malcolm and Caesar. Whereas in *Dawn of the Planet of the Apes* (the film), the two become counterparts, each trying to maneuver their individual communities toward peace, here they essentially become the same thing, just having never met. Both have a wife and child for whom they are trying to build a better world — they just happen to have worlds at polar opposites.

The newly emancipated apes have been building their society in the Muir Woods redwood forest to which they escaped at the end of *Rise*, but it is not enough.[4] Caesar recognizes that they need a home that they themselves have built, one that is larger than what they have now. At the same time, he is also dealing with fellow apes who still bear the scars, physically and emotionally, of their time in captivity. Caesar conservatively wants his kind to keep to themselves, but those close to him thirst for revenge and conquest. This brings him unknowingly into conflict with a fellow ape named Pope, whom he sends on a mission to find other apes, primarily from zoos and other places of captivity, and to bring them into the fold.

Pope decides to use this to his advantage, and quickly proves that he is willing to kill both man and ape in order to further his own ambitions. He kills a human who is protecting his farmhouse, and orders his underlings to murder the man's wife as well. Then he brutally slays an alpha male ape, thus amassing a group of less intelligent apes as his own personal army.

Pope has decided that Caesar is too weak and too much like a human for his taste,[5] and thus wishes to overthrow the king and lead all of his people to wipe out humanity. But when a chimp defects from Pope's camp and informs Caesar of what is happening, the leader sends Koba to deal with Pope, with the implication that the former is to kill the latter. Koba takes care of the matter, but having had to murder a fellow ape does not sit well with him (an irony, given his actions in *Dawn*), and as his first act of defiance, he purposefully does not inform Caesar of the humans whom Pope had locked up, effectively leaving them to starve to death.

It seems rather obvious that Pope was sent on this particular mission to make him show his true colors. What is less clear is who set him up. It is possible that Pope was becoming too militant for Caesar's comfort, and so the ape king sent him out as a test, one that Pope spectacularly failed. It could also be that Koba saw Pope as a threat to his own ranking within the community, and so played on Caesar's growing passivity to convince him to send out Pope, knowing what the other ape would attempt. Koba would know that Caesar would send him to clean up the problem, and it would further solidify his own

---

[4] A theme explored in great depth in the novel *Dawn of the Planet of the Apes: Firestorm*, by Greg Keyes.

[5] In an interesting parallel to *Battle for the Planet of the Apes*, an early-draft script of the film featured Caesar losing his hair due to radiation loss and becoming weak and human-like in appearance, which Aldo (*Dawn*'s Koba analog) cited as evidence that Caesar was no longer fit to rule.

standing with his liberator. It may be a case of reading more into what is actually there, but it just does not feel as cut and dried as presented.

At the same time, and on the other side of the country, Malcolm is trying to keep his family together as well, while also figuring out ways to keep humanity as a whole from falling completely apart. The human species has been decimated by the simian flu. As ape society has been prospering, uniting, and growing, humans are nearing extinction and turning against each other. The time clock starts for Malcolm when his wife, Rita, contracts the deadly virus and they, along with their son, Alex, set out for Austin, where there is rumored to be a cure.

Derailed by kidnappers, but ultimately assisted by a group looking to rebuild society (or, at least, to keep what's left civilized and prosperous), Malcolm ultimately learns a horrible truth: there is no cure, and any rumors thereof have been propagated by the Centers for Disease Control, to lure in the desperate in order to experiment on them. He decides it is worth the risk anyway, and plans to take his wife to Austin in the one-in-a-million chance that a cure exists. Rita, knowing that it is a fool's errand, and not wanting her son to lose both parents, takes that decision away from him by going off and dying on her own. It is a tragic end, but it speaks volumes to Malcolm's character that he doesn't let it destroy him, as we see him in *Dawn* newly remarried and still trying to save his people.

Moreci does an exceptional job of adding extra depth to characters whom we already know, and does so with a story that fits perfectly within the continuity of both *Rise* and *Dawn*. It's not always easy for those writing tie-in fiction to make their own stamp on the material while keeping the same tone as a single film, much less two. But Moreci pulls it off well, providing a very satisfactory ending while leaving readers wanting to know what happens next. Hopefully, BOOM! Studios will one day show us the next chapter, but even if the follow-up is the film *Dawn of the Planet of the Apes*, that still works well. It certainly enriches the film and brings a new appreciation of it in light of this extra knowledge of where the characters have been.

BOOM! Studios' only other recent *POTA* work has been *Star Trek/Planet of the Apes: The Primate Directive*, discussed in the following essay. As of this writing, the publisher has not yet announced plans to publish any further *Apes* comic books, either in the original or rebooted continuities. However, based solely on the high quality and ambitious stories that BOOM! has published to date, it is hoped that the company plans to explore other heretofore unrevealed segments between the original films and, possibly, to add further bridging material between *Dawn* and the third film in the rebooted franchise, the recently announced *War of the Planet of the Apes*.

What is certain is that as demand for further cinematic exploits of the apes continues, so, too, will the desire for more comic book adventures, giving collectors more new stories to add to their BOOM! box.

City on the Edge of Rebellion: IDW Takes BOOM! Where No Ape Has Gone Before

by Joseph F. Berenato

It was the comic-book announcement equivalent of dropping an Alpha-Omega Bomb into the heart of the internet.

Well, okay, maybe not... but it *was* an announcement that had several thousand of us tittering with excitement.

Star Trek. *Planet of the Apes*. James T. Kirk. George Taylor.

Neither franchise is a complete stranger to the concept of comic-book crossovers. *Star Trek* has been the subject of several intra- and inter-company crossovers (many of which have been explored in detail in another Sequart volume[1]). *Planet of the Apes*, on the other hand, has not experienced quite as many, but its inhabitants have interacted with characters and concepts from *War of the Worlds*, *Alien Nation*, and even *Tarzan*, though the latter was never published.[2] Yet despite both being pop-culture phenomena for almost fifty years (*Star Trek* premiered in 1966; *Planet of the Apes* first made its way to the

---

[1] McIntee, David A. "To Boldly Cross Over: Transporting the Enterprise to Other Comic Book Universes." *New Life and New Civilizations: Exploring Star Trek Comics.* Ed. Joseph F. Berenato. Edwardsville, IL: Sequart, 2014. 264-77.

[2] Each of these crossovers is explored in depth elsewhere in this volume.

silver screen in 1968), they each stayed away from the other's timeline, and never the twain shall meet.

Until now.

A panel at the 2014 San Diego Comic-Con heralded the coming of the five-issue *Star Trek / Planet of the Apes: The Primate Directive*. The joint effort from IDW Publishing (which currently holds the *Star Trek* comic-book license) and BOOM! Studios (keeper of the *Apes* license), written by brothers Scott and David Tipton, illustrated by Rachael Stott, and colored by Charlie Kirchoff, melded the two science-fiction franchises for the first time.[3] In addition, each issue concludes with an essay by comedian Dana Gould containing personal and insightful reflections on each franchise.

The brothers Tipton are quite familiar with the *Star Trek* universe. Besides penning tales like *Star Trek: Klingons: Blood Will Tell*, *Spock: Reflections*, and the immensely popular *Star Trek: Harlan Ellison's Original The City on the Edge of Forever Teleplay*, they were also responsible – along with artist J.K. Woodward – for giving life to *Star Trek: The Next Generation/Doctor Who: Assimilation²*, which joined the crew of the *Enterprise*-D with the Eleventh Doctor and his companions. The task of merging these two sci-fi giants for the first time – and successfully, at that – made them the logical choice for a *Trek/Apes* mash-up.

For artwork, IDW's *Trek* editor, Sarah Gaydos, turned to newcomer Stott. How, exactly, did a complete neophyte – with no mainstream credits to her name – come to land such a high-profile gig? According to Stott in an interview with the *JK's Happy Hour* podcast,[4] a full-up portfolio review at the 2014 London Super Comic Con deserves the credit. With no more openings for review, a slightly downtrodden Stott walked the convention floor and ended up in a conversation with artist Dan Slott, and ultimately showed him her portfolio. As he was looking at it, IDW editor-in-chief Chris Ryall walked up – "Just coincidence," in Stott's words – and asked to review the portfolio himself. Ryall gave Stott his business card and they started exchanging emails. Shortly thereafter, he put her in touch with Gaydos. A number of swapped images later, Gaydos offered Stott the job.

---

[3] The two franchises had met before in fan fiction – most notably in Paul Gadzikowski's "Trek to the Planet of the Apes" from the fanzine *Berengaria #5/6* (Dec. 1975), and in Greg Glick's "Beware the Beasts," published in Jean-Marc Lofficier's *Tales of the Shadowmen 3: Danse Macabre* (Nov 2006), which features Q meeting characters from Pierre Boulle's source novel – but never in licensed form.
[4] http://taylornetworkofpodcasts.com/2015/03/06/jks-happy-hour-rachael-stott/

Joining *Planet of the Apes* and *Star Trek* brought with it its own challenges. Both franchises are known for having rabid fan bases with a surgical eye for detail and an oft-immutable adherence to continuity. While the *Trek* timeline allows for a number of adventures before, during, and after the filmed missions – hence, the thousands of comics, novels, short stories, and video games during the last 48 years – the *Apes* chronology doesn't give much leeway once George Taylor and pals come crashing to the surface. Fortunately, the Tiptons were given a rather wide berth when it came to creativity within established continuity.

"There were not a lot of specific can- or can't-dos from CBS, Fox, or IDW," David Tipton said in an interview conducted for this essay,[5] "but everyone involved wanted something that made sense for both continuities."

"If I recall correctly, the only notes we were given at the outset were 'Classic *Trek* and [c]lassic *Apes*, and you have to include Taylor,'" Scott added, "which was fine by us, since we really considered Taylor to be integral."

Indeed. Charlton Heston's character in *Planet of the Apes* is iconic, and even the uninitiated associate one with the other. Without Taylor – and, by extension, Cornelius, Zira, and Doctor Zaius – this would have been like any of a number of other visits to parallel Earths for the *Enterprise*.[6]

With creative *carte blanche* from the license holders, the Tiptons were able to bring these characters together any way they saw fit. For many fans of each series, this is a dream come true. Surely this was something that the team of writing siblings has pondered for ages, no?

"To be honest," Scott admitted, "I'd never given it a thought until Chris Ryall came to us and asked if we had any ideas for how to do it."

Really?

"Yes," David agreed. "We were asked if we had ideas to do it by Chris, but it's not something we can say we have thought about previously."

All the better, then. Instead of approaching the crossover with a story that had been building and festering in their minds for decades, the Tiptons were able to come to the material with a fresh idea, one conceived specifically for the project.

---

[5] The interview also included Scott Tipton and Rachael Stott. Unless otherwise noted, any further quotations from them are the result of this interview.
[6] See the *Original Series* episodes "Miri," "Mirror, Mirror," "Bread and Circuses," and "The Omega Glory" for examples of just a few of Earth's parallels.

The Primate Directive is a result of that approach.

Buzz for *The Primate Directive* remained high for quite a while, and readers got their first glimpse of the story through an ashcan edition[7] given away at the 2014 New York Comic Con. This ashcan features the first five pages of the series, with cover art by Stott and alternate cover art (shown on the ashcan's back cover) by George Pérez. Not much by way of plot is revealed in these first five pages, but readers are treated to several teasers: a meeting between a gorilla general and a shadowed figure (who refers to a coming conflict as "glorious," a term associated with a beloved *Star Trek* villain); the introduction of said gorilla to advanced weaponry by the aforementioned shadowy figure (reminiscent of the classic *Trek* episode "A Private Little War"); and Lieutenants Sulu and Uhura, dressed as Klingons to infiltrate one of their outposts.

No other details were revealed, but that was just enough to whet appetites until the series began.

Primate Premiere

Two months later, on December 31, 2014, *Star Trek/Planet of the Apes: The Primate Directive* #1[8] premiered. Edited by IDW's Gaydos and BOOM!'s Dafna Pleban, issue #1 featured nine different covers, with art by: Stott and Kirchoff (a regular cover, a black-and-white rendering of Stott's art for the second-printing cover, and a Nerdblock.com retailer exclusive cover); Juan Ortiz; George Pérez and Len O'Grady (a subscription cover, as well as a black-and-white version of Pérez's artwork for a retailer incentive cover); Tone Rodriguez and Kirchoff (a second retailer incentive cover); and John Midgley (a Thinkgeek.com retailer exclusive cover); as well as a blank sketch cover featuring uncredited artwork of a Klingon vessel.

Besides the story teaser already shown in the ashcan, *The Primate Directive* #1 reveals the information gathered by Uhura and Sulu on their espionage mission: the Klingons, a species known for imperial conquest, have found a portal into a parallel universe and are expanding their interests there. The crew of the *U.S.S. Enterprise* investigates, travels through the portal, and finds themselves in orbit around a very familiar planet: Earth.

---

[7] A promotional comic book, usually smaller in stature and content than a standard comic book.

[8] Unlike many comic series, the individual issues of *The Primate Directive* do not have individual chapter names, so they will be referred to heretofore by their issue numbers.

By using the positioning of constellations, Spock is able to determine that they have arrived in the year 3978 (the same year, of course, that George Taylor crashes the *Liberty I*[9] in 1968's *Planet of the Apes*). Captain Kirk forms a landing party to beam down and investigate, and once there discovers Klingon Commander Kor – the shadowy figure from the first five pages – in conversation with sentient apes.

The *Enterprise's* landing party arrives in all-too-familiar territory in *Star Trek / Planet of the Apes: The Primate Directive* #2 (Jan 2015).

The first issue acts as the perfect setup to the series, but except for the first three and final pages, apes are almost completely absent from the tale. It reads like the first act of a *Star Trek* episode, with the emphasis very much on the

---

[9] Or the *Icarus*, depending on which source you accept

crew of the *Enterprise*. (One can almost hear a dramatic crescendo, *à la* Gerald Fried or Sol Kaplan, in one's head when reading the last page.) Like any good first act, it raises far more questions than it answers – Who built the portal that the Klingons found? Why are the gorillas interacting with what must surely look to them like talking humans? If Uhura can speak Klingon so well, why does she need the 23rd-century equivalent of *Klingon for Dummies* in *Star Trek VI: The Undiscovered Country*? – leaving the reader wanting plenty more for the next installment.

Damn Dirty Taylor

A month later, on January 21, 2015, *The Primate Directive* #2 was released. This issue featured three different covers: the regular one by Stott and Kirchoff, a subscription cover by Joe Corroney and Brian Miller, and a retailer incentive cover done in the style of the Gold Key *Star Trek* comics of the 1960s and '70s. The Gold Key variant was a particularly nice surprise, as those photo montage covers have been a favorite of nostalgic *Trek* comic fans for decades, the Tipton brothers among them. But given IDW's sales successes with their *Star Trek: Gold Key Archives* hardcover reprint volumes,[10] the company's affinity for the series makes sense, and a mash-up of two sci-fi icons from the same era is a logical place to show that love.

With the second issue, the series starts to feel more like a true crossover. The majority of the action takes place planetside, with only three pages occurring onboard the *Enterprise*. Kirk and crew are spotted by the gorillas and are forced to flee, stunning one of the apes with a phaser beam in the process. The as-yet-unnamed gorilla general reasons that the interlopers must be some manner of associates of Kor, who promises to handle the problem. Elsewhere, the landing party returns to the starship to digest what they've just seen, and form a new party – Kirk, Spock, Doctor Leonard "Bones" McCoy, Ensign Pavel Chekov, and biologist Lieutenant Weaver – to beam back down in a more familiar location to get their bearings.

They materialize in front of the decrepit Statue of Liberty.

Shortly thereafter, they encounter George Taylor and his mute companion, Nova, and, after an awkward first few minutes – Taylor, true to form, shoots at them – begin a dialogue about the situation facing them. Taylor believes that Kirk is there to help reestablish human dominance of the planet, but Kirk insists

---

[10] The third of which features an introduction by the writer of this essay

that it would violate their most sacred tenet, that of cultural noninterference: the Prime Directive. Taylor brings the landing party to meet chimpanzee scientists Cornelius and Zira, his only ape friends, and Kirk informs them of the Klingons' plans. The chimps, after getting over the shock of even *more* talking humans (which they do almost immediately), give a brief rundown of simian society, including recent escalations of the military sector. After Taylor tries again, unsuccessfully, to convince Kirk to help humanity, he ambushes Chekov and steals his communicator.

This issue helps to give a bit of chronological context for the series. When Kirk and Taylor meet up with Cornelius and Zira, the chimps are still at the site of the archaeological dig in the Forbidden Zone, as seen at the end of the first film. Taylor states that the site is a day's ride away from his current location, making the events of *The Primate Directive* not more than a day or two after Taylor finds his destiny in the form of Lady Liberty.

Stott really starts to shine in this issue as well. She has the ability – all the more impressive considering this is essentially her first assignment ever – to pack volumes of emotion into a single panel, via a single expression or gesture. The shock of seeing the Statue of Liberty for the landing party, for instance, is almost palpable, but it's the sight of McCoy wiping a tear from his eye that truly sells the moment. As well, when Taylor reconnects with the chimp scientists, Cornelius telegraphs exasperation, bafflement, and resignation at the thought of more talking humans with a single expression, while the soft look on Taylor's face as he holds Zira's hands is rife with affection. Stott thankfully litters such moments throughout the rest of the series.

A Piece of the Action

After a brief shipping delay, *The Primate Directive* #3 finally landed in stores on March 4, 2015. This issue featured a regular cover once again by Stott and Kirchoff, a subscription cover by Kevin Wada, and a retailer incentive cover that, like issue #2, pays homage to the Gold Key era.

Instead of jumping right into the action promised on the regular cover (which features Kirk and Taylor mid-combat on the bridge of the *Enterprise*), issue #3 opens with a journal entry by orangutan leader Doctor Zaius, who writes about failing crops and bids for expansion into the Forbidden Zone. (He also mentions deciding not to press charges of heresy against Cornelius and Zira, which explains why they were still there without police escort in the previous issue, why the site hadn't yet been destroyed, and why the couple were not in prison – or dead – in *Beneath the Planet of the Apes*.)

We then return to the main action: the landing party discovers the unconscious Chekov just as Taylor is beamed aboard the *Enterprise*. He immediately knocks out the transporter chief (Lieutenant Kyle, rocking a porntastic 'stache, just as he did in *Star Trek: The Animated Series*), and steals the man's clothes (which fit, because of course they do) so as to not draw attention by being a half-naked man (who must surely smell like a wild animal, though none of the crew seem to notice this, including a woman who flirts with him in close quarters inside a turbolift).

The landing party, minus McCoy and Weaver (who stay with Cornelius and Zira), returns to the ship, where Kirk and Spock find Taylor – a pilot in his past life – in the shuttlebay, trying to understand how to fly a shuttlecraft despite none of the buttons or dials having any kind of label whatsoever. A fight naturally ensues between the two leading men – cue the fight music from *Star Trek* episode "Amok Time" – which ends with a handshake several pages later because both men are too tired to keep beating the snot out of each other (and because, let's face it, there was no way the Tiptons would have risked infuriating either fan base by having any outcome other than a tie).

The issue ends with another scene between Kor and the gorilla leader – now identified as General Marius – with the Klingon handing the ape a disrupter pistol. Marius dons a Klingon sash and begins to ride with his men (so to speak) toward Ape City as its new conqueror.

This issue begins to futz with the chronology a bit. When we met Zira and Cornelius, they were still at the dig at the Forbidden Zone. Taylor was a short walk away from the Statue of Liberty. Logically (you'll pardon the expression, yes?), it can't be that far removed from the end of *Planet of the Apes*. Yet at the start of this issue, which takes place minutes after the last, Zaius is already back in Ape City. Clearly, this is still not long past the events of the first film – we know for certain that Brent, the human hero of *Beneath the Planet of the Apes*, has yet to arrive, since Taylor hasn't been captured by mutants, and Nova is still with him – but the exact placement is unknown.

As previously stated, Stott shows an extraordinary ability to say a lot with just a look. Perhaps the best example of that ability occurs on the third page of this issue, with a non-verbal exchange that passes between Bones and Nova. The instructions provided in the script were a bit vague: "McCoy is looking at

Nova and has one eyebrow raised."[11] Yet, by Stott's hand, what actually transpires amounts to whole lifetimes lived in a single look. McCoy looks flirtatiously at Nova, and she returns the look with every ounce of intent and heat that McCoy sends.

While Taylor meddles with Starfleet technology, McCoy catches Nova's eye in *The Primate Directive* #3 (Feb 2015).

"We did indicate the moment, but all the appeal and charm of it definitely came from Rachael," Scott said. "When I saw it, it made me wish we'd written more for those two."

This issue also provides a rarely seen view of the inside of the *Enterprise*: a bird's-eye cutaway view of the deck layout as Taylor runs through the ship. When asked about it, Rachael Stott said, "I wasn't used to drawing in an isometric perspective, but it really gives it an unusual, diagrammatic feel. It was

---

[11] Panel description courtesy of Scott Tipton

my little homage to the cutaways of the Baxter Building [from Marvel's *Fantastic Four*] that [legendary artist Jack] Kirby used to do."

Ape Shall Not Kill Editor

With shipping schedules back on track, *The Primate Directive* #4 premiered just two weeks later, on March 18, 2015. It once again featured a regular cover by Stott and Kirchoff, a retailer incentive Gold Key-esque cover, and a painted subscription cover by J.K. Woodward (the artist for both *Assimilation²* and *City on the Edge of Forever*).

Tensions are mounting in this issue. Kirk, Spock, and Taylor return to the planet with Scotty and two redshirts in tow.[12] Scotty starts to hold palaver with the chimps, but stops when Kirk admonishes him about revealing too much technological information – specifically, the slingshot time-travel maneuver.[13] After sensors reveal a gorilla army advancing on Ape City, a horrified Cornelius explains their most sacred law – "Ape shall never kill ape" – and the ramifications should that law ever be broken.

Kirk agrees to beam Zira into the city to warn Doctor Zaius, who dispatches General Ursus – the militant upstart from *Beneath* – to deal with the army. Meanwhile, a party of the renegade gorillas attacks Kirk's encampment, but are ultimately defeated, and the humans ride to try to stop the Klingons. As they do so, Ursus approaches Marius and his soldiers, but is soon in Kor's crosshairs.

There are a number of Easter eggs thrown into this issue. First and foremost, on the subscription cover, artist Woodward shows Spock sitting in what appears to be a combination cage/chair, which is actually the *Planet of the Apes* Throne released by Mego in 1975 for the company's line of 8-inch action figures. If you're squealing in delight at the thought of this, you now understand how *Star Trek* fans feel about the Gold Key covers.

As well, there's something very particular about the landing party's clothing in this issue, though Rachael Stott was reluctant to take credit for it. "Scott and David [Tipton] put in a reference to the original *Apes* TV show," she said, "in the

---

[12] In *Star Trek* vernacular, "redshirt" is an in-joke referring to any Starfleet officer wearing a red uniform (in most cases, a security officer), who is inevitably injured or killed during a mission, thereby enabling the main cast to survive from one episode to another, no matter what dangers a writer works into a story.

[13] Clearly, McCoy should not have been remotely surprised when loose-lipped Scotty, in *Star Trek IV: The Voyage Home*, had no qualms about telling a 20th-century person the formula for transparent aluminum.

outfits that the team wears when they beam down." Eagle-eyed fans will recognize the threadbare clothing as being reminiscent of that worn by Alan Virdon and Peter Burke. "I thought that was cool."

Stott also throws in quite a bit of iconic *Apes* imagery, particularly when Cornelius explains their sacred law. Be on the lookout for the crying Lawgiver statue.

Last – and perhaps least – the only redshirt injured in this issue is a man by the name of Handley. Should that name sound vaguely familiar, take a minute, bookmark this page, close the book, and look at the name that appears directly above this writer's on the cover. Yes, *The Sacred Scrolls* co-editor Rich Handley makes an appearance – at least in name – in *The Primate Directive*.

Final Contact

Three weeks later, on April 8, 2015, *The Primate Directive* #5 landed in stores. It sported a regular cover by Stott and Kirchoff, a painted subscription cover by J.K. Woodward, and a final Gold Key pastiche.

And it jumped right into the action.

A well-placed shot by Taylor disarms Kor (if, as Taylor says, one believes he was actually aiming for the gun) and the humans – and Cornelius – launch into battle with the Klingons. Kor and his men escape, but not before killing the second redshirt of the landing party...

...whose tricorder,[14] to the delight of Cornelius's scientific curiosity, is left unguarded.

Elsewhere, a one-on-one fight between the two ape generals ends in a victory for Ursus, who refuses to kill Marius out of reverence for their sacred law. Marius's army is now the victor's to command. Kirk and his officers take their leave of the chimps and then of Taylor and Nova, who decline Kirk's offer to go with them.

Once back on the *Enterprise*, Kirk finds his crew taunted by Kor, and they begin a three-day game of cat and mouse through the solar system. As they are about to give chase to their universe, they are shocked by the sight from the alternate Earth: the planet is on fire, a victim of a planet-killing cobalt bomb explosion. (This is, of course, the detonation of the Alpha-Omega Bomb, by

---

[14] In the *Star Trek* universe, a tricorder is a handheld device used for data sensing, analysis, recording, and retrieval.

Taylor's own hand, at the end of *Beneath*.) The *Enterprise* charts a course back through the portal, with plans to destroy it from the other side.

They fail to notice a small ship in orbit, containing three ape-o-nauts: Cornelius, Zira, and Doctor Milo. When Milo notes that Taylor's ship can only travel forward in time, Cornelius pulls the pilfered tricorder from his bag, containing detailed information about the slingshot maneuver on its screen.

Stop and think about that for a second. The tricorder allows the chimps to travel back in time, which is where we see them at the beginning of the third film, *Escape from the Planet of the Apes*. It is in the past that Zira will give birth to Caesar, who will ultimately lead the ape rebellion resulting in humanity's downfall and nuclear war, giving rise to the mutants who will worship the bomb that destroys the planet.

All because of the tricorder. Because of the cultural contamination expressly forbidden by the Prime Directive.

Is James T. Kirk responsible for Earth's destruction?

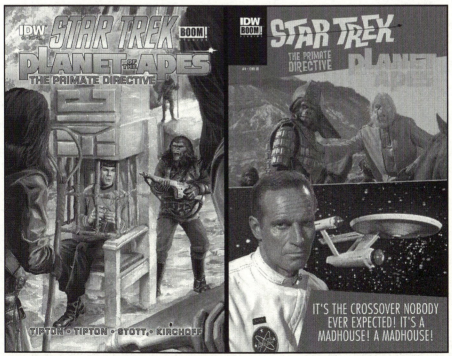

J.K. Woodward's subscription cover, featuring the Mego *Apes* Throne (left), and the retailer-incentive Gold Key homage cover for *The Primate Directive* #4 (Mar 2015)

"If you take the events to their ultimate conclusion, yeah, you could make that argument," Scott Tipton said, "but that was never our first intention."

What, then, was their intention?

"The tricorder is a way to explain the problem presented by *Escape*," David Tipton said. "Taylor's ship could go forward in time, but it's a lot harder to explain how it can move backward in time."[15]

This makes sense, since no time travel actually occurs in the original *Planet of the Apes* film. Taylor's crew does not pass through a time warp; rather, they travel in suspended animation at relativistic speeds. Time travel is not mentioned until *Beneath the Planet of the Apes*, when Brent mentions passing through a "Hasslein curve." As such, under normal conditions, Taylor's ship should not be built to travel back in time. The Tiptons' solution gets around this contradiction. Scott continued:

> We were more interested in finding ways to tie the two continuities together in a manner that complemented both. At the same time, it seemed like a clever way to patch up the one plot hole in *Apes* continuity that always seemed glaring: how exactly Taylor's ship traveled backwards in time, which was kind of glossed over in a bit of throwaway dialogue from Milo in *Escape*. The fact that it also tied into one of the main themes of *Trek* – the dangers of cultural contamination – was a nice bonus.

That still doesn't necessarily explain another glaring *Apes* plot hole: how three chimps could suddenly be interested in spaceflight, when a scant few days prior, two of those apes regarded a paper airplane as if it had been granted the gift of flight by dark wizardry. As far as ape science knew, artificial flight was impossible.[16] Yet here comes Doctor Milo, with enough knowledge of combustion, propulsion, aeronautics, avionics, and astrophysics to repair a space vessel and propel it to high-enough warp speeds to achieve time warp in the gravity well of a star. But, as Scott pointed out, "If you look at the way the *Apes* cinematic timeline works, during the events of *The Primate Directive*, and indeed much of the latter half of *Planet of the Apes*, Doctor Milo is already out there salvaging Taylor's ship, so that's already been established."

---

[15] An alternate explanation had been provided in the novel *Conspiracy of the Planet of the Apes* (Aug 2011), but that in no way lessens the impressive genius of the Tiptons' solution.

[16] It also doesn't resolve how Milo could possibly have found the requisite fuel, or how the computers and electronics of a spaceship entirely *submerged in water* for days or weeks *with an open hatch* could be made to work again using the simian equivalent of stone knives and bear skins. But *c'est la vie*.

In other words, it was already like that when the Tiptons got there.

The Primate Directive does leave some unanswered questions – Who built the portal? Why did the gorillas trust the Klingons? Seriously, did Uhura just *forget* she knew how to speak Klingon? – but ultimately, they are unimportant ones. It leaves no major plot thread dangling (Doctor Milo, Space Wizard notwithstanding) and fits comfortably and believably into the continuities of both franchises.

Except...

Zira and Cornelius now know of a whole slew of additional talking humans before Brent arrives in *Beneath*, which makes no sense since they tell Brent that they'd never met any other talking humans besides Taylor, and they tell their newfound human buddies in *Escape* that they'd only ever met two (Taylor and Brent) before going into the past. Even if the chimps agreed to stay mum about the whole thing, there would still be some earth-shattering (pun intended) consequences of their having experienced it. It's easy to accept the *Enterprise* crew going on their merry way with knowledge of yet another parallel universe tucked away in their memories (after all, that doesn't violate any *Trek* continuity in the slightest – if a Starfleet crew has discovered a parallel universe, it must be Tuesday). But Taylor, Zira, and Cornelius all going into *Beneath* with knowledge of not only entire worlds full of talking humans from other dimensions, but also *aliens* who look exactly like talking humans from other dimensions, is simply inconceivable.

Nothing is done to make them forget about it (and *Star Trek* has provided a number of options, from time travel to Vulcan mind melds), yet they seem completely unaffected in *Beneath* and *Escape* by this belief-altering experience. They never tell anyone about it in *Escape*, but more importantly, they never discuss it amongst themselves – even though it was just a few days ago.[17] Consider: They met aliens! They learned that somewhere else in the multiverse, talking humans still thrive! They traveled by transporter and saw laser-based weaponry in use! And yet, their big concern in *Beneath* is whether or not to applaud Ursus.

And how about Ursus? Since he leaves Marius alive and absorbs his troops, it's almost a given that he learns about the Klingons. So he now knows about an entire interstellar empire of talking humans (because that's definitely what the apes would assume Kor's people to be), and yet he's so fearful of the potential

---

[17] Or possibly months, given Zira's delivery of a child in *Escape*

that some *primitive* talking humans maybe, possibly, could be living in the Forbidden Zone? And neither during his "only *good* human" speech nor his private sauna excursion with Zaius does he ever mentions any of this?

Unfortunately, without the use of a *Men in Black*-style flashy-thingy mind-wiping device to make everyone on the planet forget the events that transpired in the last five issues, there's simply no easy way to explain away the lack of repercussions – beyond the aforementioned tricorder leading to the rise of the Planet of the Apes. Readers must simply accept the *Simpsons*-esque "Let us never speak of this again" tactic. If it worked for Armin Tamzarian, Snowball II, and The Shortcut, why not Cornelius, Zira, and Ursus?

This last plot point notwithstanding, *The Primate Directive* is an immensely enjoyable read. It's a well-crafted crossover by writers who clearly have an affinity for both franchises, and the artwork is absolutely exquisite – vastly superior to what readers would have a right to expect from a comics newcomer. The team of Tipton, Tipton, and Stott work exceedingly well together, and – like any good comics collaboration – seem to speak the same language, each picking up where the other left off.

"We've been so lucky," Scott said, "to have collaborators like Rachael [...] who know and love the material as much as we do and are able to really connect with the work." Added David, "We were so happy with Rachael's work on this project. She has a fantastic intuition for this material."

Indeed. They all do.

When asked how, if given two more pages, they would have written a coda with the *Enterprise*'s return to their own time and space, David Tipton demurred while Scott said, "I'll have to say no comment, just in case we ever get to return to this material."

A logical response. One can only hope that it isn't another 47 years before these franchises cross paths again.

Let's Do the Time Warp Again, and Again, and Again, and...: Time Travel to and from the *Planet of the Apes*

by Dayton Ward

Displacing characters from their own time period, either by sending them into the past or flinging them toward a distant future, has long been one of fiction's great "fish out of water" setups, dating back to such classic works as *The Time Machine* by H.G. Wells and Mark Twain's *A Connecticut Yankee in King Arthur's Court*. The concept has been used to propel stories all along the vast, millennia-spanning tapestry that is the *Planet of the Apes* saga, starting from the opening moments of the original film and continuing on into the many comic books published since its theatrical release.

As a plot device, time travel has taken many forms when depicted in the various *Apes* films, television episodes, and other media, and these presentations have, on occasion, seemed at odds with each other. The 1968 *Planet of the Apes* film, and even Pierre Boulle's original novel, *La Planète des Singes* (*Monkey Planet*), showed their central characters traveling through space and achieving relativistic speeds, resulting in a "time dilation" effect in which time progressed at a normal rate aboard their spacecraft while thousands of years passed back on Earth. In the film, astronaut George Taylor refers to this as "Hasslein's theory," but the first sequel, *Beneath the Planet of the Apes*, seems to imply that something else is at work. After crashing while apparently attempting to follow the original course charted by Colonel Taylor's ship, astronaut John Brent theorizes that his own spacecraft must have slipped through a "bend in time" or a "Hasslein curve." Knowledge of this phenomenon is later attributed to Doctor Otto Hasslein, who makes his debut in the third film, *Escape from the Planet of the Apes*. However, there's no mention of any significant length of time spent aboard Brent's ship before its crash.

Of course, Hasslein's theory is out the window by the time of *Escape*, as well as both television series, all of which depict transitions through time as something that can be affected in either direction, to the future or the past and back again. A key plot point of the live-action *Planet of the Apes* TV series is astronaut Alan Virdon's determination to somehow reverse the time warp that has deposited him and his companion, Peter Burke, more than a thousand years into their future. It makes sense that Virdon, a devoted family man, would believe this to be an achievable goal, as it's unlikely that he would have volunteered for a deep-space mission of the sort Taylor accepted in the original film, with no chance of returning home to the wife and son he left behind.

A similar phenomenon affects the crew of the spaceship *Venturer* in the animated series *Return to the Planet of the Apes*. Astronauts Bill Hudson, Judy Franklin, and Jeff Allen find themselves catapulted far into the future, which occurs after they prove the "time thrust" theory put forth by a scientist named Doctor Stanton. The *Venturer* apparently is a spaceship constructed for the express purpose of substantiating Stanton's hypothesis. In "Flames of Doom," the series' first episode, the spacecraft's internal clocks indicate that it has traveled a century forward in time before being subjected to a strange warping, and... well, you know where they end up.

Sometime later, the trio meet yet another astronaut, Ronald Brent (no relation, presumably), whose spacecraft had also been propelled into the future after departing Earth in 2109, and who had since been stranded in the Forbidden Zone for years. Brent's ship had set out almost 150 years after the *Venturer*'s launch, but had arrived nearly two decades prior to his predecessors, thanks to the timey-wimey nature of temporal travel.

Tim Burton's 2001 "re-imagined" *Planet of the Apes* introduced yet another flavor of time travel, with the film's hero, U.S. Air Force pilot Leo Davidson, being swept up in a "time storm" that propels him to the year 5021,[1] without even the courtesy of dumping him on Earth. The storm is depicted as being a "doorway" through time, with travel possible in both directions. (Was I the only one who thought about Kirk Douglas and the U.S.S. *Nimitz* from *The Final Countdown*?)

So far, the new films have yet to utilize time travel as a plot device. Given the disappearance of an astronaut team in *Rise of the Planet of the Apes*, however, it's possible that a future movie will eventually do so.

So, it's safe to say that the *Apes* films and television episodes played fast and loose with whatever "rules" may have been established for travel through space and time. When it's mentioned at all, the technology employed to make these temporal transits is described in only the vaguest terms, leaving viewers and fans to conjure their own ideas about how such feats were accomplished.[2]

Then the comics come along, and everything is up for grabs.

Despite being a staple of the filmed *Apes* adventures, time travel as a plot device is actually used quite sparingly in the comics published throughout the decades. When it began publication in the summer of 1974, Marvel Comics' *Planet of the Apes* magazine featured serialized chapters of two ongoing comics stories in each issue. While one of those segments was devoted to adapting the five original *Apes* films, the other featured piece typically was an installment of an all-new adventure.

Seven of the first eight issues included part of "Terror on the Planet of the Apes," which would continue through fifteen of the magazine's twenty-nine issues and become one of the most enduring comics storylines ever included in the ever-growing *Apes* narrative. The bulk of the original tales staked their own claims at various points along the two-millennia stretch of time encompassing the circular *Apes* chronology, with stories set in various locations around the world and offering a broader look at a future Earth (as each issue's cover boldly proclaims) "where man once stood supreme... now rule the apes!"

---

[1] According to Dark Horse Comics' film adaptation; it's indicated on a monitor.

[2] Time travel in the *Apes* universe is discussed at length in *The Planet of the Apes Chronicles*, edited by Paul A. Woods (Plexus Books, August 2001), and in *Timeline of the Planet of the Apes: The Definitive Unauthorized Chronology*, by Rich Handley (Hasslein Books, November 2008), both of which were sourced for this essay.

It wasn't until the ninth issue that Doug Moench, the writer responsible for all of the comics throughout the magazine's entire run, decided the time had come to create an all-new tale that would tie directly into plots or characters from one of the films. The result was "Kingdom on an Island of the Apes," in which Derek Zane – a would-be inventor who has studied Hasslein's theories in excruciating detail, and who followed with great interest the original space mission of Colonel Taylor and his crew – constructs a time machine (which he calls the Temporal Displacement Module) in the hopes of proving Hasslein's hypothesis. Zane attempts to convince NASA[3] that his invention might well be able to travel forward in time and ascertain the fate of Taylor and his crew, whom he believes to be stranded two millennia in the future. When his efforts are rebuffed, Zane decides to test his creation himself, and successfully propels himself forward in time to the year 3975, where he has (incorrectly) calculated that Taylor and the others arrived at the end of their own space flight.

Derek Zane's Temporal Displacement Module from *Planet of the Apes* magazine #9 (Oct 1976).

---

[3] Even though Taylor, onscreen, worked for an organization called ANSA

His time machine damaged beyond repair, Zane finds himself trapped in the distant future and sets out to find Taylor and his fellow astronauts – which, of course, brings him into contact with all manner of new characters, both human and simian. Zane eventually realizes that the current state of the planet offers him no viable means of finding Taylor and his comrades, and becomes embroiled in his own series of adventures. A popular fan assumption – one supported by the dates offered in the comic story, as well as the original *Planet of the Apes* film – is that Zane simply arrived at a point in time well before Taylor's ship returns to Earth. [4]

In addition to the two-part story (published in the magazine's ninth and tenth issues), Derek Zane would return in a later tale, "Beast on the Planet of the Apes," for issue #21. Though Moench had plotted further stories for the wayward inventor, the publication's eventual cancellation would see to it that the rest of Zane's adventures would remain untold.

Interestingly, the setup for "Kingdom" raises several questions, particularly for those fans who pay attention to the different dates thrown about across the films, television series, and other materials. First, if Zane actually does time-travel from 1974, this would mean he left *after* the return of Taylor's ship in 1973 with Cornelius, Zira, and Milo aboard, as established in *Escape from the Planet of the Apes*. Given the public scrutiny to which the three chimpanzees are subjected upon their arrival in "the present," as well as the attention Hasslein brings both to the apes and to his own theories about how they arrived on Earth – and from whence they had come – it makes no sense that Zane would be ignorant of these relevant details. However, it's apparent, during his preparations, that he knows nothing of the future world he soon will visit, and his reaction to encountering both primitive humans and advanced apes makes it clear that he has no foreknowledge of future events as recounted by Cornelius and Zira in *Escape* – or that talking apes even exist.

In one of his planned but unpublished stories for the magazine, "Journey to the Planet of the Apes," Moench developed a tale in which another set of time travelers (cleverly dubbed "tempnauts") is dispatched on a mission to the future in search of Derek Zane. Doctor Krigstein, the same NASA official who originally rejected Zane's claims about having built a time machine, discovers

---

[4] Moench set the Zane storyline in 3975, the same year in which he'd set his adaptation of the first movie (based on the date cited in Michael Wilson's shooting script), unaware that this had been changed to 3978 in the final film.

that the prospective inventor and his theories were right. Using Zane's own plans, NASA constructs a second Temporal Displacement Module and sends a pair of rescuers, Mara Winston and Jackson Brock, after the missing Zane.

Following a planned flurry of adventures, Zane would have returned to his own time in later issues. Moench even had an inventive twist waiting in the wings for that story's conclusion, with the inventor finding himself no longer suited for life in the 20th century, and thus building *another* time machine and flinging himself once more into the distant future (shades of Jonathan Swift's thematically similar *Gulliver's Travels*). Like the original "Kingdom on an Island of the Apes," a potential continuity glitch would seem to be introduced in this latter storyline as well, which was originally planned to take place in 1977 or 1978, well after the events of *Escape from the Planet of the Apes*.

As Marvel Comics was winding down its run of *Planet of the Apes* magazine, a Spanish-language comic published only in Argentina, *El Planeta de los Simios*, began offering new tales featuring astronauts Alan Virdon and Peter Burke, along with their chimpanzee companion, Galen, continuing the adventures begun in the live-action television series. The trio is still on the run from Councilor Zaius and Security Chief Urko, moving from place to place and trying to stay one step ahead of the gorilla army that continues to hunt them. (The comic is at odds with the TV series in a number of ways, though, most notably in how it relocates the fugitives from southern California to the East Coast.)

"The Star Gods," which appeared in the comic's fifth issue, features the astronauts and Galen learning of the existence of another spacecraft, which apparently crashed shortly before Virdon's and Burke's arrival. This is likely not the same spacecraft to which Zaius alluded in the TV series' pilot episode, "Escape from Tomorrow." According to Zaius, that ship landed ten years earlier, with at least two astronauts surviving its crash. Urko, believing their advanced knowledge might incite the local human population to insurrection, killed the astronauts and destroyed all evidence of their spaceship. The vessel found by Virdon, Burke, and Galen, known as the *Blue Star*, crashed with no survivors near an outlying village, and Arpo, the local ape prefect with designs on one day overthrowing Zaius and the Central City council, has declared the wrecked craft a religious object.

When Arpo captures the renegades and learns of their true identities, he forces the astronauts to repair the damaged ship so that he might use it as a weapon against Central City. Unable to utilize the vessel to return to his own era, Virdon instead manages to sabotage the ship and force its destruction.

While the story explains that Virdon and Burke knew of the *Blue Star*'s mission and disappearance prior to their own departure from Earth, we are never given any real information about the craft's original crew, or the circumstances surrounding their arrival from the past.

Another story for the comic that was never published, "Encounter with Edison," would have shown the astronauts meeting Thomas Edison, who arrives in the year 3085 after constructing his own time machine and traveling from an unknown point in the late 19th or early 20th century. According to research that Rich Handley compiled for his book *Timeline of the Planet of the Apes*, for which he interviewed writer Jorge Claudio Morhain, Virdon and Burke would have tried to utilize Edison's invention to travel to their own time, but would have ended up stranded in the future when Edison returned home.

Though *El Planeta de los Simios* ceased publication after seven issues, the adventures of Virdon, Burke, and Galen continued elsewhere. In addition to a set of children's audio dramas produced by Power Records in 1974,[5] British publisher Brown Watson produced three "annuals" – hardcover tomes aimed at young readers, featuring comics and prose stories with illustrations – between 1975 and 1977. These annuals contained artwork rivaling the best of the Marvel magazines, but only the third volume featured a comic strip involving time travel. In "From Out of the Sky," the fugitives witness the crash-landing of a spacecraft and soon find it along with its lone survivor, a female astronaut named Verina Bolton, who happens to be a friend of Burke's.

The astronauts' initial excitement at the possibility of using the craft to get back to their own era is quickly dampened when Virdon discovers a fuel leak that – even if repaired – will only allow one passenger to hopefully make the transit back to the 20th century. The decision is made to send Verina back with her ship so she can alert others from their own time of Virdon's and Burke's plight, and the vessel makes a last-second getaway as gorilla soldiers close in. Unfortunately, the story ends without telling readers whether Verina made it home, or if she was able to convince someone to mount a rescue mission for

---

[5] One of which, *Battle of Two Worlds*, features a would-be Nazi dictator named Trang, possibly a time traveler, who tries to take over the ape-controlled planet. Virdon and Burke once again hope to use his spaceship (developed by NASA in the 1970s) to return home... which, as expected, does not go as planned.

Burke and Virdon. In a final odd twist, the story is also the last to feature the astronauts and Galen, whose final fates have yet to be officially revealed. [6]

Planet of the Apes as a comics property would lie dormant for more than a decade until a small, independent comics publisher, Malibu Graphics, acquired a license from 20th Century Fox in 1990. Under its Adventure Comics imprint, Malibu launched a monthly ongoing *Apes* title, while also producing several companion miniseries and single-issue stories. With few deviations, the monthly title's various tales progressed in mostly linear fashion during a period approximately one hundred years after the events depicted in the film *Battle for the Planet of the Apes*, with the miniseries tales inserted at various points along this stretch of time.

Like its Marvel predecessor, Malibu's *Apes* comics did not resist the lure of employing time travel in order to bring even more 20th-century humans to the future, ape-dominated Earth. *Ape City*, the first of Malibu's miniseries projects, gives readers a look at how the simian revolution has unfolded elsewhere around the world. In this case, Ape City is in Europe, where the fall of humanity and the rise of the apes have taken a markedly different turn than what we saw in North America in the decades after Caesar led the initial uprising in *Conquest of the Planet of the Apes*. Humans in this part of the world fell in much more rapid fashion, and in such great numbers, that in less than two centuries, very few (if any) can even be found on the continent. Infrastructure survives, however, leaving the burgeoning ape population with the makings of a modern society that they embrace – if only so they can teach themselves to understand the various technologies that humanity has left behind.

It is into this future that a spacecraft arrives from 1990, carrying a team of assassins with a single objective: to kill as many apes as possible in a desperate bid to give humanity a fighting chance at altering its destiny, and perhaps prevent Earth's eventual destruction. It's basically *The Dirty Half-Dozen on the Planet of the Apes*, as the group includes four convicted murderers (known as Scab, Devon, Moriah, and π) who have been offered amnesty in exchange for successfully completing their mission. Leading the team for this undertaking is

---

[6] In 2005, writer Mike McColm penned "Return to Yesterday," a fan comic (archived online at potatv.kassidyrae.com/yesterday.html) that provided a sequel to "From Out of the Sky," revealed Bolton's fate, and offered closure to the show's main characters. In addition, ABC filmed several "aged Galen" clips for its five TV movies repackaging the show (potatv.kassidyrae.com/galenslastappearance.html), which revealed that the fugitives *did* return home, though not how they did so.

none other than Jo Taylor, daughter of Colonel George Taylor. After following in his footsteps and joining the space program, Jo discovers the truth about her father's ultimate fate, as well as that of Earth itself. When she learns of a top-secret government program designed to prevent those future events from coming to pass, she volunteers to lead the "Vindicators" and avenge her father.

In *Ape City* #1 (Aug 1990), the Vindicators prepare to kick some monkey butt.

The whole idea seems misguided. If the government had put this plan into motion based on what had been learned from testimony provided by Cornelius and Zira in *Escape*, then they might have been basing their actions on the assumption that the ape uprising would not occur for centuries to come. However, by 1990, it would be obvious to some – as it was to Governor Breck in *Conquest* – that apes were gaining intelligence much more rapidly than the chimpanzees had described.

As for the Vindicators, in *Ape City* #2, Jo Taylor believes she's landed on Earth "several decades" before her father's arrival – according to calculations made by scientists prior to her departure from 1990 – by which time humans have devolved to a point that reclaiming their society from the apes would be far beyond their grasp. Why not target an earlier time, when humanity still has the ability to forestall or at least mitigate the events that will bring about its own downfall? For that matter, why not travel to the past, and kill Cornelius and Zira before she can give birth to the ape who one day would lead the revolution, or try to prevent Taylor and his ship from leaving in the first place? The idea of altering past events that have already been influenced by future history is fascinating all on its own, though, and it's a potential aspect of the *Apes* saga that's never explored with any real depth.

Questions like this ultimately saw to it that a similar storyline proposed for one of Malibu Comics' single-issue or "one-shot" *Apes* stories never went forward. Writer Mike Valerio, who later would pen the one-shot *The Sins of the Father*, also had pitched a story titled *Manhunt on the Planet of the Apes*, in which the government, following the events of *Escape*, puts into motion a plan to send someone forward through time in an attempt to alter the course of future events. The top-secret initiative, dubbed "Operation Hasslein," would create a time travel vehicle capable of dispatching an assassin to the distant future to hunt down Taylor and stop him from triggering the Alpha-Omega bomb and destroying Earth. In an interview conducted by Handley, excerpts of which were included as supporting material in his *Timeline of the Planet of the Apes*, Valerio said that while the idea seemed feasible at first, story problems quickly surfaced.

"If you're going to send somebody into the future to kill Taylor," Valerio said, "why wait until Taylor arrives when you could kill him before he ever goes on his mission? Alternatively, if you do have a time machine, why not send that assassin to kill Caesar before he ever leads the revolt? Or to kill Zira before she can give birth to Milo/Caesar?" As the tale would've begun soon after the third film's events, many details remained unknown with respect to Caesar's rise to power and the precise timeframe of ape ascension and humanity's downfall. Also a problem was how anyone – even Cornelius and Zira – knew for certain that Taylor himself was responsible for detonating the bomb, since everyone who witnessed that event died in the explosion. Such questions and plot logic problems began piling up, to the point at which Valerio and Malibu co-founder Tom K. Mason eventually deemed the story unworkable. There was also the fact that *Ape City* had already tackled the similar premise, and had introduced many of the same issues.

What's interesting is how stories from the different publishers use as their point of departure the desire or need to follow after Taylor and his crew, either to help him avoid his tragic fate or to prevent him – by any means necessary – from triggering Earth's destruction. Yet, in both Marvel's "Kingdom on an Island of the Apes" and Malibu's *Ape City*, no mention is made of Brent or his ship from *Beneath the Planet of the Apes*. While it's possible, though unlikely, that Derek Zane had no knowledge of Brent's mission while building his Temporal Displacement Module, surely Jo Taylor and those spearheading the Vindicator project would have been aware of him, given that they were working for the U.S. government.

Another notable aspect of the various time-travel elements from the films, TV series, and comics is that the details of the technology are never fully explained. The closest we get to any real "understanding" of time-travel fundamentals comes from Hasslein in *Escape* (albeit in vague terms), from Virgil's philosophizing in *Battle for the Planet of the Apes*, and from Zane's work in "Kingdom on an Island of the Apes." Generally speaking, and at least within the realm of the *Planet of the Apes* mythos, developing time-travel technology would seem to be incredibly easy – although NASA, in particular, seems to have a terrible track record so far as employing it without disastrous side-effects. (Or, should we blame ANSA?)

Another of Malibu's miniseries to carry a time-travel element was *Urchak's Folly*, which took the well-worn concept and offered it with a new twist. Instead of an astronaut arriving in the future via a time warp, Sebastian Thorne instead is a mute inmate committed to an "institute for mental incurables." The facility's owner, an unethical doctor named Foucault, has spent enormous time and effort attempting to prove, once and for all, that Charles Darwin's theories of evolution are false, and that biblical creationism is the true origin of Earth and the human species. To this end, he constructs a time machine in order to travel to the future and see for himself how humans will advance in the centuries to come. Thorne is the unwilling participant in Foucault's first test of his creation, and soon finds himself catapulted forward hundreds of years in time, with no memory of how he got there. He encounters a human woman named Miranda and a group of human resistance fighters who call themselves "Taylorites," and is caught up in their fight against an army of gorillas led by the sadistic silverback Colonel Urchak.

The story is an interesting take on the well-used "man out of time" premise that drives many *Planet of the Apes* stories, all the more so because of its

Doctor Foucault's time machine from *Urchak's Folly* #4 (Apr 1991).

obvious tips of the hat to H.G. Wells' classic science fiction novel *The Time Machine*. However, the most interesting aspect of the tale, Foucault's motivations for constructing his machine with his intention to visit the future, is left largely unexplored except as brief exposition to drive Thorne's story. One has to wonder why Foucault, driven as he is to disprove Darwin's theories, wouldn't first want to travel to the distant past and bring back proof of mankind's origins as recorded in the Bible.

Another tease left to readers without any real follow-up comes after the gorilla Urchak is unwittingly transported back to Foucault's era at the conclusion of the story. How did the Victorian-age physician deal with the abrupt appearance in his laboratory of a sentient, talking ape? Though we know Urchak's final fate – he appears stuffed and mounted in a display case in Foucault's lab – it would have been fascinating to see the Malibu Comics writers devise at least one tale revolving around the gorilla's brief time spent in the 19th century. What if Urchak had lived long enough to make some greater impact on the world in which he found himself? Shades of General Thade from Tim Burton's *Planet of the Apes* remake, anyone?

Getting back to those pesky time warps, they apparently aren't just problems plaguing human and simian astronauts. Lest one think that only Earth is harassed by such spatial phenomena, Malibu also provided readers and fans with *Ape Nation*. Inspired by the classic "crossover" comics of the 1970s, such as Marvel and DC's *Superman vs. Spider-Man* and *Batman vs. The Incredible Hulk*, along with more recent offerings such as *Aliens vs. Predator*, this miniseries brought together the universes of *Planet of the Apes* and *Alien Nation*, another cult-classic science fiction film.

Like *Apes*, *Alien Nation* also had spawned its own short-lived yet fondly remembered television series, along with several tie-in works, including novels as well as comics published by Malibu. Using *Alien Nation*'s basic setup as a launching point, *Ape Nation* posits a future in which a spacecraft carrying Tenctonese slaves travels through a time warp and arrives on Earth not in 1991, as depicted in the original film, but instead in the ape-dominated future as already envisioned in Malibu's *Planet of the Apes* comics.

With both properties owned by 20th Century Fox, it was a simple matter to convince the studio's licensing department to allow the crossover, which begins as something of an "alien invasion" story with the Tenctonese "newcomers" and their leader, Danada, forming an alliance with disgraced gorilla General Ollo and the infamous human known as Simon the Slaughterer. Together, they launch a campaign of conquest, while Heston, a well-respected special officer serving the apes' High Council (named, of course, after Charlton Heston), and Caan (named for *Alien Nation*'s James Caan), who had led the Tenctonese before being usurped by Danada, forge an alliance in order to marshal resistance against the coming invasion of Ape City.

Yes, it sounds odd, but it *works*. Like all such crossovers, *Ape Nation* succeeds mostly because the writers and artists, who obviously were fans of both properties, were enjoying themselves with every panel of this odd tale. The manner in which the Tenctonese are brought to Earth is no more implausible than any of the other bizarre events that brought all those astronauts and other travelers from the 20th century into the ape-dominated future, and care is taken to ensure that the storytelling rules established for each "universe" are respected.

Another crossover which was planned though never realized involved the Lord of the Jungle himself, Tarzan. Since 1996, Dark Horse Comics has held a license to produce Tarzan stories, which have included reprints of earlier works from previous publishers, as well all-new tales. In addition to encountering Edgar Rice Burroughs's other famous hero, John Carter, Tarzan has also found himself face to face with Superman and Batman, as well as the alien hunters from the *Predator* franchise. In 2006, comics writer Lovern Kindzierski and artist Alan Weiss pitched to Dark Horse *Tarzan on the Planet of the Apes*. Unlike the publisher's previous *Apes* comics, which took their cue from Tim Burton's 2001 film, this story would have sent Lord Greystoke to the far future of the original *Apes* timeline, thanks to a time machine built by none other than famed 19th-century author H.G. Wells.

According to Kindzierski, from an interview conducted by Handley in 2009, Tarzan would have arrived at a point several years before Colonel Taylor's crash. There, he would have found a tribe of humans that included a young girl whom Taylor would later name "Nova." Also in the mix would be Doctor Zaius, whose encounter with Tarzan would later provide the justification he harbors to fear intelligent humans and what they might do, given the chance. Additionally, Tarzan faces off against Alexander, a gorilla soldier who, through the tale's twists and turns, would be sent back to 1991, the time of Caesar and the first ape uprising.

Tarzan on the Planet of the Apes certainly sounds as though it might have made for a rousing tale. The idea of H.G. Wells inventing a time machine would seem to be a tip of the hat to Karl Alexander's fanciful novel *Time After Time* and the more well-known film of the same name.[7] On the surface, Tarzan seems a better crossover fit for *Planet of the Apes* than *Alien Nation*, with far fewer logistical obstacles to navigate in order to bring the two properties together. Of course, one can't ponder this road not taken without also wondering what it might be like to see the Warlord of Mars himself, John Carter, return from Barsoom to find Earth in the grips of ape domination.

Since acquiring the license for *Planet of the Apes* comics in 2011, BOOM! Studios has seemed content to refrain from utilizing time travel to drive any of its stories. Instead, the publisher has chosen to set its monthly title and assorted miniseries at various points in time before Taylor's arrival, or in the newly rebooted continuity. As of this writing, the sole exception to that storytelling strategy is a collaboration with fellow independent comics publisher IDW for *The Primate Directive*, a special crossover event by Scott and David Tipton and Rachael Stott that brings together characters from the 1968 *Planet of the Apes* film with Captain James T. Kirk and the crew of the U.S.S. *Enterprise* from the original *Star Trek* television series.

How are two such disparate future histories brought together? It seems the Klingons have acquired advanced technology that allows them to access portals to other dimensions. The resulting portals cross not only space, but time as well. When the *Enterprise* follows a Klingon warship through one such portal, Captain Kirk and his crew find themselves orbiting an alternate Earth, and Spock determines the current year in this "alternate reality" to be 3978, the year of the first *Planet of the Apes* film. Kirk and a landing party beam down to investigate, and what do they find? Why, those damned, dirty apes, of course. Complicating matters is Kor, a Klingon commander[8] who is arming the apes with weapons far more advanced than their own simple rifles and pistols. Of course, things get seriously crazy when Kirk encounters an astronaut from the 20th century who now calls this bizarre, upside-down Earth home. Guess who?

---

[7] In both the novel and the film (directed by Nicholas Meyer), Wells constructs a time machine which is used by his good friend, Doctor John Leslie Stephenson, to escape to the year 1979 as a means of eluding the police when it's discovered that he is the infamous serial killer "Jack the Ripper." Wells pursues Stephenson into the future to apprehend him, where he meets the woman he will marry, Amy Robbins. It's implied that this adventure would inspire Wells to write *The Time Machine*.
[8] Portrayed by John Colicos in the original *Star Trek* series' "Errand of Mercy," and later in three episodes of *Deep Space Nine*, as well as by James Doohan in the animated episode "The Time Trap."

Cue hijinks.

After more than fifty years – going all the way back to the initial publication of Pierre Boulle's novel – time travel remains an integral component of the *Planet of the Apes* saga. With two thousand years of mostly circular history in which to play, why should writers bother with such tales at this point? Perhaps because it's still fun to insert characters into the singularly outlandish setting that is a planet where intelligent apes have risen from the ashes of what once was human civilization. That the trope has been used only sparingly may contribute to the enduring appeal of such stories, and with luck, we've not seen the last of them.

Damn Them All to Hell: The Unpublished *Apes* Comics

by Rich Handley

Despite the immense popularity of the *Planet of the Apes* films, fans have become accustomed to cancellation when it comes to licensed spinoff comic books. In 2013, BOOM! Studios' ongoing *POTA* storylines by Daryl Gregory, Carlos Magno, Gabriel Hardman, and Corinna Sara Bechko were prematurely canceled despite being deservedly well-received. Those who have long followed *Apes* comics were likely not surprised. Long before BOOM! entered the arena, Marvel Comics, Malibu Graphics, Dark Horse Comics, Metallic Rose Comics (Mr. Comics), and Argentina's Editorial Mo.Pa.Sa. all saw their *Planet of the Apes* runs prematurely aborted as well, resulting in a number of proposed titles from each publisher never seeing the light of day.

In 2008 and 2009, while conducting research for a pair of *Planet of the Apes* reference books,[1] I reached out to numerous *POTA* comics writers, from Marvel to Mr. Comics, asking them to share their unpublished lore. In 2013, I then spoke with BOOM!'s creative teams while preparing a series of online articles

---

[1] *Timeline of the Planet of the Apes: The Definitive Chronology* (2008) and *Lexicon of the Planet of the Apes: The Comprehensive Encyclopedia* (2010), from Hasslein Books.

for the 13thDimension.com comics culture blog.[2] What I received during all of these e-mail interviews was illuminating: not just brief descriptions but, in some cases, entire outlines or even scripts – and from every single writer, no less. Thanks to the generosity of these creative minds, let's take a look back at several time-lost comic books from *Planet of the Apes*.[3]

Marvel Comics

"Future History Chronicles VI: The Captive of the Canals"

One of the most popular storylines of the Marvel run was Doug Moench's five-part "Future History Chronicles." Illustrated by Tom Sutton, "FHC" presented a new take on *Planet of the Apes*, in which humans and simians traveled the oceans on vast city-ships. The story focused on a human couple, Alaric and Reena, their friend Starkor, and gorilla architect Graymalkyn, whose adventures brought them face to muzzle with great dangers both above and below sea-level.

The final issue ended on a cliffhanger, with the group escaping Her Majesty's Cannibal Corps – ape mutants astride giant frogs – and discovering a great city on land, known as Sexxtann. For thirty years, their fate and the nature of the city remained a mystery to fans – but not to Moench. The writer had already outlined a sixth chapter in the saga, titled "The Captive of the Canals,"[4] when Marvel opted to drop the *Apes* license after APJAC Productions upped the licensing fee. (Although it has long been assumed that the series ended due to low sales, Moench said interest from readers and Marvel remained high, with only the increased fee necessitating cancellation.)

Initially, Moench had conceived the tale as a *King Kong* riff, with a captured giant ape transferred to the ruins of Manhattan – an irony, in that this Kong would have been taken from civilization to primitive ruins, rather than the other way around. As Moench described it, "The giant ape was not only a nuclear freak from the radiation, but was also insane from radiation sickness. He was

---

[2] That five-part series, titled "Unpublished on the *Planet of the Apes*" (hassleinbooks.blogspot.com/2013/12/apes-week.html), formed the basis for this essay, along with another article by yours truly from 2007, titled "Time-Lost Tales from the Planet of the Apes," published in *Simian Scrolls* issue 15.

[3] The quotes cited throughout this essay come from the above-noted interviews.

[4] This and Doug Moench's other "lost" scripts and outlines are archived at Hunter Goatley's *Planet of the Apes* Archive (pota.goatley.com/moench.html), with Moench's permission.

intelligent, but he was crazy and destructive, and had to be appeased with sacrifices of human beings. He was a berserker."

Moench's final concept was quite different, in terms of both storyline and the giant ape's gender. Upon arrival at Sexxtann, Alaric's team met the Industrialists, descendants of citizens from several African nations who blamed apes and Caucasian humans for the planet's devastation and decided to form their own isolated civilization. The city, a 42-level hexagonal fortress, contained a vast canal system filled with giant amphibians that were used for amusement, transportation, and sustenance.

The Industrialists employed non-"green" methods of commerce, thus endangering the natural world. This angered the Cannibal Corps, ape environmentalists whose queen had been subjected to radiation and genetic experimentation, causing her to reach immense size, and damaging her brain in the process. Banished from Sexxtann, Alaric's team found the giant ape in a jungle at the city's center. Her Majesty, lonely for her own kind, took a liking to Graymalkyn and gave her life to save his when the Industrialists torched the jungle. Her death throes toppled the walls, flooding the trees and drowning the childlike behemoth.

The outline specified an 18-page story, though an endnote urged editor John David Warner to consider twenty pages so Sutton could "heighten the drama, broaden the scope, increase the sweep, embolden the action, add a few more big blockbuster panels for the appropriate scenes, and in general make for a better story." It's unclear if Moench wrote a complete script based on the outline, but he was unable to locate one in his archives.

"Terror on the Planet of the Apes, Phase 2: To Meet the Makers"

Arguably the trippiest of Moench's *Apes* storylines was "Terror on the Planet of the Apes." This long-running serial starred Jason, an angry human teen, his chimp friend Alexander, eccentric human wayfarer Lightning Smith ("Lightsmith"), his mute gibbon companion Gilbert, a sexy human gypsy named Malagueña, and racist gorilla military leader Brutus, the saga's main villain.

As with "Future History Chronicles," "Terror" ended without resolution. Thaddeus, the Lawgiver's attendant, was captured and cyborged by the insane Makers, whose berserker creations, the Gorilloids, tried to help Brutus destroy Ape City in issue #29. Had Marvel kept the title running, Moench had planned a 38-page "double-length special" titled "To Meet the Makers." Herb Trimpe, who'd drawn "Terror" following the departure of artist Mike Ploog, was assigned to illustrate it.

In Moench's outline for "To Meet the Makers," Thaddeus, now controlled by the Makers, tried to kill Lightsmith, forcing him to impale the young ape with an ancient rusty hypodermic needle, making him deathly ill. The wayfarer tried to cure the Lawgiver – who'd been dying since the previous storyline – by consulting an old medical text citing glycerin as a treatment for heart ailments. Unfortunately, Lightsmith mistook the explosive form of nitroglycerin for the medication and nearly blew up the Lawgiver while trying to save his life.[5]

If such a scene seems a bit wacky, that's because it was. But given Lightsmith's personality, it was fitting and worked quite well. Far more over the top was the Makers' latest creation: Smashore, a nine-foot-tall albino Gorilloid with a hole in his head to propel bombs, as well as a utility belt, bionic eyeballs able to shoot death rays, and fingertip laser-shooters – a reminder that although it was set in the *Planet of the Apes* mythos, Marvel's "Terror" was, first and foremost, a comic book.

Defeating Smashore with the help of his old friends Steely Dan and Gunpowder Julius, Jason learned that Alex's house had been burned down by human racists wearing black hoods, just as Brutus's Ape Supremacists had killed his family in the first issue. This made the youth realize he'd been wrong to hold onto hatred and, in what would have been a turning point had "Terror" continued, Jason decided to make peace with Brutus – only to find that the gorilla had escaped.

"Journey to the Planet of the Apes"

Moench's third storyline, involving inventor and time traveler Derek Zane, was also unfinished. Had Marvel continued beyond #29, Zane's saga would have become the magazine's mainstay. With Marvel's film adaptations completed, Moench needed a new focus for issue #30 onward, and Zane fit the bill. Originally titled "Return to the Planet of the Apes," this storyline – which he described in his script as "John Chimper of Mars," referencing Edgar Rice Burroughs' John Carter novels – was renamed "Journey to the Planet of the Apes" to avoid conflicting with the animated series.

The script for "Journey" began in 1974, with NASA's Doctor Krigstein (from issue #9) investigating Zane's disappearance. Krigstein found Zane's scientific papers, including plans for his time machine, the Temporal Displacement Module. Using Zane's equations, NASA built its own model – the *Chronos I* – so it could rescue Zane from the year 3976. Two "tempunauts," Mara Winston and

---

[5] Nitroglycerin is, in fact, used to treat heart ailments in the real world.

Jackson Brock, were chosen for the mission, though Brock only volunteered in order to profit from knowledge of the future.

In that future, Zane befriended Faron, a chimp scientist who'd found a bubble-domed human city now inhabited by apes. Branded a heretic, Faron was hunted by Jurando, a gorilla conceived as a new recurring villain. Brock would also have become an ongoing nemesis, as his attempt to strand Winston in the future would have caused the time machine's destruction and the loss of his own eye. The opening chapter would have concluded with Jurando capturing the two travelers.

While Marvel's monthly magazine was published in the United States, a weekly, serialized version was released in Britain, requiring additional covers. Issue #117's cover, by artist Val Mayerik, appeared unconnected to the stories within, as it featured two astronauts in an arena setting, surrounded by gorillas. Moench's handwritten notes for "Journey" offer a clue to the story behind that cover, as his outline began with the following notation:

> VAL: Since this is our effort to 'continue' the adaptations with an original 'adaptation' of our own... the series should bear a stamp similar to the previous movie adaptations – emphasis on movie-type schtick & settings – episodic cliffhanger chapters – a feeling of broad sweep & scope – greater reliance on dialogue, etc., etc. In fact, this new series should seem more like the movie stuff than like the previous appearances of its major character in *Apes* #9, 10, & 21.

This could indicate that Mayerik's #117 cover had, indeed, been intended for the "Journey" storyline.

"Beyond the Planet of the Apes"

A second note to Mayerik and Warner laid out Moench's plans beyond the opening script, with Zane and Faron befriending Winston and meeting a chimp woman from the civilized ape city, providing love interests for both males. Brock would have amassed a renegade army of gorilla followers, and Zane would have ultimately been reunited with his wife Andrea in Avedon.

This, Moench told me, would have segued into "a number of successive 'movie' sequels." After eight or ten chapters of "Journey," he planned to launch into a new ongoing storyline titled "Beyond the Planet of the Apes," in which Zane's group would have blasted off for another planet. "And think about it," Moench said. "If 20th [Century] Fox had continued with more movies, wouldn't such a plotline have become inevitable...? Apes in spacesuits – up against aliens (instead of more mutants) with rayguns, etc.?"

Inevitable? Well... maybe not. Intriguing, though? Certainly.

Ultimately, Moench wrote in his outline, "Our characters would be ready for a return to Earth – but maybe a return (via Charlton Heston's original astronaut time-jump) back to 1976... rather than their intended 3976. After that, of course, Zane would decide he's still a misfit in his own milieu, get homesick for Lady Andrea back in Avedon circa 3976, build himself yet another time machine, and... ad infinitum." This, he noted, would have occurred around issue 60, indicating that his plans for *Apes* stretched far into the future, well beyond Marvel's 29th issue.

"Forbidden Zone Prime"

Although Moench maintains archives of his past work, he was unable to shed light on another mystery. In March 2006, a page of original Marvel *Planet of the Apes* artwork was discovered for sale online that had not come from any of Marvel's published tales. That single page featured a chimp architect named Viraga, who was furious at her husband Julius for some vague offense. Apologizing for his actions, Julius admitted that he'd grown cynical and bitter in his old age, unable to accept the cruelty that ape society inflicted on humans. As he spoke, the young-at-heart chimp executed acrobatic flips and jumps around the town square.

Attempts to locate additional portions of this story yielded a handful of pages (including, as luck would have it, the title spread), thanks to art collector Edward Haber, but to date, the story remains incomplete.[6] Moench himself cannot recall any additional details, but admitted, "Viraga is just the sort of name I would come up with." This story, he said, was likely slated for a 30th issue that was created but never printed, though he could not locate the script or the completed issue in his files.

The additional material provided *some* context to that first page of Viraga and Julius: a respected chimp architect, she felt humiliated that he publicly belittled her adherence to strict architectural forms (which, I guess, makes him a bit of a jerk, though he's clearly the story's hero). Although she loved Julius, she had little respect for his non-acceptance of ape-dominance rhetoric, or his fondness for archaic poetry. Plus, his bond with a primitive human woman named Steena widened the rift between them. More intelligent than other humans of her era, Steena wished apes could let go of their hatred and learn to love humans – and each other. Eventually, a gorilla soldier named Zandor nearly

---

[6] The pages found to date are also available at Goatley's *Apes* site (pota.goatley.com/moench.html).

killed Steena just for being human. Julius risked his life to save hers, but knew their bond would be unable to change the hatred of society.

Julius and Steena make an interspecies connection, but the outlook for their friendship is grim in Marvel's unpublished "Forbidden Zone Prime."

Bob Larkin created a stunning cover painting for this story, but no more has been unearthed regarding the content, including its ending. The real mystery of this tale, however, involves the artwork. Although that initially found page is credited to the late Sonny Trinidad, the Filipino artist denied having produced any such illustrations when I emailed his children, Norman and Cherry Trinidad, to inquire about it. It's possible that Trinidad may have forgotten about this particular assignment – or that the name on the art page was erroneous, and that it was, in fact, illustrated by someone else. Sadly, we may never know.

Apes Down Under

When Australian publisher Newton Comics began offering Marvel reprints in 1975, editor John Corneille hoped to see Newton produce original comic strips as well. Corneille suggested *Planet of the Apes* since it was Newton's best-selling reprint at the time. Newcomer Philip Bentley was slated to write the script, with art by penciller Colin Paraskevas and inker Greg Gates. "It was the closest thing we felt we were likely to get to working in the industry," Bentley explained at the pulpfaction.net message forum in 2007,[7] "and [we] welcomed the opportunity to approach a strip from a commissioned perspective."

Bentley posted the six-page script he came up with, which starred Byron, a thirty-something chimp branded a heretic for attempting to teach humans how to read. Byron's wife betrayed him to authorities, but when the orangutans excused his crime due to his being related to a famous scientist, the arresting gorilla became furious and vowed to kill him. He wrote on the forum:

> I make no claims as to the strip's quality, and present it here, firstly, because others expressed an interest in seeing it and, secondly, because it is yet another of those curious sidelights that the Australian comics scene seems peppered with – indeed, I might suggest that aspects of the scene are almost entirely made up of sidelights, more's the pity. I admit that it is little more than what a fan might have come up with, but given that none of us were great devotees of *POTA* (does that make fans 'Apeies' or 'Potties'?) I think we did bring a sense of detachment to the project that helped our proto-professional stance.

Ultimately, Newton Comics pulled the plug on the concept. As Bentley explained on the forum:

> I don't think we knew whether it was hit on the head here or in the States. From what I know now, I am sure that it never was run by Marvel. From all reports, publisher Maxwell Newton, who was using that unholy triumvirate of comics, pop magazines, and porn to run a recently acquired 'über printing press' 24-7, only ever made one down-payment for the reprint rights and then conveniently was 'never in' when Marvel rang trying to get him to cough up the rest.

Bentley could not recall where the story would have gone had it been allowed to proceed, but posted, "My notes made during our initial conference don't really align with the story as it came together. According to these, we were thinking of using child apes as the protagonists, as 'kids seem to like

---

[7] Bentley's post is available at forums.pulpfaction.net/viewtopic.php?f=19&t=3246.

pretending being apes' (those of us with a grumpy-old-man disposition may well agree with that, although not in the way we meant it at the time)."

Battle for the Planet of the Apes

Three pages of artwork were cut from Marvel's adaptation of *Battle for the Planet of the Apes*, which surfaced online a few years ago. These pages involved General Aldo rallying his gorilla soldiers to rebel against Caesar, and repeatedly yelling "Guns! Guns! Guns! We need guns!" like a crazed, hairy Charlton Heston. Featured on one page were several panels of Caesar's son, Cornelius, bidding farewell to his pet toad and then sneaking off into the night to be killed by the bloodthirsty general.

These pages wouldn't have added much to the adapation, other than a lot of guns, so it's not surprising that they were removed.

Malibu Graphics

Manhunt on the Planet of the Apes

In the 1990s, Malibu Graphics' Adventure Comics imprint picked up the *Planet of the Apes* license, releasing both an ongoing title set a century after Caesar's death, and also a string of miniseries and one-shot specials set in various eras. One such special was *Sins of the Father,* by the late Mike Valerio and artist Mitch Byrd. Originally titled *Murder on the Planet of the Apes*, *Sins* revealed a hard lesson learned by a young Doctor Zaius regarding integrity, justice, and the importance of preserving ape society, no matter the cost.

Sins of the Father was not the only *Planet of the Apes* story that Valerio proposed. As the author told me via e-mail in late 2009:

> We're going back seventeen or so years, so my memory's a little fuzzy, but I know that I pitched one other *Apes* idea to [editor and co-founder] Tom Mason at Malibu. I know that he and I talked about it some, but never wrote anything down, aside from some brainstorming e-mails. And I don't recall if we were talking about this as another comic book special or taking it directly to 20th Century Fox with it as a new movie pitch (though I seem to recall Tom suggesting that).

As Valerio described it, *Manhunt on the Planet of the Apes* would have been both a sequel to *Escape* and a "prequel/continuation" of *Planet* and *Beneath*. The story, he explained, would have started after the deaths of Zira, Cornelius, and Otto Hasslein.

> Knowing that the Earth is doomed because Taylor will destroy it in the future, the U.S. government and military create 'Operation: Hasslein,' a shadow program dedicated to developing a time travel device that will send an assassin into the future sometime before Taylor's arrival.

The assassin's objective: to wait for Taylor to arrive, then track him down and kill him before he met Brent and detonated the Alpha-Omega Bomb.

According to Valerio, Mason liked the idea, but as the two began developing it further, they soon realized there were "all kinds of plot-logic problems inherent to the time travel set-up." For instance, he said, "If you're going to send somebody into the future to kill Taylor, why wait until Taylor arrives when you could kill him before he ever goes on his mission? Or, if you do have a time machine, why not send that assassin to kill Caesar before he ever leads the revolt? Or to kill Zira before she can give birth to Milo/Caesar?" In addition, it's unlikely anyone in the 20th century would have known it was Taylor who triggered the detonation.

Such "plot complications and conundrums" began to overwhelm them, Valerio admitted, which meant "either the core idea was dumb, or we were too dumb to figure out how to make it work." What's more, he added, there were too many similarities to the *Terminator* films – as well as to the *Alien* movies, once they decided to make the assassin female.

"The more we tried to change the idea to make it fresh," Valerio said, "the more unworkable it became. Ultimately, we just abandoned the idea and walked away."

It's interesting to note that, despite this, Malibu had already explored a similar premise in Charles Marshall's *Ape City* miniseries – and the same logic problems applied. Not having read *Ape City*, however, Valerio was unaware of the similarities and was surprised to hear about them during our interview.

Ape Nation

The four-issue *Ape Nation* miniseries featured a crossover between *Planet of the Apes* and TV's *Alien Nation*, written by Marshall and illustrated by M.C. Wyman and Terry Pallot. Several years ago, a page of artwork cut from that series surfaced online, featuring a tender scene between heartbroken ape scout Heston and a Tenctonese woman, Elysa. The page was certainly not crucial to the story, but its removal is unfortunate, as it was quite effective. In addition, a sequel to Ape Nation was planned and announced, and Marshall plotted out the entire story, but for whatever reason, the series never saw print.

"Back from the Future"

Marshall served as the regular writer on Malibu's monthly *Apes* series and, like Moench and Valerio, also had story ideas that remained unrealized. "I don't have a lot of specific memories about those last few issues," Marshall told me, regarding the final four-parter in which the spirit of Governor Breck killed many of the characters created during his tenure. "Obviously, it was an attempt to 'clean house'... I think it was also an attempt to leave the *POTA* world the way I found it, without a lot of unnecessary clutter. We knew the series was going away, and that I was moving on."

Although Marshall recalled no "big themes or ideas left for the characters who didn't bite it at the end of the series," he did cite two stories he "fleshed out and never got a chance to tell."

The first, titled "Back from the Future," featured Jojo and Frito, his two comedic, dimwitted gorilla guards. Marshall described the story as "a farcical time-travel piece that probably would have gone God-knows-where." He cited the brawling best friends as his favorite characters from his work on the series, stating, "Those two knuckleheads were the easiest characters to write that I ever used; I'd just clear my head and let them go wherever they wanted. It was always pretty ridiculous stuff, but it never ceased to entertain me, and I figured I could be sure I was at least entertaining one person."

Although Gary Chaloner, the writer and artist of Malibu's *Urchak's Folly* miniseries, recalled no scripts of his that Malibu rejected, an unpublished cover he drew has surfaced online. It is unclear whether it was created for a published or unpublished tale (Chaloner no longer remembers), though the two apes depicted in the image appear to be Jojo and Frito. This may indicate it was created for "Back from the Future."

"The Most Dangerous Animal"

The other tale was an arc that Marshall dubbed "The Most Dangerous Animal" – referencing Richard Connell's short story "The Most Dangerous Game" – which he described as "an ambitious time-travel story where a group of humans (possibly government) discover that the world has been lost to the apes and stage a huge attack that's actually a Trojan horse for an attempt to destroy all apekind with a manmade plague."

In the course of the story, Marshall said, the disaster would have been averted for the apes, but not for humanity. "The story ends with an *Escape from the Planet of the Apes* nod as a human is born who will be destined to lead his people in revolt. It never really came together for me – at least, in part, because I never knew whether I was rooting for the humans or apes." Marshall could not recall any further details of either concept.

Redemption of the Planet of the Apes

Lowell Cunningham, the author of Malibu's *The Forbidden Zone*, proposed an additional *Apes* tale that ended up in limbo. During our e-mail interview, the

Men in Black creator offered this glimpse into *Redemption of the Planet of the Apes*: "There was a story idea I had, but which wasn't used because it was thought to touch on elements which were off-limits due to the *Planet of the Apes* remake which was in the works at the time."

The basic idea, he explained, involved a Cornelius clone and an attempt to prevent the world's future destruction. "A scientist manages to recover Cornelius's memories and discovers the fate of the Earth, then sets a plan in motion to make sure Earth survives the [Alpha-]Omega bomb."

According to Cunningham, "Redemption" took place before and during *Conquest of the Planet of the Apes*, and during the climax of *Beneath the Planet of the Apes*. A scientist studying how memory is stored and passed down through generations used genetic material from Cornelius's corpse to create a clone, whom he named Janus. The clone retained the chimp's knowledge and, thus, knew of the planet's future destruction at Taylor's hands. (Cornelius, it should be noted, would have had no way of knowing about the Alpha-Omega Bomb, or about Taylor's part in detonating it, having been in space when the Earth melted.)

Unlike other tales involving characters changing the future via time travel, the scientist hoped to ensure the planet survived the detonation, but without otherwise altering the timeline. "He had an energy device that was developed as a defense against the Alpha-Omega Bomb," Cunningham said, "and would allow the bomb's energy to be shunted into space."

The scientist planned to hide both the device and Janus in a cryotube for two thousand years, at which time the clone would awaken and activate the machine before the explosion. But as his plan was put in motion, Caesar's rebellion erupted. "Fighting his way through the battles of *Conquest*, he placed the device in the Statue of Liberty, along with a cryotube protecting Janus, until the proper time."

In the end, Cunningham told me, the plan would have succeeded and Earth would have survived the detonation — but from space, it would still have appeared to Cornelius and Zira that the bomb had melted Earth's rim. This, he explained, would have saved the world from destruction, while preserving the timeline for posterity.

Unfortunately, the inclusion of a Cornelius clone "killed" the concept, according to Cunningham. "It wasn't so much the cloning as it was which character was cloned," he explained. "A clone of Cornelius would be considered the same as Cornelius, I was told. So far as I know, there was never any intention to use cloning in any *Planet of the Apes* film."

Sky Gods

Malibu's final trio of unpublished tales, each a four-issue miniseries, were submitted by *Blood of the Apes* author Roland Mann. The first of these, *Sky Gods*, would have been one of Malibu's most unusual *Apes* offerings, as the first issue would have featured no apes whatsoever. "Tom [Mason] mentioned to me that he wanted to see a proposal for an ape story that would be something James Cameron would do if he were making the next *Apes* movie," Mann told me during a telephone interview.[8]

The concept involved a time-lost colony spaceship – launched in the 20th century in an effort to preserve mankind, given Earth's fated destruction – that entered a Hasslein Curve and was thrown forward to the year 5000. The survivors set out to establish a colony, only to discover the planet populated by a race of sapient, horse-riding... tigers! Mutated by radiation, the beasts had evolved into a vicious warrior race that preyed on apes (mankind being extinct by then). Nick, one of the colonists, would have befriended an ape named Teryl, and their people would have formed an ape-human alliance to fight the tiger tribe together.

According to Mann, Mason greenlighted *Sky Gods* (a working title, along with *Second Coming*) and "kicked it back" for revisions. However, he said, "before I could send him the revision – and get a contract – Malibu pulled back on *Apes* stories." Like *Blood of the Apes*, set in Memphis, Tennessee, *Sky Gods* would have taken place in the southern United States – specifically, former New Orleans. "What I wanted to do with my *Apes* stories," he stated, "was to keep the spirit of the *Apes* property, but take them to a different *geographical* location – primarily the South."

Mann re-watched all five *Planet of the Apes* movies and read Marshall's comics, searching for a unique spin on the mythos. "Different was the key thing, to me," he said, "I wanted my stories to be just a little different than other *Apes*

---

[8] In 1996, Cameron almost did make a *Planet of the Apes* film, as he was in talks with Fox to executive-produce and write a sixth movie in the series – starring, unbelievably, Arnold Schwarzenegger – though he declined to direct it since he was busy filming *Titanic* at the time. Cameron chose *Capricorn One*'s Peter Hyams as director, but when Fox rejected Hyams, Cameron stepped down, as did Schwarzenegger.

books Malibu was doing/had done. That's why I brought the tigers into *Sky Gods*, and tried to shift the relationship between man and ape."

Henry the Ape

Henry the Ape, while not as unusual an *Apes* concept as sapient felines, would certainly qualify as different, since it involved European royalty. This miniseries would have starred a young ape prince reluctantly in line for the throne of England, embarking on an adventure of discovery throughout former Europe. (Malibu's *Ape City* miniseries had revealed Europe to be home to a thriving simian society, free of the human race.)

In the course of his travels, Henry would have encountered a wide array of ape cultures, set in a comedic motif. "For *Henry*, I wanted to do something more light-hearted, and the prince who doesn't want to be king and thus travels the post-apocalyptic world. Well," Mann laughed, "it seemed interesting to *me* anyway!"

He recalled little else about *Henry the Ape*, but noted, "What I remember about it was I wanted Henry to be a youngish ape." Although Mason liked the idea, Mann never submitted anything in writing, nor fleshed out the story beyond a single paragraph relayed over the phone, as Malibu had opted to scale back its *Planet of the Apes* titles by that time.

Indiapes

Mann's final unpublished work, *Indiapes*, is one he barely recalled when we spoke. Looking back on it, he joked, "That *may* have been one meant for my 'private files!'" In fact, he'd forgotten about it entirely, with only the following brief description from his notes remaining:

> Start off with Ape-Indians at a war dance. Show some of them good, some bad. Shift to them attacking an ape-city. The apes there have a few guns. Not many, but some. This is somewhere in the Texas area. The Indiapes take food, a gun or two, and some women. Back to the Indiape camp we focus on one ape and his captured woman. Tension! Humans are slaves in the Indiape camp. Woman makes comment about this and asks do any of the other humans talk. Our Indiape laughs: a talking man! That's funny. He gets another man and makes fun of him because he can't talk. Woman doesn't think it's funny.

Mann laughed while telling me about this, admitting, "Yeah, I know. I don't see where it was going either."

Nova Comes Along

Christopher Sausville's *Planet of the Apes Collectibles: Unauthorized Guide with Trivia & Values* referenced an unpublished Malibu tale titled *Nova Comes Along*. According to Mason, however, no such story was ever planned, and none of the publisher's *Apes* writers recalled having ever pitched a Nova-centric tale. When I asked Sausville about this via e-mail, the author indicated that he had received the information from a fellow collector, though he could not recall who it was, and acknowledged that this individual may have been in error.

Editorial Mo.Pa.Sa.
El Planeta de los Simios

In 1977, Argentina publisher Editorial Mo.Pa.Sa. published a series of seven original Spanish-language comic books based on the *Planet of the Apes* TV series. Like most of the company's titles, its *Apes* series, *El Planeta de los Simios*, was unlicensed. Thus, these tales have never been officially published in English, though fan-produced translations are available for download at Kassidy Rae's *Planet of the Apes*: The Television Series website.[9]

In addition to the stories presented in these issues, author Jorge Claudio Morhain wrote five more scripts that did not see print. Series artist Sergio Alejandro Mulko never illustrated most of these tales, as Editorial Mo.Pa.Sa. halted the series after only seven issues due to financial difficulties. Mulko did, however, eventually create artwork for "The Queen" two decades later, during an attempt to resurrect the series as a fan-based project that unfortunately faltered. Morhain and Mulko provided me with the script and art to "The Queen," along with synopsis of the other four unpublished (and, to this day, unillustrated) tales from *El Planeta de los Simios*.

"The Queen"

A legendary being called the Queen of the Caves, said to be neither ape nor human, is prophesied to one day unite both species in equality. A human named Bethia assumes the Queen's identity in order to become the leader of a cult of humans and apes who worship the cave goddess. Fugitives Galen, Peter Burke, and Alan Virdon encounter her followers when Burke becomes romantically involved with Bethia's sister, Mariaan.

"The Killer"

A human hunter shoots apes at a school until Virdon, Burke, and Galen risk death to stop him.

"Cain"

A human survivor, resistant to radiation, struggles to live in the ruins of New York City, which has grown decrepit from the passage of time (apparently,

---

[9] Translations can be downloaded at potatv.kassidyrae.com/simios.html.

Morhain was unaware that the TV series was set not in New York, but in California; his published *Apes* comics made the same mistake).

"Encounter with Edison"

Thomas Edison arrives from the past in a time machine of his own design. Virdon and Burke try to use it to return to their own era, but it only take Edison home, predictably stranding them in the future.

"The Archeologist"

A human village, mobilized by a brainwashing device, digs up a lost civilization in New York's John F. Kennedy Airport. As the astronauts flee, they see the semi-buried Statue of Liberty.

Dark Horse Comics
Issue #7 and Beyond

Dark Horse's comic based on Tim Burton's *Planet of the Apes* remake surpassed the film in terms of storytelling and characterization. The film's critical failure, however, resulted in the title's cancellation before writers Ian Edginton and Dan Abnett could bring their long-term plans to fruition. At the end of issue #6, Attar's motley band faced the Ultimar in a bloody battle that left the revered simian assassin Keyser dead. After burying him, the others continued on their quest to find Ari – with no apparent resolution to any of the series' continuing threads.

Had the title continued, the authors revealed, it would have taken the form of "an epic quest as Essau, Seneca, Crow, and Attar went in search of the older Ari, who would have gradually been built up as a sort of mythic figure as the story progressed." Kharim, anxious to dispel the dishonor that his grandfather, Attar, had brought to their family, would have continued to plague the rebels. Abnett and Edginton planned to "use the opportunity to explore more of the world, encounter other ape cities and so on." Specifically, they hoped to explore the myth of Semos, revealing how apes rose to power and how humanity reverted to intelligent, articulate primitives.

"We would also find that there were native inhabitants of the planet – sort of that world's equivalent of the mutants in the original movies – who are not well pleased at the apes taking over the prime ecological niche," Edginton noted. Though no design had yet been decided upon for the look and back-story of these natives, the writers recalled, "They most certainly would have been humanoid, though – probably a product of parallel evolution. The same goes for the whole planet, which would explain how come they had horses."

One aspect the duo intended to explore was the fates of such film characters as Attar, Ari, and Thade. "After the events of the film," they explained, "Attar began to question his faith following the arrival of Pericles and the evidence that the apes were once the humans' servants, etc." Attar's association with Thade, now in disgrace, had led to his exile. "The ape senate was wary of Thade's growing ambition, and used the failure of his military expedition into the Forbidden Zone as a means of stripping him of his rank and power." Thade vanished soon thereafter.

Ari, meanwhile, would have changed from "a middle-class, liberal, 'hug-a-human' animal activist into a full-fledged radical and heretic." Like Attar, Edginton told me, "she's searching for the truth and has been on the run for years." He was also tempted to have Daena join forces with Ari, and said, "In the twenty years or so since the events of the film, both women would have changed and matured. Ari wouldn't be so dewy-eyed and idealistic, while Daena would have mellowed a little – she wouldn't be so angry all the time. I'd like to think that they'd be friends, but in a sarcastic, sparring kind of way."

Another character the duo hoped to revisit was Limbo, whom Edginton deemed "too good a character to ignore." The aged orangutan, he said, would "probably have been living a quiet life somewhere when Seneca and Essau arrive and turn his life upside down!"

Attar's team would have found Ari living on a remote island among a community of human-friendly apes and the descendants of the *Oberon* crew. "They hadn't stayed with the station when it crashed," the writers explained, "but had ventured out to explore their new world and found somewhere safe to live, the apes not liking water. They'd also raised the rapidly evolving apes as equals." These humans would have been a highly technological community, having taken the station's technology with them, including space pods. The story would have ended with Kharim's forces laying siege to the island and the others escaping through time in the pods. "We would have found out where and when they ended up in the next series," Edginton said.

Crossing Over

Dark Horse founder Mike Richardson axed the *Apes* title after the film failed to impress, but talks soon began regarding a new series based on the classic movies. "I don't think the idea was run by Fox," Edginton recalled. "I think the crossing over of the Tim Burton and classic *Apes* movie worlds was just an idea thrown out there by Dark Horse as a possible way of keeping the comic going."

To that end, he and Abnett looked for a way to relocate their characters from Burton's world (known as Ashlar in the movie's script) to Caesar's Earth. Edginton said he saw the "magnetic storm/spatial/temporal anomaly thing — the McGuffin in the Burton movie" — as a means of accomplishing this feat, adding, "It would send the pods skimming across time, space and parallel universes, which is how we'd end up in the classic movie *Apes* world."

Ultimately, the writers had hoped to have the story jump to an ape world similar to Soror, from Pierre Boulle's *Monkey Planet*, which Edginton described as "a contemporary world but populated by apes, which is where they'd see the Thade version of the Lincoln Memorial. It wouldn't have been the original Thade, though — by then, the name would have become the family surname of a powerful ape dynasty, like the Kennedys or the Rothschilds." In the end, however, "the plug was simply pulled, and that was that."

Tarzan on the Planet of the Apes

Ever since Dark Horse Comics released its first *Alien vs. Predator* series, franchise crossovers have become increasingly popular. From Archie Andrews encountering a superhero vigilante (*Archie Meets the Punisher*) and a sci-fi monster (*Archie Meets Predator*) to *Freddy vs. Jason, Superman vs. The Terminator*, and *The League of Extraordinary Gentlemen*, a variety of unlikely team-ups have hit stands. *POTA* has gotten into the game three times: first in Marvel's "Apeslayer" saga, which merged *Apes* with Marvel's *War of the Worlds* spinoff *Killraven*; and then in Malibu's *Ape Nation* miniseries. Most recently, BOOM! Studios and IDW joined forces for a *POTA* and *Star Trek* crossover titled *The Primate Directive*, boldly taking the apes where none have gone before.

However, had Lovern Kindzierski and Alan Weiss been allowed to pursue a project they proposed to Dark Horse, a fourth (or third, chronologically) *Apes* crossover would have occurred in 2006. The two creators pitched *Tarzan on the Planet of the Apes* to Richardson, with Kindzierski as writer and Weiss as artist.

Tarzan on the Planet of the Apes would have seen Edgar Rice Burroughs' iconic ape-man propelled into the ape-controlled future in a time machine built by H.G. Wells. Tarzan would have befriended Nova's tribe and encountered a simian hunting party, including a younger Doctor Zaius. One gorilla on the expedition, Phaestus, would have sympathized with the human savages and helped Tarzan protect them. Zaius, considering the ape-man a threat, would have set out to destroy him. Tarzan would have faced an angry gorilla — Alexander, the hunting party's leader — who would have been thrown back in time to the era of Caesar's rebellion. The comic would also have featured U.S.

President Theodore Roosevelt, whom Tarzan had previously met in *The Legend of Tarzan* episode "Tarzan and the Rough Rider." Kindzierski said via email:

> This was something I talked about with [*Revolution on the Planet of the Apes* co-writer] Ty Templeton, and he said 'You know, the rights are going to be up.' So I guess this was in 2006. Ty said, 'Mr. Comics is just about to give up its rights to it, so maybe you can still salvage it with Richardson, if he picks up the rights again.' So I said, hey, that would be a great thing. Mike *loved* the idea. I don't know how it got shot down – I believe, from the conversation I had with Mike later, that he went to some kind of Burroughs site or chat room for fans, and the Burroughs people didn't like it.

Mr. Comics
Combat on the Planet of the Apes

Mr. Comics raised the bar on *Planet of the Apes* comics when it published its highly lauded miniseries *Revolution on the Planet of the Apes*, written by Templeton and Joe O'Brien. However, Templeton's original script, titled *Combat on the Planet of the Apes* (alternate title: *War on the Planet of the Apes*), was quite different.

In *Combat*, Templeton had intended to have Thade and Caesar co-existing on the same Earth. "There's nothing in the Burton movie," he maintained, "that rules out the original films, since all of his movie takes place on another planet that is not Earth, until the very end, when we discover Earth has been taken over by Thade's followers, years in the past, because of a time loop."[10]

Had *Combat* seen print, Templeton would have revealed Thade's apes to have been an offshoot of Aldo's genetically enhanced ape pilots.

> There was nothing that said the Earth that Thade went back to couldn't have been the very same Earth that Milo, Cornelius, and Zira went back to. And, in fact, they arrived at similar times. So in our original script, the ape revolution on the West Coast, with Caesar, was going to create a small Ape Nation, leaving the rest of America ruled by humans – no nukes, no big fight for America.

In fact, Templeton said, Caesar's apes would have attempted to live in peace with humans, as he'd promised at the end of the theatrical version of *Conquest of the Planet of the Apes*.

---

[10] It should be noted that the opening scenes of Burton's film would seem to negate the classic movies, as Earth was not yet ape-dominated despite the film being set in 2029, almost forty years after Caesar's 1991 revolution in *Conquest*.

A decade later, Thade would have arrived on Earth with a squad of soldiers, to discover a world with both human and ape governments, living side by side. "Thade originally lands on the East Coast," Templeton stated, "and is taken in to see the human government, as Zira and Cornelius originally were. He eventually tires of the humans prodding him, asking questions about his ship and his story, so Thade [escapes] and makes his way to California, to meet up with Caesar, proposing to create a vast ape army and take over the world for apekind."

Caesar would have been intrigued by Thade, Templeton said – "a creature from the future, like his parents, but from a colony world instead of Earth itself" – but would have declined the offer, preferring peace. "Thade won't hear of it, and starts preaching violence and human hatred to the inhabitants of Ape City, eventually causing a schism of the population (mostly amongst the gorillas) who form an army and head out from the valleys into the hills of California."

Thade's splinter group would have secured the state's military installations, seizing jets, tanks, ships, and other vehicles to defeat the humans still running the United States. "A few of the ideas made it into the miniseries anyway, with Aldo stepping into the role of Thade for the whole subplot involving the attack on the East Coast," Templeton noted. "Taking over the White House, for instance, was a scene almost intact from the original script, where Thade lights a cigar sitting in the oval office, rather than Aldo."

The apes' reverence for Thade would have grown with each victory against mankind, culminating in a civil war between Thade and Caesar for control of simian society. Caesar would have won, killing Thade but giving him a special place in history to heal the rift caused by the conflict – and, thus, explaining his statue replacing the Lincoln Memorial. Templeton's intention had been for Thade to become the Lawgiver who wrote the scroll warning against "the beast, man," and an offshoot of apekind would thereafter have revered him as the true spirit of apedom, rather than Caesar. "The legacies of Thade and Caesar become intertwined," he said, "as the spirit of peace and war that permeate the ape adventures."

Artist Richard Pace had created a promotional poster, cover art, and several interior pages for the Thade-Caesar version. In the end, however, Fox nixed such a crossover, and Templeton altered *Revolution* to focus on Aldo rather than Thade. "When we moved to a new storyline," Templeton told me, "Richard was too busy to work on the book, and we, sadly, had to go with other creators." Pace's artwork was slated to appear in a trade-paperback compilation of *Revolution*, but Mr. Comics never released that promised

Unused artwork for *Revolution on the Planet of the Apes* by Richard Pace (Dec 2005).

collection. A fanzine, *The Forbidden Zine*, later presented the artist's unused materials to fans, with Templeton's and Pace's permission.

Also altered was artist Dennis Rodier's original painted cover for *Revolution* #1, which Fox rejected out of concern over its depiction of a burning U.S. flag. Templeton eventually posted the original version at his blog.[11] It's interesting that despite Fox's protests over the cover, a similar image recently appeared in the film *Dawn of the Planet of the Apes*.

According to Templeton, a scene ultimately cut from *Revolution* would have taken place within a presidential bunker located inside Abraham Lincoln's nose at Mount Rushmore. The base was first featured in Marvel's "Terror on the Planet of the Apes" saga as the home of Lightsmith and Gilbert, and the author had intended to pay homage to that storyline, until space constraints necessitated its removal.

"The Believer"

One major loss to fans caused by Mr. Comics' failure to release the trade paperback of *Revolution* was a five-page story written and illustrated by Sam Agro, originally slated to appear as a back-up tale in issue #4. Titled "The Believer," it would have tied into both the miniseries and the first *Apes* film, featuring parallel storylines set during Caesar's rebellion and Zaius's revocation of Cornelius's travel permit.

In one timeframe (1991), while watching footage of the revolution on the Internet, a priest prayed before his altar, stunned that any animal but man could have "the divine spark" of intelligence. The clergyman sought Christ's guidance, wondering if he should accept speaking apes as his brothers. As he did so, a gorilla crashed into the room, but rather than embrace peace, the priest beat the ape to death with a large crucifix, ignoring its utterance of a single plea, "Mercy."

Two millennia later, Cornelius met with Zaius to ask why his permit had been canceled after finding a cave of artifacts. The orangutan told him he'd hoped to spare Cornelius "an exercise in futility," for science must never supplant the Sacred Scrolls and their warnings of mankind's danger. To that end, he urged Cornelius to put aside his discovery, re-read his scriptures, and trust the Lawgiver's wisdom.

Agro submitted fully penciled and lettered artwork to Templeton for his consideration. "I did think the story was a strong one," Agro told me during a

---

[11] tytempletonart.wordpress.com/category/planet-of-the-apes-2/

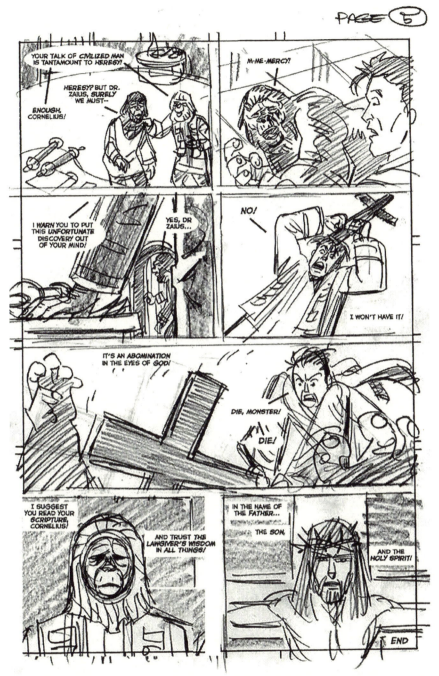

A sketched page from the unpublished backup tale "The Believer," created for *Revolution on the Planet of the Apes* (Dec 2005).

2010 email interview that I conducted for *Simian Scrolls* issue 16,[12] "and very much in keeping with the fundamental themes of the original series of films: religion, repression, prejudice, ignorance, and violence." The use of a Catholic setting, he noted, was deliberate. "I felt the Catholic religion, which leans somewhat more toward the Old Testament than some other Christian faiths, helped to set up the priest's final choice to go all medieval on the gorilla's ass. And, the priest is bludgeoning the ape into submission literally, whereas Zaius is pummeling Cornelius into submission verbally, with well-chosen quotations and threats of heresy."

Templeton, however, foresaw a backlash over the religious overtones of the story – particularly the final panels, which juxtaposed the Christian and simian saviors. Agro explained:

> In the final two panels, I drew a direct visual comparison between the Lawgiver and Jesus. Ty felt this was a bit too 'hot' for our publisher, Steve Ballantyne, and probably for Fox as well. And he also felt, perhaps rightly so, that some readers might find it offensive. I think he said something along the lines of 'People don't want to see their god compared to a monkey.'

What's more, Agro said, there was also a disagreement about the use of parallel panels, as well as the lack of action in the Zaius / Cornelius scenes:

> I felt that the use of coloring – sepia tones for Zaius and full-color for the priest section – would clarify the two continuities sufficiently to avoid confusion, and that for a five-page story, there was plenty of action in the main sequence. Plus, I liked the idea that the story could be read three ways – from beginning to end, or either continuity alone. Considering those points of contention, and the fact that I felt the story would lose about fifty percent of its punch without the direct comparison of the final two panels, I ultimately decided to pursue another idea I'd come up with earlier.

That idea was "Paternal Instinct," which appeared in its place as a back-up tale in *Revolution* issue #4.

Despite his reservations at the time, Templeton praised the story and its author. "*Planet of the Apes* succeeds when it pushes the envelope," he said, "and this is a strong story. I think it absolutely deserves to be seen by people." In 2010, the tale appeared in *Simian Scrolls* #16.

Empire on the Planet of the Apes

Following the first miniseries' critical success, Templeton and O'Brien began discussing a proposed sequel, titled *Empire on the Planet of the Apes*. However,

---

[12] This issue is archived at pota.goatley.com/scrolls/simianscrolls_16.pdf.

that follow-up title never came to pass for reasons unknown even to Templeton. Had *Empire* been published, Templeton said, he and O'Brien intended to chronicle the building of Ape City (as seen in *Battle for the Planet of the Apes*), explaining how the gorillas and chimpanzees came to lead separate lives following that film, with different civilizations and separate Lawgivers – a topic briefly explored in "Ape Shall Not Kill Ape," a backup story in *Revolution* issue #5. Their goal, he explained, would have been to fix the "continuity glitches" they saw between the first three films.

Although Templeton kept no detailed notes outlining his plans for *Empire*, he did recall some of what he and O'Brien had in mind.

> The schism between chimps and gorillas came from the gorillas' wish to see all humans killed, and the chimps wished to live *with* us lowly people. This was mostly because of the terrible treatment gorillas suffered before the Night of the Fires.[13] Chimps, bonobos, and orangutans were usually domestic servants, gorillas were laborers, and the memory never went away.

Following the break-up of apes into two camps, Templeton said, orangutans and bonobos lived in both nations, as "the smart apes in society, taking over the sciences and schooling." The bonobos, he noted, died out in a few generations and did not survive, as they were "too small and gentle a race, even for the ape civilization." (The bonobo species also featured in "Ape Shall Not Kill Ape," as well as in William T. Quick's "Burtonverse" novels *The Fall* (2002) and *Rule* (2003), and onscreen in both *Rise of the Planet of the Apes* and *Dawn of the Planet of the Apes*, in the form of Koba.)

One of Templeton's goals was to reconcile Aldo's role as a hero of ape history in *Escape* with his nature as a "monstrous villain" in *Battle*. The groundwork, he said, was laid with "Ape Shall Not Kill Ape," in which an army of apes – descendants of those who had left Ape City three centuries earlier to protest humanity's place in society – returned to rewrite history.

"There's more than one history of this civilization," Templeton revealed. "It splits up at some point, to come together again. Anthropology is full of that stuff – Phoenician / Egyptian / Nubian cultures all have the same root languages and religious icons, but they clearly become different cultures at some point."

Templeton said he might also have explored a "puzzling" aspect of the first two films. "I had always wondered about the lack of non-Whites in Zauis's time. There *is* something fascinating there, but it would have to be a hideous period

---

[13] As seen in *Conquest of the Planet of the Apes* (1972).

of history that one would cringe in the reading of it. I assume they [non-Whites] were hunted to extinction five hundred years back."

In fact, it was the idea of non-Caucasians not living in North America that interested him most:

> I always had it, in the back of my head, that there were *many* human colonies – survivors, mutant, semi-mutant, all sorts of different kinds of versions of ape-like creatures living on this planet.[14] Maybe there's a baboon colony in Spain, and who knows how the monkeys fared in South America. The brief snapshot of civilization that Taylor and Brent get is so myopic that you could play in this world forever and still stay true to Boulle's and Serling's and Dehn's land.

Empire would have been the first spinoff since Marvel's "Quest for the Planet of the Apes" to feature Mandemus, Caesar's "conscience" in *Battle for the Planet of the Apes*. In a posting at the POTA Yahoo Group,[15] Templeton said he saw the orangutan as having performed in Armando's circus, thus acquiring the power of speech from Caesar (according to *Revolution*, the apes learned to speak so quickly because Caesar mentally willed them to do so).

Where's the Moon?

While conceiving *Revolution*, Templeton decided to plant seeds for a future storyline based on an idea suggested in the original film but never explained[16] – that Earth's lunar satellite was absent in 3978. Thus, Caesar experienced visions of his grandchildren involved in a global war with humans, destroying the Moon in "an orgy of violence and madness." Caesar wrote about this and other visions in a series of journals in *Revolution*, presented as backup features to the main story, but no further details were provided.

The conflict, according to Templeton, would have occurred about a century after *Conquest of the Planet of the Apes*. Though he never worked out the specifics for such a war, his notes included the detonation of an Alpha-Omega Bomb on a lunar colony. "I wanted to plant the idea in Caesar's Journal," he said, "simply as a nod to what was one of my original thoughts about storylines." According to Templeton, this story would have been a separate tale, not part of *Empire on the Planet of the Apes*, which would have occurred about a hundred years before that event.

---

[14] As it happens, this basically describes Doug Moench's tenure on Marvel's *Planet of the Apes* magazine.

[15] groups.yahoo.com/neo/groups/pota/info

[16] Until BOOM! Studios explored that very idea in *Planet of the Apes: Cataclysm*.

The first, first, first thing I wrote down for the briefest notes about storylines was the destruction of the Moon. It's the biggest aspect of history that's never touched upon in any of the subsequent movies, and probably a forgotten, throwaway line to future writers. But it's stuck in my head for decades that something destroyed the Moon, and we're never told what.

Moreover, Templeton considered writing a story about a "very small colony of apes, living in Australia, who survive the Earth's destruction at the end of *Beneath*," which he described as "sort of an *Omega Man* with apes (to keep it all in the Heston zone)." This story, Templeton noted, would have suggested that ape civilization did not actually end with the bomb's detonation in *Beneath*, but rather merely changed as a result.

BOOM! Studios
Planet of the Apes Monthly Series

In 2011, BOOM! entered the arena with the launch of a new monthly comic series simply titled *Planet of the Apes*, written by Daryl Gregory and illustrated by Carlos Magno. Set after the book-end Lawgiver scenes from *Battle for the Planet of the Apes*, it explored a civil war between the granddaughters of the Lawgiver: Alaya (a chimp) and Sullivan (her adopted human sister).

Gregory's monthly run ended after sixteen issues, but the author continued the story in four one-shots, titled *Planet of the Apes Annual*, *Planet of the Apes Special*, *Planet of the Apes Spectacular*, and *Planet of the Apes Giant*. He said:

> I was able to tell the entire story I wanted to tell. BOOM! gave me a year's advance notice to plan an ending, so I was able to bring it to a conclusion. That doesn't always happen in comics, but I'm happy to have been given the chance to exit gracefully.

Digital Apes

Gregory also penned an online prequel comic to *Rise of the Planet of the Apes* in which a pair of wild African chimps, Alpha and Bright Eyes, were captured by poachers and sold into captivity. Bright Eyes was sent for scientific experiments at Gen-Sys Laboratories, where she would later give birth to Caesar. Although rumors persisted that BOOM! might also offer a hardcopy version of the *Rise* prequel, no such print edition was forthcoming, and the serial has since been removed from its website, www.apescomics.com.

BOOM!'s second online comic, *Before the Dawn* (apes2014.com), was part of an early marketing campaign for *Dawn of the Planet of the Apes* and was released in print as a 2013 San Diego Comic Con exclusive.

Terror on the Planet of the Apes

In 1991, Malibu Graphics reprinted the first four chapters of Marvel's "Terror" saga, but not the rest of that story. Thus, twenty years later, when BOOM! announced plans to reprint the entire story and previewed the first four covers online, readers were ecstatic at the idea of having quality reprints – and at (apparently unsubstantiated) rumors that Doug Moench might pen new chapters after more than three decades. Unfortunately, all plans regarding the "Terror" reprints appear to have been quietly dropped, as no further mention was made, and no issues were ever released.

Beyond *Cataclysm*

In discussing their work, Corinna Bechko and Gabriel Hardman recalled, in an e-mail interview, "We didn't submit any story arcs that didn't get used, since BOOM! told us, one issue into our last arc [of *Planet of the Apes: Cataclysm*], that the series was drawing to a close." The duo had hoped to go beyond their 21-issue stint on *Apes*. "We had plans that would have made it a longer arc, and further stories to tell in the *POTA* universe, but it wasn't meant to be."

As Hardman explained, "Since our series was heading toward Taylor's arrival [in the 1968 film], we'd hoped to be able to develop Cornelius's and Zira's relationship more, and show how they became the couple we know and love from the films. We'd also had plans for an epic covert mutant human-ape war that only Zaius and a few apes knew about." This, he said, would have shown why the orangutan agreed with Ursus's plan to invade the Forbidden Zone in *Beneath the Planet of the Apes*. "Sadly," Bechko lamented, "none of this got to the stage of scripting, much less artwork – but at least we did get to lead up to it over the year that we were on the book."

Following *Dawn of the Planet of the Apes'* theatrical release, BOOM! published several new *POTA* titles, including a one-shot called *Contagion*, a *Dawn* prequel miniseries, and the above-noted *Apes/Trek* crossover, with more in the works. Hardman's and Becko's plans seem to be on permanent hold, however, and it's unknown if the couple – or Daryl Gregory – will ever revisit the upside-down world.

Since 1974, a great many *Apes* comics have been shelved. Though some of these abandoned concepts were stronger than others, all were borne out of the writers' love for *Planet of the Apes*. As fans anxiously await word regarding what BOOM! Studios plans to do next, we can only wonder what might have been had any of these time-lost tales come to fruition.

The Moon Goes BOOM!: An Afterword

by Dafna Pleban

I'm going to tell you a secret: I'm an impostor.

Or more specifically, I am not the true-blue, deeply read, fully immersed *Planet of the Apes* fan you've spent the last few hundred pages hearing from. I have not read every single comic in the *Planet of the Apes* pantheon, I have not (much to my shame when I admitted this to Rich Handley on the phone, early in this process) seen every episode of the TV show or the animated series, and, until I began to edit the books for BOOM! Studios, I hadn't even seen all of the movies. Sure, since beginning on the books, I've spent many an hour (a day, a week) neck-deep in the annals of the *Planet of the Apes* wiki, The Sacred Scrolls,[1] which has helped me to research names and dates that are important to our comics – but I didn't (and still don't) feel comfortable claiming any sort of true authority. My first exposure to the franchise was the Tim Burton reboot. My first *enjoyable* exposure to the franchise was the 2011 reboot, *Rise of the Planet of the Apes*. Maybe "impostor" is the wrong way to put it; maybe a more accurate way would be "late as hell to the awesome party."

I had been an editor at BOOM! Studios for roughly a year when *Rise* came out. The editor at the time (of a comic simply titled *Planet of the Apes*, written by Daryl Gregory and illustrated by Carlos Magno) was Ian Brill. He had been a

---

[1] http://planetoftheapes.wikia.com, managed by Neil Moxham

friend of mine before my time at BOOM! Studios, and had undertaken the unenviable task of bringing me up to speed with all the pop culture I had missed in my childhood.

Comic books and science fiction became my own personal teenage rebellion (cheaper than drugs, and easier to acquire, too), so I wasn't entering the ring completely unarmed. I had managed the canny trick of convincing my parents that *Star Trek* was an educational program (thank you, *Reading Rainbow*!). Available in practically every second-hand bookstore on the planet, *Star Trek* was my formative influence — in all forms, whether books, comics, TV, or movies. It was the perfect gateway drug to anything with a social conscience and a penchant for time travel.

By the time I came to BOOM! and admitted I had never watched a John Carpenter film, or gone to a ballgame, or seen a *Planet of the Apes* movie that didn't have talking humans in it, Ian took it upon himself to bring me up to the appropriate cultural speed. When a little movie called *Rise of the Planet of the Apes* came out, I dutifully went on opening night. I had helped proof the first few issues of the comic, after all, so it was the least I could do.

And. Well. Things were a little different after that.

I'm not sure what I expected going into the film that first time, but coming out, I knew one thing: I couldn't get enough. Subtle but searing commentary on the power of dehumanization? The destructiveness of the well-meaning and kind-hearted? How even on the eve of the destruction of an entire species, two people can still recognize the other's right to exist? In the moral universe of *Planet of the Apes*, the right to exist is never questioned, even if the means to that existence become increasingly impossible.

It was heady, dizzying stuff. So, of course, I couldn't get enough of it.

When BOOM! got the license, one thing was clear: we wanted to do it right. *Rise of the Planet of the Apes* was on the horizon, and we faced the difficult task of crafting content long before we had a chance to experience the final work ourselves. We could read the screenplay, yes, but as so much of the final work exists in that liminal space between script and screen, we wanted to find a place where we could tell the best story. Set anything before *Rise*, and there aren't many talking apes at your disposal. Set anything afterward, and you risk stepping on the toes of any potential sequel Fox may have planned. Set it during *Rise* without having seen the film, and you set anyone up, even the best writer, for potential hardship.

That left the original 1968 canon. Not only was the original continuity a closed loop (literally and figuratively), but Fox let us have free rein, of sorts. The story was finished, the timeline well-defined. We had no restrictions within the established parameters, as long as all characters hit their marks when they were supposed to. That's where writers like Daryl Gregory (*Planet of the Apes*) and Corinna Bechko and Gabriel Hardman (*Betrayal of the Planet of the Apes, Exile on the Planet of the Apes,* and *Planet of the Apes: Cataclysm*) came in.

Matt Gagnon, our editor-in-chief, loved what Daryl Gregory had done with Kurt Busiek's world in *Dracula: The Company of Monsters*, and knew that Daryl was a *POTA* fan from his work on the online *Rise of the Planet of the Apes* prequel comic we did for the lead-up to that film. Whereas the prequel had a small timeframe, Daryl wanted the widest possible canvas to work with. And what better canvas than literally hundreds of years at your disposal?

Daryl set his storyline 1,300 years before George Taylor fell from the stars. In so doing, he chose arguably the most important point between Caesar's rise and Taylor's fall: the generation of humans who lived right before the species lost its capacity for speech. Apes were the ruling class, while humans were second-hand citizens in their flourishing utopia. Daryl came into the story in the same way that all great writers do, by finding the characters at the heart of the conflict. His approach was brilliant, embodying the schism between man and ape within one family: the adopted children of the Lawgiver – one chimpanzee, the other human.

Through these two siblings, Daryl created a stage on which the best stories (more specifically, the best *Planet of the Apes* stories) could be told. There was intergenerational conflict – between Sully, the human sister, and the next generation of mankind who were born mute, as well as between the chimpanzee Alaya and the next generation of apes who saw humans in an increasingly hostile light. There was a class conflict between the slums of Skintown, where humans were allowed to make their homes, and the richly ornate City Tree, where the richest and most powerful apes lived and where humans worked as servants. There was a familial conflict, with Alaya and Sully unwittingly embodying both the conflict and the promise between their peoples. When they eventually find common ground and work together in a last-ditch effort to save their city, the bond is deeply earned. They've been through everything together, and Daryl made sure we were with them every step of the way.

Just as Daryl crafted the emotional core of the story, Carlos Magno brought the script to life. But artists do more than simply bring a writer's world to life – they are true collaborators. They're a whole film crew: director of photography, location scout, set designers, actors, extras, and more. Carlos wasn't simply responsible for the richly detailed world of Mak (everything from the costumes to the architecture and the forests – all Carlos). I can find no better example of what he brought to the book than the two-page splash in issue #10 of *Planet of the Apes*. The script called for, simply, three panels, detailing a meeting of humans versus apes on a winter battlefield. What took up about half a script page became two pages of at least thirty-plus characters duking it out on the battlefield. Five characters sharing a single panel is some of the toughest work a comics artist can do. Now picture thirty or more characters (apes, humans, and horses) per panel, locked in a fierce battle, with the action tracking perfectly to convey the intent of the script. It's incredibly hard, even on a good day, but Carlos managed to create a beautifully detailed world every month, on time, for sixteen issues.

The final key to the puzzle is the coloring, and I lucked out with an amazing run of people. When Ian Brill put the book together, Juan Manuel Tumburús was the colorist, imbuing the world of Mak with a dusty, lived-in palette of tans, oranges, and reds, giving Carlos's line art weight and surface for light to refract off of. Juan was followed by Nolan Woodard, who brought a palette that, at once, was familiar and different – acid greens and striking pinks were interwoven into the dusty, familiar landscape, bringing bright pops of color to the action. After Nolan was Darrin Moore, who brought an incredible eye to an environment, bringing mist to an early morning scene, or refracting moonlight on an illicit midnight meeting.

Whereas Daryl's *Planet of the Apes* plumbed the depths of thousands of years of unexplored canon, Corinna Bechko and Gabriel Hardman aimed their sights a little closer to home. Their project was set up while Ian was editing the books, and I was lucky enough to carry it across the finish line. Gabriel and Corinna knew they wanted to tell a story in the classic Ape City setting, and to have access to classic characters like Doctors Zaius and Milo, but they also wanted to find a space to tell their own story.

With *Betrayal of the Planet of the Apes*, Corinna and Gabriel struck on the perfect synthesis of courtroom drama, political thriller, and killer classic sci-fi – we billed it as "Doctor Zaius: Year One," but really, what they put together was their own brilliant cast of characters to explore the classic *POTA* universe. The two had the knack of creating characters and places that felt like they had always existed in the *Apes* universe – characters like General Aleron, the disgraced soldier who begins to unravel the conspiracy at the heart of Ape City; Doctor Cato, the kindly orangutan scientist who tries to teach humans sign language; Prisca, Cato's student and a scientist in her own right, who works tirelessly to help the humans in any way she can; and so many more.

The series was drawn by Gabriel Hardman himself, and was colored by the brilliant Jordie Bellaire. When *Betrayal* wrapped, we knew we couldn't leave the story there. As much as I had campaigned to kill Aleron in the end – not because I disliked the character, mind you, but rather because I always look for an opportunity to hammer in that underlying nihilism of the *POTA* universe (a note they wisely ignored) – I was glad that most of our major characters were relatively intact.

Instead of turning *Betrayal* into an ongoing title, we wanted to give the books a chance to draw in new readers, as well as retain those we earned with the first miniseries. It also gave us a natural break in the narrative to jump ahead a couple of years. Whereas *Betrayal* took place twenty years before the 1968 film, we moved up a couple of years for the next miniseries, giving time within the world of the story for the landscape to shift, and for new dynamics to arise. It also gave us a chance to come up with a new title, which is always both daunting and a complete blast. There's an elegance to it, and after a few tries (*Menace of the Planet of the Apes, Vengeance of/on the Planet of the Apes, Peril on the Planet of the Apes*, etc.), Corinna and Gabriel came up with a pitch-perfect title just as they had done before: *Exile on the Planet of the Apes* – which was fitting, because with Aleron self-exiled to the Forbidden Zone, *Heart of Darkness* very much became the touchstone for the story and world.

While Gabriel would continue to provide covers, he wanted to focus on writing, so we brought in Marc Laming, an incredibly talented artist from the United Kingdom. Marc had worked previously with BOOM! on *The Rinse*, a gritty crime book about money laundering. While a modern, all-human-cast comic might not immediately a proper *POTA* artist make, Marc's love of the films, as well as his incredible ink work, made him perfect for *Exile*. With Jordie setting the palette for the new series, and *The Rinse* colorist Darrin Moore picking up the baton for the rest of the run, *Exile* became a fitting continuation of the world that Corinna and Gabriel had created.

Franchises are always a delicate tight-rope to walk – you want to explore the existing canon while not overwriting it, and you want to extend the story

Phil Noto's cover to *Planet of the Apes: Cataclysm* #1 (Sep 2012), the first of a twelve-part series leading up to the events of the 1968 film.

without stepping on potential future storylines. I usually enjoy the challenge, as the limitations act as a form of self-editing, forcing us to discover the heart of the story. But sometimes, to put it plainly, you just want to blow shit up.

I remember having dinner at one San Diego Comic Con with Corinna and Gabriel, and they had something important to tell me. We were gearing up to turn their excellent run of miniseries into an ongoing comic, and we had tasked Gabriel and Corinna with coming up with what they wanted to do next. They had built an incredible world for themselves, bringing to life the state of Ape City mere decades before Taylor would arrive. Doctor Zaius was still a young politician, Ursus was a soldier still making his way up the ranks, and... Earth still had a lunar satellite. They wanted to fix that in the only way comics with an unlimited special-effects budget could.

They wanted to blow up the Moon.

Corinna and Gabriel envisioned what would eventually be called *Planet of the Apes: Cataclysm* as an opportunity to set the stage for the upcoming films. This would involve all the key players – bringing Zaius to the point at which his view of humanity and the risks mankind represented would be cemented firmly, Milo to the mindset at which he would be open to entertaining the idea of intelligent humans, and Ursus to the place where there would be no answer but putting Taylor in the ground. Most of all, they had the mutants consolidating power and biding their time until *Beneath*.

Even better, Corinna and Gabriel had access to all the groundwork they laid down with *Betrayal* and *Exile*, with Aleron's acolytes still out there; Prisca older and wiser (and more careful for it); and Timon still trapped in the Forbidden Zone. It was the perfect mix of ingredients, and with Damian Couceiro (previously an artist on *Dracula: The Company of Monsters* – for Daryl Gregory, no less!) on board, alongside Darrin Moore as colorist, we had a well-seasoned team who worked effortlessly together. Throw in the fact that we were able to get covers for the first four issues from Alex Ross himself, and you couldn't have asked for a better book.

And did I mention we got to blow up the Moon? Because holy hell, we got to blow up the Moon! Then we got to rain pieces of the Moon down on Ape City, and then kick off a tsunami and eventually burn half of Ape City to the ground.

Which brings me to *Dawn of the Planet of the Apes*.

For the first time in the direct market, BOOM! Studios' comics were playing extensively in the new films' canon. Written by Michael Moreci (*Hoax Hunters*), illustrated by Dan McDaid (*Vandroid*), and colored by talented newcomer Jason Wordie, *Dawn* gave us the perfect space to explore – since it's set between the first and second movies in the rebooted continuity, we had the opportunity to examine those missing 10 years as Caesar starts to bring the threads of his society together, and Malcolm and his family struggle to survive their own society falling apart. The key difference between *Dawn* and our other *POTA* titles is that for the first time, we had to put the toys back where we found them. With the story set between the two films, we had the start and end points for our characters, but the middle was all ours to play with. Our usual tool set (like blowing up the Moon, for example) was off the table. With the Moon set firmly in the sky, Moreci and I worked closely to find the story that he wanted to tell in this fixed universe.

The way licensed comics production works, we have to start the process of approvals and pitches long before the first issue is scripted, which necessitated starting before the actual film came out. With Moreci not in California, I had to go to Fox Studios and hunker down with the screenplay. Effects work aside, the bulk of the film was there, and I can honestly say it was an incredibly enjoyable read. The characters and action were electric on the page, but I was faced with a problem – how would I convey this to Moreci, who still hadn't seen the film, much less read the script himself?

Extensive notes and multiple drafts later, we had our first issue's script. And it was a good one. It was about Caesar and Malcolm, and their respective post-*Rise* stories. It touched on the classic *POTA* themes of survival and the cost thereof, of what you find yourself willing to sacrifice for the people you care for, and of the lines you can't bear to cross, not even for the greater good. And then the *Dawn* movie came out.

Despite my having read the script multiple times, nothing really could have prepared me for how much I loved the actual film. Thrilling and affecting in equal parts, the CG work on Caesar and Koba, the heart that Jason Clarke brought to Malcolm – everything came together as more than the sum of its parts. There was a depth of emotion and weariness suffusing the film which brought a reality to the world that the script could never impart. Michael, my excellent assistant editor Alex Galer, and I came out of the film all on the same metaphorical page: a rewrite was in order. Not because the first draft was bad, but because we suddenly had so much more to work with: Koba's slowly fracturing loyalty, Malcolm's slow realization that there may not be anything left worth fighting for, and Caesar's own realization that good intent may not be enough. It was heady, thrilling stuff, and what we had in that first draft was not going to be enough.

But change is easy when you're eager to make it, and the next draft encompassed everything we wanted to explore after coming out of the film. We had all the themes of the first draft, but now we had real stakes: Malcolm had a family to lose, Caesar had one to start, and we had the whole of the world to start slowly degrading, morally and physically. Even better, we had our villain – the jealous, angry Pope, a darker mirror to Koba, his hate for humans extending even to Caesar, an ape whom he sees as someone who was raised and groomed by the very people who experimented on him.

In an attempt to bring Pope into the fold, Caesar sends him out into the world for reconnaissance; with their community quickly taking root, Caesar must know if there are other threats to their existence. What Pope does with that power – enslaving apes alongside humans – sets the stage for Koba to enact Caesar's will in a way that sets up their relationship by the time *Dawn* happens. Thus, we had the script we loved, and now we needed the artist to bring that world to life.

After an extensive search, we reached out to Dan McDaid. His excellent work on *Vandroid* told us that he could do the kinetic, affecting action we'd need for the story, but it was his test page with Caesar and his family that told us he could capture the true essence of the film: the eyes. Being able to capture the depth of Caesar's and Koba's eyes was essential to capturing their characters, and Dan was able to do it in spades.

With artist Chris Mitten bringing the degraded world to vibrant color on covers, colorist Jason Wordie bringing the palette of the film to Dan's linework, and letterer Ed Dukeshire finding a canny solution to conveying the apes' sign language, versus when they choose to physically speak, our *Dawn of the Planet of the Apes* miniseries came together relatively quickly. I'm incredibly proud of the final story. I hope the fans enjoy reading the miniseries as much as we enjoyed making it.

More than anything, beyond just being proud of the excellent work I've been lucky to be a part of, I'm so glad to have discovered the world of *Planet of the Apes*. The fanbase and the culture are incredibly welcoming, and I can't wait to be a part of that world for years to come. It's a rare thing that such a long-running franchise can be open to newcomers, but I don't think it's an accident – for as nihilistic and cynical as *Planet of the Apes* can be about the direction of the human race, the mythos maintains that, innately, we always *mean* to do good, even if we occasionally screw it up a little.

Well, a lot. The planet *did* explode, after all. (And so did the Moon... but I helped a bit on that one.)

About the Contributors

Sam Agro is a writer, illustrator, and some-time performer. In his day job as a storyboard artist, Sam has worked on such animated series as *Teenage Mutant Ninja Turtles, Ewoks, Droids,* and *The Ripping Friends.* He has also created storyboards for live-action films like *Fly Away Home* and the *Saw* horror movie franchise. In addition, Sam writes and draws for the comics industry, including DC's *Looney Tunes*, Mr. Comics's *Revolution on the Planet of the Apes*, and Alterna's *Horror in the West* and *Monstrosity*. "Madhouse of Ideas: Marvel Terrorizes the Planet of the Apes" is Sam's first published essay. His first published prose fiction, "We Apologize for the Delay," appeared in *Gods, Memes and Monsters*, from Stone Skin Press UK. When all this other stuff isn't enough to keep him busy, Sam writes and performs improv, sketch comedy, and short plays with the comedy group The Canadian Space Opera Company. Sam lives in Toronto, Canada, with his beautiful, patient wife, Beth, and their wacky cat, Little V.

Jim Beard, a native of Toledo, Ohio, was introduced to comic books at an early age by his father, who passed on to him a love for the medium and the pulp characters who preceded it. After decades of reading, collecting, and dissecting comics, Jim became a published writer when he sold a story to DC Comics in 2002. Since that time, he has written official *Star Wars* and *Ghostbusters* comic stories, and has contributed articles and essays to several volumes of comic book history. His work includes *Gotham City 14 Miles*, a book of essays about the 1966 *Batman* TV series (also from Sequart Organization); *Sgt. Janus, Spirit-Breaker*, a collection of pulp ghost stories featuring his own

Edwardian occult detective; *Captain Action: Riddle of the Glowing Men*, the first pulp prose novel based on the classic 1960s action figure; *Monster Earth*, a shared-world anthology of giant monster tales; and a GI Joe Adventure Team novella for Kindle Worlds, *Mystery of the Sunken Tomb*. Currently, Jim provides regular content for Marvel.com, the official Marvel Comics website, and is a regular columnist for *Toledo Free Press*. Please visit him at sgtjanus.blogspot.com and on Facebook at facebook.com/thebeardjimbeard.

Corinna Bechko has been writing comics since her horror graphic novel *Heathentown* was published by Image/Shadowline in 2009. Since then, she has worked for numerous comics publishers, including Marvel, DC, BOOM! Studios, and Dark Horse, on titles that include co-creating *Invisible Republic* for Image Comics and co-writing *Planet of the Apes, Star Wars: Legacy Volume II, Savage Hulk*, and *Sensation Comics*. She is a zoologist by training and has worked closely with (nonverbal) orangutans and chimpanzees.

Joseph F. Berenato obtained a B.A. in English and spent four years as *The Hammonton Gazette*'s entertainment editor before returning to his roots at his family's blueberry farm in Hammonton, N.J. Joe was a contributor to *Gotham City 14 Miles*, and is contracted to author *Something Strange: The Unauthorized Ghostbusters Encyclopedia* and co-author *It's Alive! The Complete Universal Monsters Encyclopedia* for Hasslein Books, with Jim and Becky Beard. In 2014, he conceived, edited, and contributed to *New Life and New Civilizations: Exploring Star Trek Comics* (also from Sequart Organization). Joe wrote the introduction for IDW Publishing's *Star Trek: Gold Key Archives Volume 3*, and also contributed to ATB Publishing's 2015 *Star Trek* anthology *Outside In: TOS 110*. He is an editor at Hasslein Books and an adjunct professor with Salem Community College (through which he teaches Freshman Comp to inmates at South Woods State Prison), and recently received a Master of Arts in Writing from Rowan University. You can find Joe at jfberenato.wordpress.com and on Twitter at @JFBerenato.

Joe Bongiorno is the owner and founder of The Royal Publisher of Oz and the creator of The Royal Timeline of Oz (oztimeline.net), the *Star Wars* Expanded Universe Timeline (starwarstimeline.net), and the *X-Files* Chronology (xfilestimeline.net). He has published several books, including *The Law of Oz and Other Stories, The Magic Umbrella of Oz, Queen Ann in Oz*, and *Adolf Hitler in Oz*. Currently, he is hard at work on his own book, titled *Black Sabbath: The Illustrated Lyrics*, which analyzes every song by the original Black Sabbath. Joe has also contributed to Lucasfilm's licensed *Star Wars* universe. In his spare time, he lives on Long Island with two humans, two dogs, and five cats.

Pat Carbajal, a cover and interior illustrator for Hasslein Books, started as a political cartoonist for national newspapers in Argentina, then created realistic portraits for financial newspaper *Ambito Financiero*. He started producing art for the U.S. market in 2007, with covers for Adamant Entertainment's *Tales of Fu Man Chu* and *Foe Factory: Modern*. In 2009, Pat painted the cover of Bluewater Productions' *Female Force: Sarah Palin*, followed by biographical comics on Barack Obama, George W. Bush, Bill Clinton, Ronald Reagan, Richard Nixon, Al Gore, Ted Kennedy, and Colin Powell, in the *Political Power* series. Rock stars were next, including Bob Dylan, Jim Morrison, and Jimi Hendrix, in *Rock and Roll Comics: The Sixties*, as well as Ozzy Osborne, AC/DC, and Guns n' Roses, in *Rock and Roll Comics: Rock Heroes*. The first graphic novel illustrated by Pat was Bluewater's *Allan Quatermain*, written by Clay and Susan Griffith. Together with the Griffiths, he created "The Raven" for Bluewater's horror comic, *Vincent Price Presents*, in which he debuted as a writer.

Joseph Dilworth, Jr., was born at a very young age in a small hospital the day before episode six of the *Doctor Who* serial "The War Games" aired. He's been hooked ever since. A lifelong writer, he served for six years as the founder, editor, and lead writer of Pop Culture Zoo. At PCZ, Joe wrote numerous reviews, conducted many highly acclaimed interviews, and offered fair and balanced opinions about numerous topics. He is currently a co-host of The Flickcast's weekly podcast and a staff editor at Hasslein Books, and he writes a regular column about TV for *Long Island Pulse Magazine*. He firmly believes that *Doctor Who* is the greatest show ever created, period, and *Cinema Paradiso* is his favorite film. Joe resides in the Pacific Northwest, where he spends time with his family, brews beer, writes, reads, and expresses his opinion to whoever will listen. Just be warned: He has little regard for the laws of space and time.

Dan Greenfield is the editor and co-creator of 13thDimension.com, a website devoted primarily to comics and pop culture, past and present. To him, the basic food groups are Batman, *Planet of the Apes*, *Star Trek* (the original series), James Bond, the Beatles, and the Rolling Stones. Dan is married to his remarkably patient wife, Wendy, and his best sidekick is his son, Sam. They have two cats, Lex and Zod.

Edward Gross is a veteran entertainment journalist who has been on the editorial staffs of a wide variety of magazines, among them *Geek*, *Cinescape*, *SFX*, *Starlog*, *CFQ*, *Movie Magic*, and *Sci-Fi Now*. He is the author or co-author of such non-fiction books as *Planet of the Apes Revisited, Above & Below: A 25th Anniversary Beauty and the Beast Companion, Captains' Logs: The Complete Trek Voyages, Superhero Confidential*, and the forthcoming *Fifty Year Mission: The Complete Uncensored Unauthorized Oral History of Star Trek*.

Rich Handley is the editor of Hasslein Books (hassleinbooks.com) and the managing editor of *RFID Journal*. He has written or co-written five books to date, including *Timeline of the Planet of the Apes, Lexicon of the Planet of the Apes, Conspiracy of the Planet of the Apes*, and two *Back to the Future* reference books, and is currently hard at work on others, as well as assisting BOOM! Studios on several upcoming *Apes* comics projects. Rich has contributed numerous works to Lucasfilm's licensed *Star Wars* franchise, and is co-editing a trio of *Star Wars* essay books for Sequart, as well as a sequel to the book you now hold, titled *Bright Eyes, Ape City: Examining the Planet of the Apes Mythos*. He has penned essays for IDW's *Star Trek* newspaper strip reprint books, ATB Publishing's 2015 *Star Trek* anthology *Outside In: TOS 110*, and Sequart's *New Life and New Civilizations: Exploring Star Trek Comics*, and has also contributed to numerous other publications, including *Star Trek Communicator, Star Trek Magazine, Simian Scrolls, Cinefantastique, Sci-Fi Invasion, Toons, Movie Magic, Cinescape*, and *Dungeon / Polyhedron*.

Gabriel Hardman is the co-writer and artist of *Invisible Republic*, from Image Comics. He has also co-written (with Corinna Bechko) and drawn *Savage Hulk* for Marvel Comics, *Star Wars: Legacy* for Dark Horse Comics, and *Planet of the Apes* for BOOM! Studios. Gabriel has drawn *Hulk, Secret Avengers*, and *Agents of Atlas* for Marvel, as well as the original graphic novel *Heathentown* for Image / Shadowline. In addition, he has worked as a storyboard artist on movies such as *Interstellar, Inception, Tropic Thunder, The Dark Knight Rises, Superman Returns*, and *X-Men 2*. He lives with his wife, writer Corinna Bechko, their cats, a bunny named Clyfford Still, and their dog.

Zaki Hasan was born and raised in Chicago—with a decade-long detour in Saudi Arabia—before settling in the San Francisco Bay Area. He is a professor of communication and media studies, and a co-founder of Mr. Boy Productions, an L.A.-based independent film and video company. A lifelong *Planet of the Apes* fan, Zaki self-published an *Apes*-themed fanzine called *The Sacred Scrolls* in the mid-1990s, while he was still in high school. He is currently a co-host of the MovieFilm Podcast and a co-author of Quirk Books' *Geek Wisdom: The Sacred Teachings of Nerd Culture,* and his work has been featured in *Q-News, Illume*, and *The Huffington Post*. In addition, he has appeared as a panelist on Al

Jazeera America's *The Stream*, and is a contributing editor at Altmuslimah.com. Since 2004, his blog, *Zaki's Corner*, has been his one-stop forum for musings on news, media, politics, and pop culture.

Dafna Pleban is the editor of the *Planet of the Apes* titles for BOOM! Studios. She has worked on a wide variety of titles, including *Lumberjanes*, *Sons of Anarchy*, *Suicide Risk*, and more, and is also contributing to the sequel to this book, *Bright Eyes, Ape City: Examining the Planet of the Apes Mythos* (also from Sequart). You can find her on Twitter, talking about her cat and *Star Trek*, at @DafnaDOOM.

John Roche suspects that his first exposure to *Planet of the Apes* was actually a U.K. television advert for the launch of the Marvel *Apes* weekly in 1974, featuring Bob Larkin's glorious cover to the second issue of the U.S. magazine. John was, therefore, utterly powerless in Fate's decision to immediately render him a lifelong *Apes*, Marvel, and Larkin fan. John's imagination was ignited by the *Planet of the Apes* TV series in 1974, and by the wonderful bounty of trading cards, novels, and action figures that blazed the trail for other franchises. John lives in Wales, U.K., with his very own Welsh Dragon of a wife, Gill, and a ridiculous amount of *Apes* and Marvel memorabilia. He is a co-editor of *Simian Scrolls: The U.K. Apezine*. John still recalls a bitter, tragic day in 1977 when, having read the final page of "Future History Chronicles V" in *Mighty World of Marvel* #246, he realized it was "over." Little did that sad young boy dream that, one day, decades later, *Apes* would be topping the box office again, new *Apes* merchandise would be plentiful, and he would enjoy the privilege of being part of this wonderful book. "APES RULE!!!"

Lou Tambone is an independent musician, freelance writer, and Web designer from northern New Jersey. A lifelong fan of pop culture, he was an early HTML adopter, creating and maintaining some of the first *Star Wars* fan sites located under the starwarz.com banner. As for non-Web writing, he has previously been published in magazines like *Sci-Fi World*, and looks forward to making plenty more contributions to the writing world after *The Sacred Scrolls: Comics on the Planet of the Apes*. When he's not reading or writing stories, Lou is usually writing music or rehearsing with one of his many bands. During his "spare" time, he tries to remember to eat and breathe. You can visit Lou online at loutambone.com or facebook.com/loutunes.

Dayton Ward is a *New York Times* bestselling author or co-author of numerous novels and short stories, including a whole bunch of stuff set in the *Star Trek* universe, and often works with friend and co-writer Kevin Dilmore. He has also written (or co-written) for *Star Trek Communicator, Star Trek Magazine,* Syfy.com, *StarTrek.com, and* Tor.com, and is a monthly contributor to the Novel Spaces writers blog (novelspaces.blogspot.com). Dayton is known to wax nostalgic about all manner of geek and sundry topics over on his own blog, *The Fog of Ward* (daytonward.com).

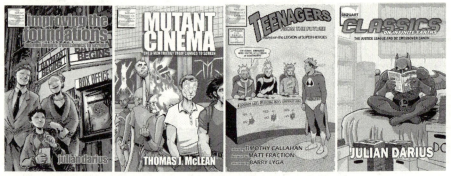

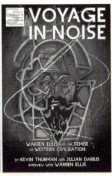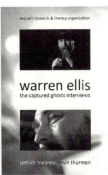

SHOT IN THE FACE: A SAVAGE JOURNEY TO THE HEART OF *TRANSMETROPOLITAN*
KEEPING THE WORLD STRANGE: A *PLANETARY* GUIDE
VOYAGE IN NOISE: WARREN ELLIS AND THE DEMISE OF WESTERN CIVILIZATION
WARREN ELLIS: THE CAPTURED GHOSTS INTERVIEWS

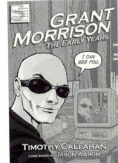

GRANT MORRISON: THE EARLY YEARS
OUR SENTENCE IS UP: SEEING GRANT MORRISON'S *THE INVISIBLES*
CURING THE POSTMODERN BLUES: READING GRANT MORRISON AND CHRIS WESTON'S *THE FILTH* IN THE 21ST CENTURY
THE ANATOMY OF ZUR-EN-ARRH: UNDERSTANDING GRANT MORRISON'S BATMAN

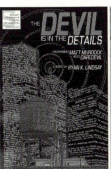

MINUTES TO MIDNIGHT: TWELVE ESSAYS ON *WATCHMEN*
AND THE UNIVERSE SO BIG: UNDERSTANDING *BATMAN: THE KILLING JOKE*
THE DEVIL IS IN THE DETAILS: EXAMINING MATT MURDOCK AND DAREDEVIL
THE FUTURE OF COMICS, THE FUTURE OF MEN: MATT FRACTION'S *CASANOVA*

For more information and for exclusive content, visit Sequart.org.

Made in the USA
Middletown, DE
06 November 2016